Collins

AF661148

Maths EXPERT

3

Author | Prabha Sethy

Components of DigiSuite

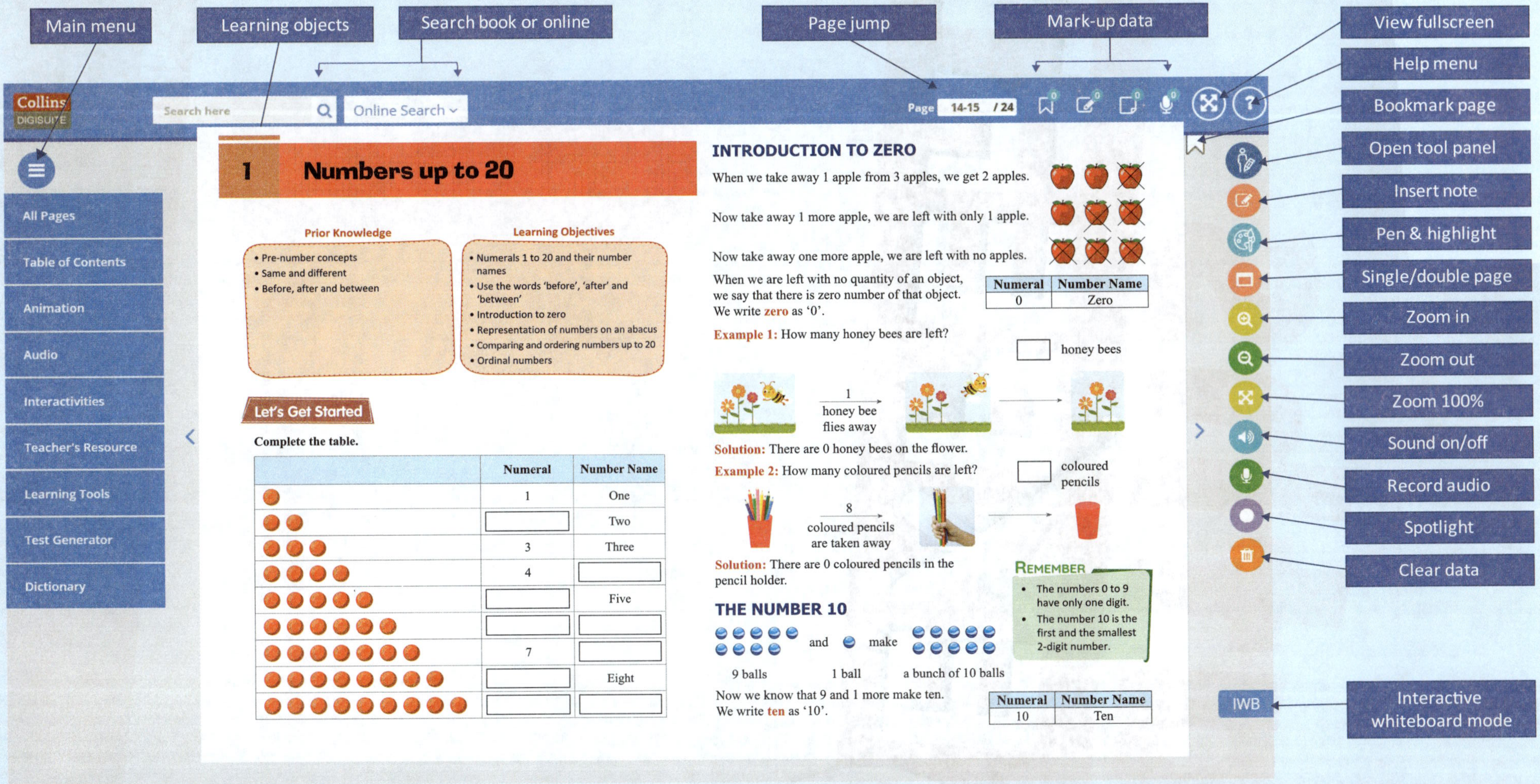

Student + Teacher			Teacher-only	
animations	activities	games	lesson plans	teacher's notes
ilt instructor-led tutorials	w worksheets	v videos	w worksheets	ak answer keys
	audio			

(icons: ia activities, g games, lp lesson plans, tn teacher's notes)

Preface

Collins Maths Expert is a series of eight books for Classes 1 to 8. The series adheres to the guidelines of the **National Education Policy (NEP) 2020** and aligns with the vision of the ***National Initiative for Proficiency in Reading with Understanding and Numeracy* (NIPUN Bharat)**.

In this series, the approach is **"Less Is More"** and **"Drill and Practice"**. It provides all the basic information considered essential in attaining the objectives of mathematics education. All concept explanations are *simple* and *concise* with more *focus on Solved Examples*. The content has also been organized in a horizontal and vertical progression. The language used is child friendly and age appropriate.

This series aims to provide adequate opportunities to help students develop problem solving and critical thinking skills through solved examples, practice questions, formulas, tables, images and illustrations. Most of the solved examples are constructed from daily life situations requiring the student to apply mathematical principles and formula for their solution. Varieties of questions have been included to cater to all level of students. Sufficient provision for practice, revision and review have been provided through adequate number of questions. While citing examples from real life, an effort has been made to make the content inclusive with respect to race, gender, regions, religion, food, flora, fauna, festivals, etc.

We would like to take this opportunity to thank all the teachers who reviewed the books and provided their invaluable feedback, which helped in improving the quality of the content. Any suggestions or constructive criticism from the users are welcome. We shall try to incorporate those in the future editions.

Authors

About the Features

The key features of ***Collins Maths Expert*** series are completely aligned with National Education Policy (NEP) 2020.

Let's Recap!

A variety of questions based on the previous grade for quick recapitulation

Prior Knowledge:

List of topics to help construct connections between old and new knowledge

Learning Objectives:

List of main topics that will be covered in a chapter

Let's Get Started:

Interactive exercise to begin a chapter with real-life connect and addressing 21st Century Skills

Solved Examples:

A variety of worked out examples based on each topic

Alert:

Snippets to clear common misconceptions and mistakes

Exercise:

Purposefully designed in-text exercises

Remember:

Important points for quick reference

Word Problems:
Textual questions based on real-life situations

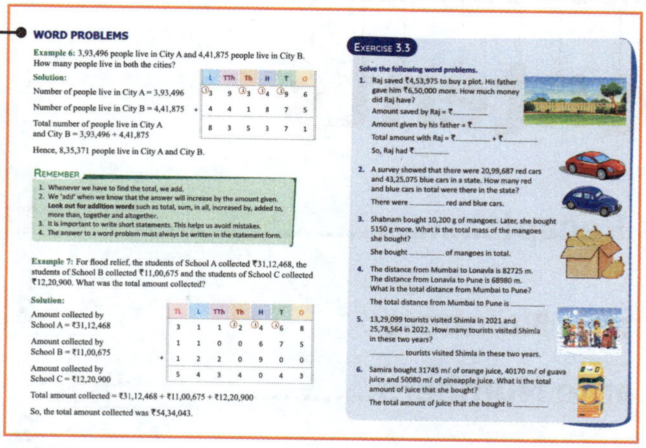

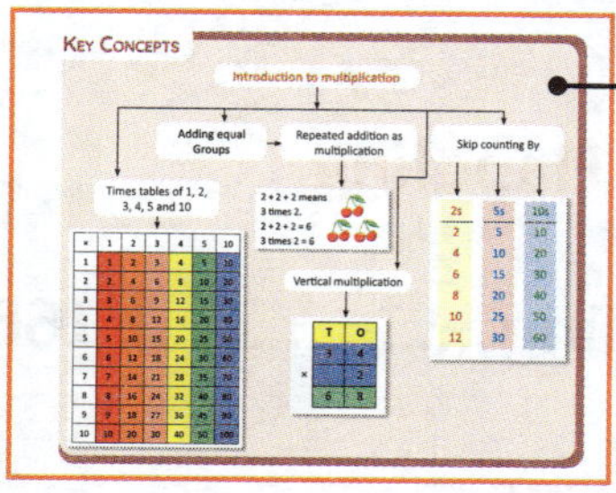

Key Concepts:
A graphic organizer to recap the chapter

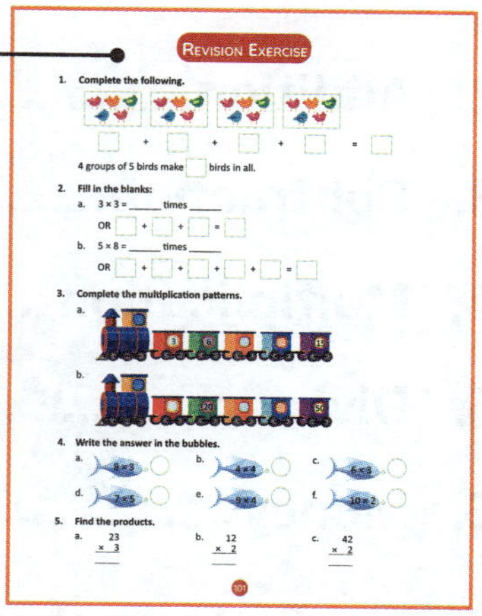

Revision Exercise:
Variety of questions based on the topics covered in the chapter

Test Paper:
Variety of questions based on the entire book

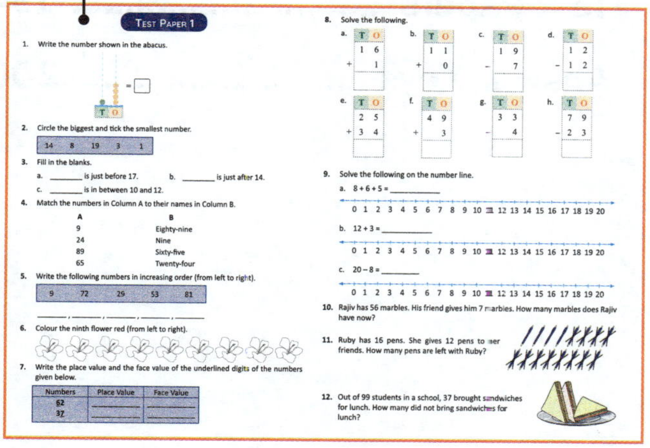

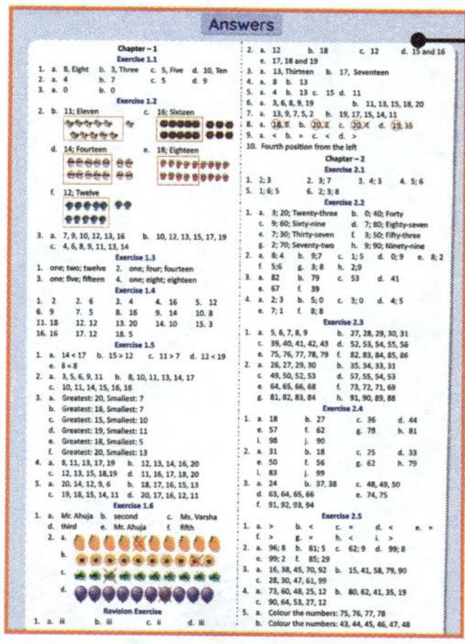

Answer Keys:
Solution to Exercises and Revision Exercise

Poster:
Hands-on/STEAM-based activities to develop 21st Century Skills

Contents

Let's Recap!

1. Choose the correct option.

a. The number after 728 is ______.

i. 725 ii. 729 iii. 727 iv. 730

b. What is the expanded form of 498?

i. 4 + 9 + 8 ii. 400 + 90 + 8 iii. 40 + 90 + 8 iv. 4 + 90 + 8

c. If 38 students attended an Arts class on Monday and 39 students on Tuesday, how many students attended the class on both these days?

i. 77 ii. 78 iii. 79 iv. 80

d. A baker baked 150 loaves of bread and sold 128 loaves. How many loaves of bread were left unsold?

i. 25 ii. 28 iii. 50 iv. 22

e. $38 \times 5 =$

i. 180 ii. 190 iii. 380 iv. 390

f. Samik had 30 sweets. He distributed them equally in 6 packets. How many sweets did he put in each packet?

i. 3 ii. 4 iii. 5 iv. 6

g. In $24 \div 4 = 6$, the dividend is

i. 24 ii. 4 iii. 6 iv. 2

i. Which one of these shapes has no corner?

i. Circle ii. Triangle iii. Rectangle iv. Square

j. Which container has the largest capacity?

A

B

C

D

i. C ii. D iii. A iv. B

k. The time on the clock is

i. 7 o'clock

ii. 7:30

iii. 7:15

iv. 7:45

l. There are ________ months in a year.

i. 10 ii. 11 iii. 12 iv. 24

m. Philip wants to buy a book for ₹780. He has only ₹590 with him. How much more money does he need?

i. ₹180 ii. ₹290 iii. ₹280 iv. ₹190

n. If each  = 10 apples and the shopkeeper sold 

 apples on Monday, how many apples did he sell?

i. 50 ii. 60 iii. 70 iv. 80

o. What would be the next number in the pattern 60, 50, 40, 30, 20?

i. 20 ii. 10 iii. 30 iv. 40

2. Fill in the blanks.

a. 589 is _____ than 728.

b. 140 + 526 = _____

c. In $4 \times 8 = 32$, the multiplier is______, the multiplicand is _____ and the product is _____.

d. 25 apples are shared equally among 5 children. Each child gets ______ apples.

e. If yesterday was Monday, then today is __________.

3. State true or false.

a. Objects that look like a sphere have curved surface.

b. The distance from the tip of your little finger to the tip of your thumb makes a cubit.

c. The money used by a country is called its rupee.

d. Collection of information is called data.

e. A pattern is a repeated arrangement of shapes, numbers or letters.

1 Large Numbers

Prior Knowledge

- Numbers up to 999
- Place value and face value
- Ordering of numbers
- Forming numbers up to 3 digits

Learning Objectives

- 4- and 5-digit numbers
- Comparison of numbers
- Ascending and descending order
- Successor and predecessor
- Forming numbers out of given digits
- Even and odd numbers

Let's Get Started

A. Write the numbers shown on each abacus. How many digits do these numbers have?

i. ii. iii. iv. v.

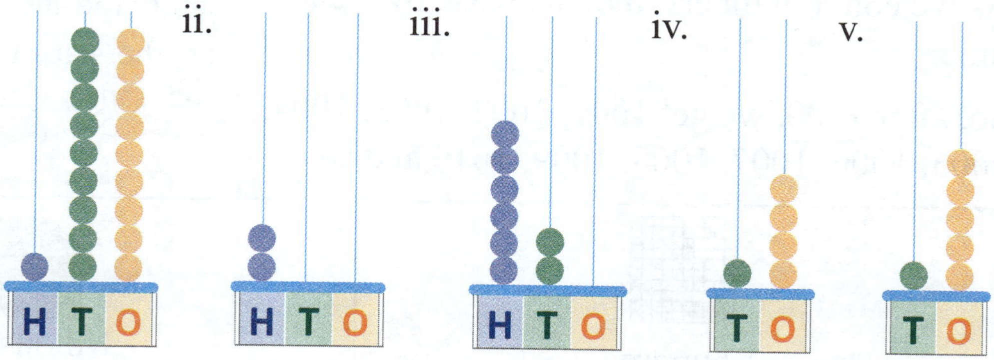

Number:

Number of digits:

B. Complete the table.

Numbers	Smallest	Greatest
1-digit numbers	0	
2-digit numbers		99
3-digit numbers		

Note that 1 more than the greatest 1-digit number is the smallest 2-digit number.

9 + 1 = 10

Greatest 1-digit number — Smallest 2-digit number

In the same way, 1 more than the greatest 2-digit number is the smallest 3-digit number.

4-DIGIT NUMBERS

We have learnt in the previous class that 999 is the greatest 3-digit number.

On adding 1 to it, we get a 4-digit number. 999 + 1 = 1000. Its number name is one thousand.

1000 is the smallest 4-digit number. It introduces the **thousands** period to us.

In 4-digit numbers, we use the following place values. Ten hundreds make 1 thousand.

Thousands	Hundreds	Tens	Ones
↓ Th	↓ H	↓ T	↓ O

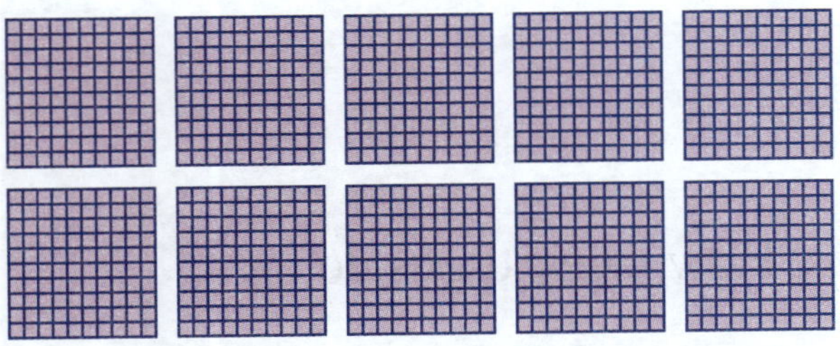

= 1000

As we count numbers, they increase by 1 each time.

So, after 1000, we get 1001, 1002, 1003, 1004, 1005, 1006, 1007, 1008, 1009, 1010 and so on.

REMEMBER

How many hundreds are there in one thousand?

Thousands	Hundreds	Tens	Ones
1	0	0	0
Th	**H**	**T**	**O**
1	0	0	0

Draw a line after hundreds. On the left of the line, we get 10.

So, there are 10 hundreds in one thousand.

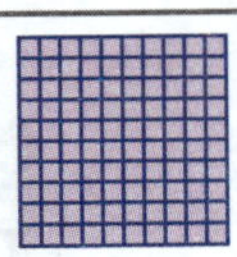 1 hundred	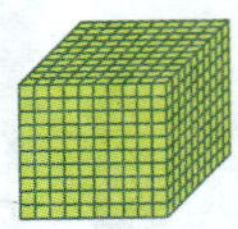 1 thousand
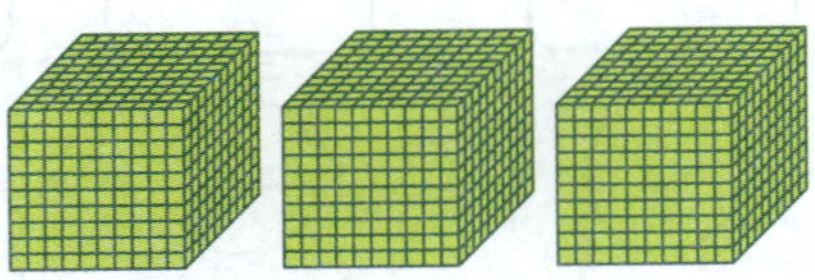 3 thousand	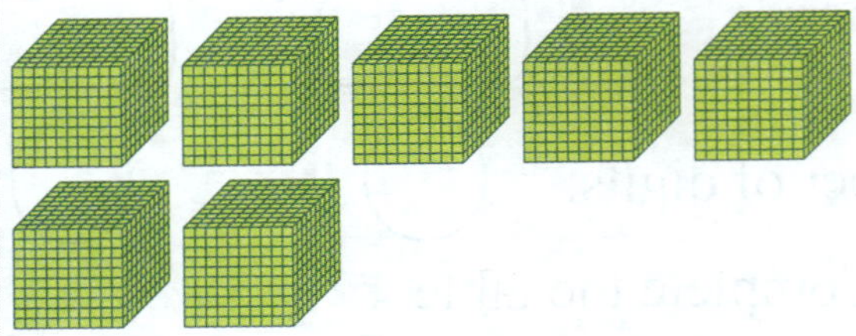 7 thousand
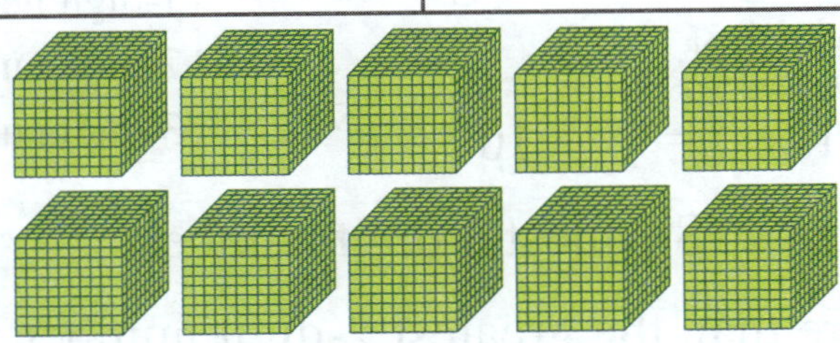 10 thousand	

Reading 4-digit Numbers

Consider a 4-digit number, 1563. To read a 4-digit number, read the thousands first, then hundreds and finally the number formed by the tens and ones digits.

TH	H	T	O
1	5	6	3

One thousand five hundred sixty-three

So, 1563 is read as one thousand five hundred sixty-three.

Similarly, the 4-digit number 5644 is read as five thousand six hundred forty-four.

Writing Numerals for Number Names

Consider the number name: five thousand two hundred eighty-one. The numeral for it is 5281.

Similarly, the numeral for the number name nine thousand one hundred thirty is 9130.

TH	H	T	O
5	2	8	1

Understanding 4-digit Numbers and Expanded Form

Example 1: Express 1254 in different ways. 1254 is a 4-digit number. It can be shown as given below.

Solution:

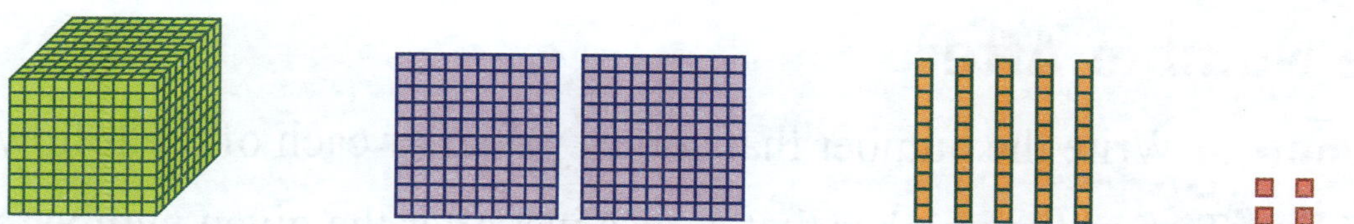

1 Thousand **2 Hundreds** **5 Tens** **4 Ones**

Abacus

Place Value Chart

TH	H	T	O
1	2	5	4

It can also be written as

Number name

One thousand two hundred fifty-four

Expanded form

1254 = <u>1</u> thousand <u>2</u> hundreds <u>5</u> tens <u>4</u> ones

or

1254 = 1000 + 200 + 50 + 4

REMEMBER

Once we put the number in the place value chart, we understand the number better.

Example 2: Express 4639 in different ways.

Solution: 4639 is a 4-digit number. It can be shown as follows.

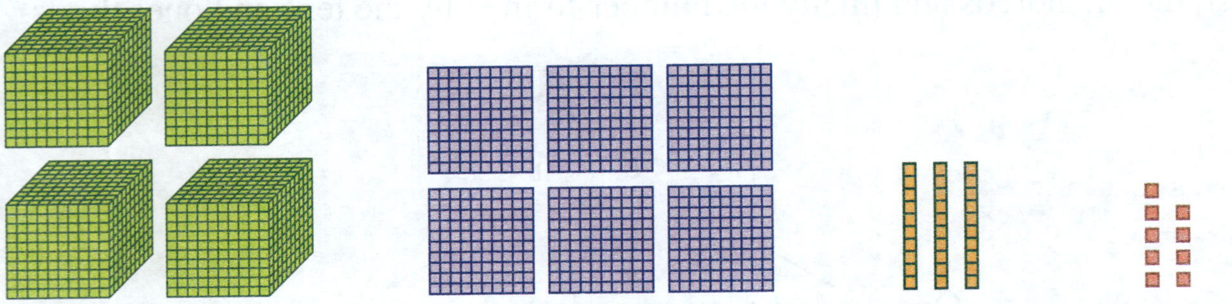

4 Thousands **6 Hundreds** **3 Tens** **9 Ones**

Abacus

Place Value Chart

TH	H	T	O
4	6	3	9

Number name

Four thousand six hundred thirty-nine

Expanded form

4 thousands 6 hundreds 3 tens 9 ones

or

4000 + 600 + 30 + 9

The Number After

Example 3: Write the number that comes just after each of the following.

Solution: To find the number that comes just after the given number, we add 1 to the given number.

a. 3485 3486 b. 6148 6149 c. 7259 7260

The Number Before

Example 4: Write the number that comes before each of the following.

Solution: To find the number that comes before the given number, we subtract 1 from the given number.

a. 3283 3284 b. 5195 5196 c. 8728 8729

Exercise 1.1

1. Write the answers for the following.

a. Write the number represented by the following.

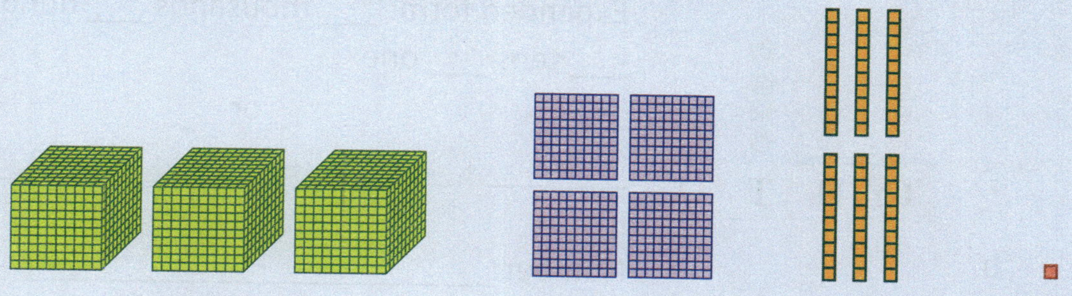

Thousands Hundreds Tens One

____

Represent the same number on the abacus.

For the same number, write the following.

Number name: ________________________

Expanded form: ___ thousands ___ hundreds ___ tens ___ one

or

________ + ________ + ________ + ________

b. Write the number represented by the following.

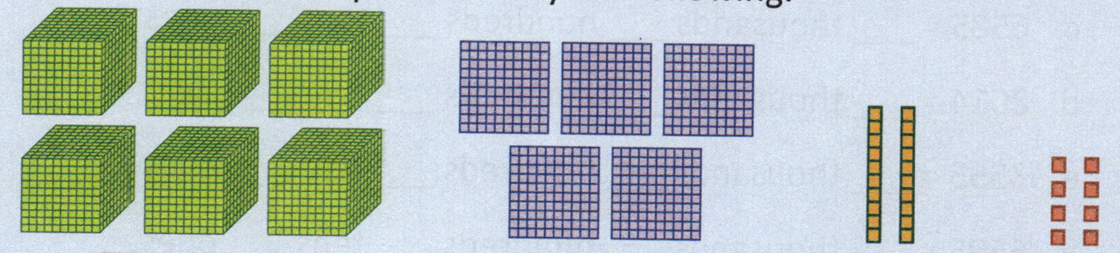

Thousands Hundreds Tens Ones

____

Represent the same number on the abacus.

For the same number, write the following.

Number name: ________________________

Expanded form: ___ thousands ___ hundreds ___ tens ___ ones

or

________ + ________ + ________ + ________

2. **Look at each abacus and write the answers.**

a.

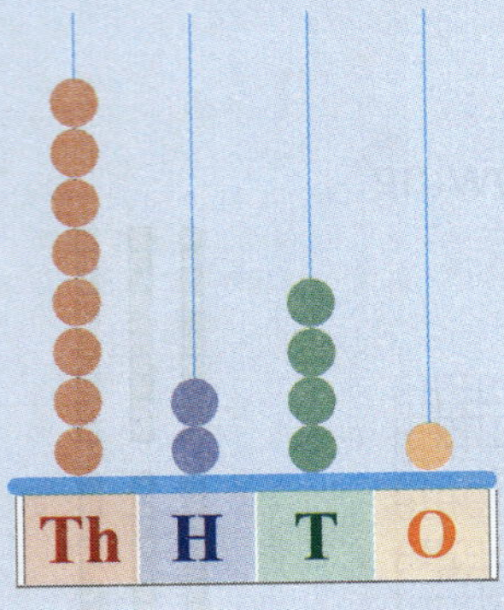

Number: ____________________

Number name: ____________________

Expanded form: ___ thousands ___ hundreds ___ tens ___ one

or

________ + ________ + ________ + ________

b.

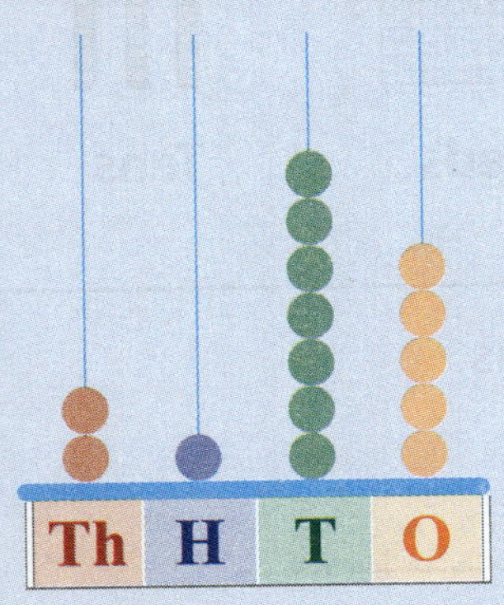

Number: ____________________

Number name: ____________________

Expanded form: ___ thousands ___ hundred ___ tens ___ ones

or

________ + ________ + ________ + ________

3. **Write the expanded form of the following numbers.**

a. 1464 = ___ thousands ___ hundreds ___ tens ___ ones

b. 3545 = ___ thousands ___ hundreds ___ tens ___ ones

c. 6585 = ___ thousands ___ hundreds ___ tens ___ ones

d. 8014 = ___ thousands ___ hundreds ___ ten ___ ones

e. 3555 = ___ thousands ___ hundreds ___ tens ___ ones

f. 6595 = ___ thousands ___ hundreds ___ tens ___ ones

g. 9769 = ___ thousands ___ hundreds ___ tens ___ ones

4. **Write the next four numbers for each of the following. One has been done for you.**

a. 1000, 1001, 1002, 1003, 1004

b. 1153, ________, ________, ________, ________

c. 2450, ________, ________, ________, ________

d. 7869, ________, ________, ________, ________

5. **Write the numerals for the following number names. One has been done for you.**

a. Two thousand four hundred seventeen 2417.

b. Nine thousand six hundred twenty ________.

c. One thousand five hundred seven ________.

d. Seven thousand twenty-eight ________.

6. **Write the number that comes just after each of the following.**

a. 2508 ________ b. 4185 ________ c. 6379 ________

7. **Write the number that comes just before each of the following.**

a. ________ 1845 b. ________ 7389 c. ________ 6120

5-DIGIT NUMBERS

The greatest 4-digit number is 9999. By adding 1 to it, we get the smallest 5-digit number.

9999 + 1 = 10,000

Its number name is ten thousand.

> In a 5-digit number, we put a comma after the third digit from the right.
>
> For example, 10,000, 20,000, 30,000 and so on.

In 5-digit numbers, we use one more place value, which is **ten thousands**.

Ten Thousands	Thousands	Hundreds	Tens	Ones
↓ TTh	↓ Th	↓ H	↓ T	↓ O

Given below are some number names from ten thousands.

Numeral	Number Name
10,000	Ten thousand
20,000	Twenty thousand
30,000	Thirty thousand
40,000	Forty thousand
50,000	Fifty thousand
60,000	Sixty thousand
70,000	Seventy thousand
80,000	Eighty thousand
90,000	Ninety thousand

Reading 5-digit Numbers

Consider the 5-digit number 59,726.

TTh	Th	H	T	O
5	9	7	2	6

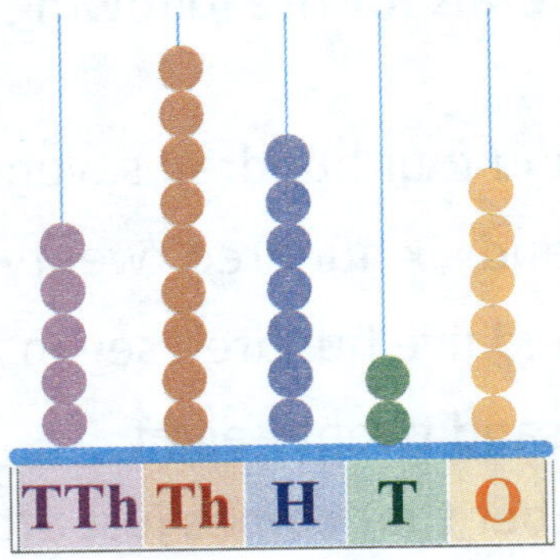

Club the digits of thousands and ten thousands places.

So, 59,726 is read as fifty-nine thousand seven hundred twenty-six.

Similarly, 12,001 is read as twelve thousand one. It is represented on abacus as shown alongside.

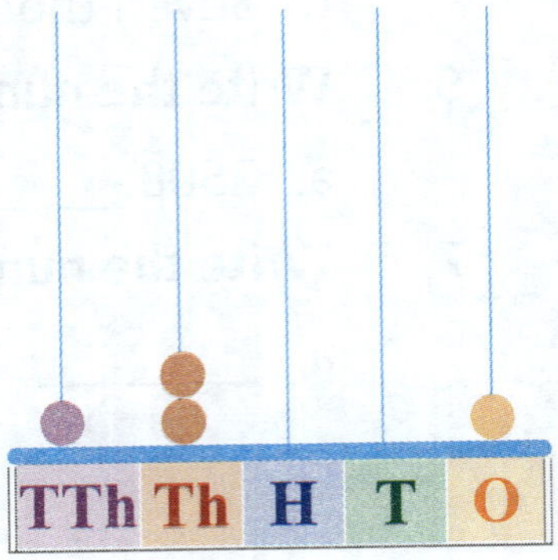

Writing Numerals for Number Names

Consider the number name: twenty-five thousand seven hundred eighty-two. The numeral for it is

TTh	Th	H	T	O
2	5	7	8	2

Similarly, the numeral for the number name eighty-two thousand four hundred twenty is 82,420.

PLACE VALUE AND FACE VALUE

The place value of a digit is the digit followed by as many zeros as the number of digits on the right side of the digit concerned in the number.

The face value of a digit is the digit itself.

Example 5: Find the place value and face value of each digit in

a. 7329 b. 34,872.

Solution: a. In 7329,

Place value of 7 = 7000 [Write the digit, 7 and then, write as many zeros as the number of digits after it.]

Face value of 7 = 7

Similarly, Place value of 3 = 300 Face value of 3 = 3

Place value of 2 = 20 Face value of 2 = 2

Place value of 9 = 9 Face value of 9 = 9

b. In 34,872

Place value of 3 = 30000 [Write 3, and then, write as many zeros after it as the number of digits after 3.]

Face value of 3 = 3 [The digit itself]

Similarly,

Place value of 4 = 4000 Face value of 4 = 4

Place value of 8 = 800 Face value of 8 = 8

Place value of 7 = 70 Face value of 7 = 7

Place value of 2 = 2 Face value of 2 = 2

COUNTING NUMBERS IN 10s, 100s AND 1000s

Counting Numbers in 10s

When we count numbers in 10s, we add 10 each time.

Example 6: Write the next four numbers by counting in 10s.

a. 5620 b. 17140

Solution:

+10 +10 +10 +10

a. 5620 5630 5640 5650 5660

+10 +10 +10 +10

b. 17140 17150 17160 17170 17180

Counting Numbers in 100s

When we count numbers in 100s, we add 100 each time.

Example 7: Write the next four numbers by counting in 100s.

a. 4370 b. 15291

Solution:

+100 +100 +100 +100

a. 4370 4470 4570 4670 4770

+100 +100 +100 +100

b. 15291 15391 15491 15591 15691

Counting Numbers in 1000s

When we count numbers in 1000s, we add 1000 each time.

Example 8: Write the next four numbers by counting in 1000s.

a. 2497   b. 25400

Solution:

a. 2497 →(+1000) 3497 →(+1000) 4497 →(+1000) 5497 →(+1000) 6497

b. 25400 →(+1000) 26400 →(+1000) 27400 →(+1000) 28400 →(+1000) 29400

Count and Write the Numbers in the Boxes:

Count in 10s	3589				
Count in 100s	3589				
Count in 1000s	3589				

Exercise 1.2

1. Draw beads to represent each number on the abacus.

a. 56,134

b. 10,267

2. Write the number names for the following numbers.

a. 12,847 ____________________

b. 29,354 ____________________

c. 35,461 ____________________

d. 46,007 ____________________

e. 58,209 ____________________

f. 20,203 ____________________

3. Write the numerals for the following number names.

a. Sixty-three thousand five hundred seventy-one ________

b. Thirty-four thousand twenty-nine ________

c. Eighty-seven thousand ________

d. Ninety-four thousand two hundred sixty ________

e. Seventy thousand four ________

f. Forty-four thousand four hundred forty-four ________

4. Write the next four numbers.

a. 4949, ________, ________, ________, ________

b. 3020, ________, ________, ________, ________

c. 7697, ________, ________, ________, ________

d. 20,000, ________, ________, ________, ________

e. 32,491, ________, ________, ________, ________

f. 53,042, ________, ________, ________, ________

5. Write the number that comes after each of the following.

a. 32,564 ______ b. 60,248 ______ c. 51,003 ______

6. Write the number that comes before each of the following.

a. ______ 43,715 b. ______ 72,628 c. ______ 51,009

7. Write the place values and face values of the underlined digits.

a. 6786 Place value = ______ Face value = ______

b. 16,379 Place value = ______ Face value = ______

c. 4629 Place value ______ Face value = ______

d. 1038 Place value ______ Face value = ______

e. 7650 Place value ______ Face value = ______

f. 9218 Place value = ______ Face value = ______

g. 5342 Place value ______ Face value = ______

h. 7160 Place value ______ Face value = ______

8. Fill in the blanks by counting in 10s.

a. 6320, ________, ________, ________, ________

b. 17,450, ________, ________, ________, ________

c. 45,657, ________, ________, ________, ________

9. Fill in the blanks by counting in 100s.

a. 3244, ________, ________, ________, ________

b. 48,530, ________, ________, ________, ________

c. 33,333, ________, ________, ________, ________

10. Fill in the blanks by counting in 1000s.

a. 3003, ________, ________, ________, ________

b. 4522, ________, ________, ________, ________

c. 75,099, ________, ________, ________,

COMPARISON OF NUMBERS

Comparing Numbers With Different Number of Digits

When we compare numbers with different number of digits, the number with more number of digits is greater.

REMEMBER

The symbol for 'greater than' is >.
The symbol for 'less than' is <.
The symbol for 'equal to' is =.

Example 9: Sunita has 2678 coins and Ekta has 12,345 coins. Who has more number of coins?

Solution: Here, 2678 is a 4-digit number, while 12,345 is a 5-digit number.

So, 12,345 > 2678.

Hence, Ekta has more number of coins.

Comparing Numbers With the Same Number of Digits

Comparing 4-digit Numbers

Let us learn to find whether a number is greater than, smaller than or equal to another number with the same number of digits. Look at some examples.

Example 10: Write >, < or =.

Solution:

a.

TH	H	T	O
5	9	4	2

______

TH	H	T	O
6	3	8	2

Check the digit in the thousands place. 5 < 6, so 5942 < 6382.

b.

TH	H	T	O
9	2	7	6

______

TH	H	T	O
9	1	8	0

First, check the digits in the thousands place. As both the digits are equal, check the digits in the hundreds place. 2 > 1, so 9276 > 9180.

c.

TH	H	T	O
6	7	5	3

______

TH	H	T	O
6	7	9	1

The digits in the thousands and the hundreds places in both the numbers are the same. So, check the digits in the tens place. Since 5 < 9, 6753 < 6791.

d.

TH	H	T	O
8	2	1	9

______

TH	H	T	O
8	2	1	7

The digits in the thousands, hundreds and tens places in both the numbers are same. So, check the digits in the ones place. Since 9 > 7, 8219 > 8217.

e.

TH	H	T	O
4	5	9	3

______

TH	H	T	O
4	5	9	3

The digits are exactly the same in both the numbers, so, 4593 = 4593.

Comparing 5-digit Numbers

To compare 5-digit numbers, we apply the same method used in comparing 4-digit numbers. First, check the digits in the ten thousands place. The number with the greater digit is greater.

If the digit in the ten thousands place is the same in the given numbers, then check the digits in the thousands place and so on.

Example 11: In one week, a food outlet sold 34,211 sandwiches and 34,121 burgers. Which food item was sold in more quantity?

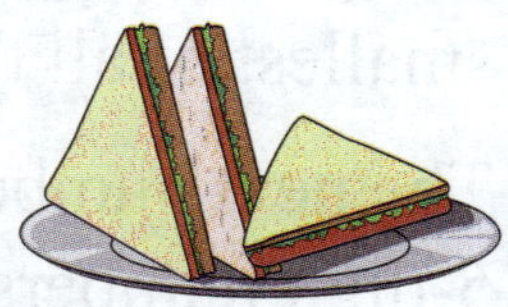

Solution: Let us compare 34,211 and 34,121.

Step 1: Check the digits at the ten thousands place of both the numbers. The digits are equal. So, move on to the thousands place.

Step 2: The digits at the thousands place are also the same. So, move on to the next digit.

Step 3: The digit at the hundreds place in 34,211 is 2 and that in 34,121 is 1. Since 2 > 1, 34,211 > 34,121.

Hence, sandwiches were sold in more quantity.

EXERCISE 1.3

1. Compare the following numbers and put the correct signs <, > or =.

a. 6131 ☐ 6313

b. 8702 ☐ 8761

c. 7878 ☐ 8787

d. 2002 ☐ 2066

e. 56,666 ☐ 5666

f. 9999 ☐ 99,999

2. Write >, < or =.

a. 5678 ☐ 5786

b. 3655 ☐ 4564

c. 45,567 ☐ 45,675

d. 11,112 ☐ 11,122

e. 65,776 ☐ 67,556

f. 56,129 ☐ 56,129

ASCENDING ORDER

Ascending order means arranging the numbers from the smallest to the greatest.

To write numbers in the ascending order, compare them and then write them from the smallest to the greatest.

Example 12: Write the following numbers in the ascending order.

3496 2719 53,281 14,789

Solution: We observe that there are two 4-digit and two 5-digit numbers. It is clear that the 4-digit numbers are smaller than both the 5-digit numbers. So, we compare the 4-digit numbers first. Since 2 < 3,we have 2719 < 3496. Hence, the smallest of all the given numbers is 2719.

The next number in the ascending order will be 3496. Now, we compare the 5-digit numbers. Since 1 < 5, we have 14,789 < 53,281. So, on arranging the numbers in the ascending order, we get:

2719 < 3496 < 14,789 < 53,281

DESCENDING ORDER

Descending order means arranging the numbers from the greatest to the smallest.

To write numbers in the descending order, compare them and then write them from the greatest to the smallest.

Example 13: Write the following numbers in the descending order.

12,397 8427 1738 66,249

Solution: There are two 4-digit and two 5-digit numbers. It is clear that 5-digit numbers are greater than 4-digit numbers. So, we compare the 5-digit numbers first.

Since 6 > 1, we have 66,249 > 12,397. Hence, the greatest of all the given numbers is 66,249. The next number in the descending order will be 12,397.

REMEMBER

	Smallest	Largest
1-digit number	1	9
2-digit number	10	99
3-digit number	100	999
4-digit number	1000	9999
5-digit number	10,000	99,999

Now, we compare the numbers with 4 digits. Since 8 > 1, we have 8427 > 1738. So, on arranging the numbers in the descending order, we get:

66,249 > 12,397 > 8427 > 1738

SUCCESSOR AND PREDECESSOR

Successor of a number is the number we get after adding 1 to the original number. **Predecessor** of a number is the number we get after subtracting 1 from the original number.

Example 14: Find the successor of 4298.

Solution: The successor of 4298 is

$$\begin{array}{r} 4298 \\ +\quad 1 \\ \hline 4299 \\ \hline \end{array}$$

Example 15: Find the predecessor of 32197.

Solution: The predecessor of 32197 is

$$\begin{array}{r} 32197 \\ -\quad 1 \\ \hline 32196 \\ \hline \end{array}$$

EXERCISE 1.4

1. **Circle the greatest number in each of the following.**

a. 3942	3973	8427	8489
b. 4928	9001	4998	9073
c. 39,281	39,273	39,879	35,729
d. 15,829	21,738	21,329	21,702

2. **Circle the smallest number in each of the following.**

a. 4392	4351	4359	4729
b. 6732	9183	9291	6987
c. 48,403	48,399	48,058	48,287
d. 65,394	67,729	65,418	67,412

3. **Rewrite the following numbers in the ascending order.**

a. 2407	6138	1890	1987
b. 4989	8273	10,729	3462
c. 71,103	61,812	2304	9001
d. 16,294	11,832	5038	4279

4. **Rewrite the following numbers in the descending order.**

a. 7008	7801	4612	6298
b. 5293	18,824	7963	8451
c. 99,621	59,819	22,793	61,723
d. 98,173	98,035	98,461	4920

5. **Write the successor of the following.**

a. 2890 b. 4019 c. 45,091

d. 9999 e. 99,991

6. **Write the predecessor of the following.**

a. 4000 b. 7999 c. 10,090

d. 89,001 e. 10,000

FORMATION OF NUMBERS

We can form different numbers with the given digits by arranging them in different places. To make a new number from the existing, just shift the places of digits.

There are two conditions under which numbers can be formed: without repetition of digits and with repetition of digits.

Formation of Numbers Without Repetition of Digits

In this case, we have to use the given digits only once and form the number.

> **REMEMBER**
>
> To form the greatest number, arrange the digits in the descending order.
>
> To form the smallest number, arrange the digits in the ascending order.

To make the largest number from a given number of digits, keep the largest digit at the highest place, keep the second largest digit at the second highest place and so on.

To make the smallest number from a given number of digits, keep the smallest digit at the highest place, keep the second smallest digit at the second highest place and so on.

Example 16: Form the greatest 4-digit number using the digits 2, 6, 5 and 3.

Solution: To form the greatest 4-digit number, arrange the digits in the descending order.

$6 > 5 > 3 > 2$

Therefore, the greatest 5-digit number formed is 6532.

Example 17: Form the smallest 5-digit number using the digits 2, 8, 4, 9 and 1.

Solution: To form the smallest 5-digit number, arrange the digits in the ascending order.

$1 < 2 < 4 < 8 < 9$

Therefore, the smallest 5-digit number formed is 12,489.

Example 18: Form the smallest 5-digit number using the digits 7, 9, 3, 0 and 6.

Solution: If there is 0 among the given digits, never put it in the highest place. Always put 0 in the second highest place.

So, using digits 7, 9, 3, 0 and 6, the smallest possible 5-digit number will be 30,679.

Formation of Numbers With Repetition of Digits

In this case, we can use the given digits as per the repetition rule provided in the problem and form the number.

Example 19: Form the greatest possible 4-digit number using the digits 5, 8, 1 assuming that any one of the digits can be repeated once.

Solution: As we have to form the greatest possible number, we will repeat the largest digit, 8. Put 8 in the highest place, and 8 again in the second highest place. Then, put the next smallest digit (5) in the next place. Finally, put the smallest digit (1) at the end.

The greatest possible 4-digit number formed is 8851.

Example 20: Write the smallest 4-digit number that can be formed by the digits 3, 1, 6, repeating 3 once.

Solution: We need to form the smallest number. So, put 1 (smallest of the given digits) at the highest place. Put the next smallest digit, that is 3 in the next place. Repeat the digit 3 in the next place again. Put the greatest digit, that is, 6 at the end.

The smallest 4-digit number formed is 1336.

EVEN AND ODD NUMBERS

Even numbers are numbers that can be arranged in pairs, without leaving any object unpaired. Numbers that end with 0, 2, 4, 6 or 8 are even numbers. For example, 8, 28, 364 and 2456 are even numbers.

Odd numbers are numbers that cannot be paired completely. In case of odd numbers, one object will always remain unpaired.

Numbers that end with 1, 3, 5, 7 or 9 are odd numbers. For example, 21, 85, 789 and 3457 are odd numbers.

EXERCISE 1.5

1. Write the greatest and the smallest numbers formed by the given digits.

	Greatest	Smallest
a. 2, 4, 8, 1	________	________
b. 1, 5, 6, 2	________	________
c. 4, 2, 3, 8, 1	________	________
d. 9, 5, 7, 3, 2	________	________
e. 8, 2, 1, 6, 0	________	________
f 2, 5, 0, 8	________	________
g. 7, 3, 9, 0	________	________
h. 6, 0, 1, 4, 5	________	________
i. 2, 9, 3, 7, 8	________	________
j. 6, 5, 0, 9, 1	________	________

2. Form the numbers as indicated.

a. The smallest 4-digit number with digits 2, 3, 7, repeating 2 once. ______

b. The largest 4-digit number using digits 9, 2, 5, repeating 5 once. ______

c. The largest 4-digit number with digits 2, 3, 7 repeating 2 once. ______

d. The smallest 4-digit number using digits 9, 2, 5 repeating 5 once. ______

e. The smallest 4-digit number using digits 8, 6, 1 repeating 6 once. ______

f. The smallest 4-digit number using digits 2, 5, 7 repeating 7 once. ______

g. The largest 4-digit number using digits 5, 8, 0 repeating 8 once. ______

3. Circle the even numbers and tick the odd numbers.

12 40 1278 4 5 9 27

7389 236 10 8 51 593

4. State True or False.

a. The smallest 2-digit number is even. ________

b. The largest 3-digit number is odd. ________

c. The smallest 4-digit number is odd. ________

d. The largest 2-digit number is 90. ________

e. 2200 is an even number. ________

f. The successor of 99 is an odd number. ________

g. The predecessor of 1000 is an odd number. ________

5. **Write the greatest and the smallest 4-digit numbers using the given digits, if repetition of digits is allowed.**

	Digits	Greatest Number	Smallest Number
a.	5, 8, 9	________	________
b.	2, 7, 3	________	________
c.	1, 0, 8	________	________
d.	4, 9, 6	________	________
e.	2, 5, 3	________	________
f.	7, 1, 8	________	________
g.	6, 0, 9	________	________
h.	1, 5, 0	________	________
i.	4, 3, 2	________	________
j.	8, 0, 7	________	________

Key Concepts

Large Numbers

Read and write 4- and 5-digit numbers

Even numbers: 246, 6530
Odd numbers: 245, 6531

Place Value: The value indicating the position or place of a digit in a number
Face Value: The number itself

Expressions:
- Number names
- Numerals
- Expanded form

Comparing numbers
- greatest and smallest numbers
- ascending and descending order

- Successor: The next number
- Predecessor: The previous number

Revision Exercise

1. Write the number represented by the following.

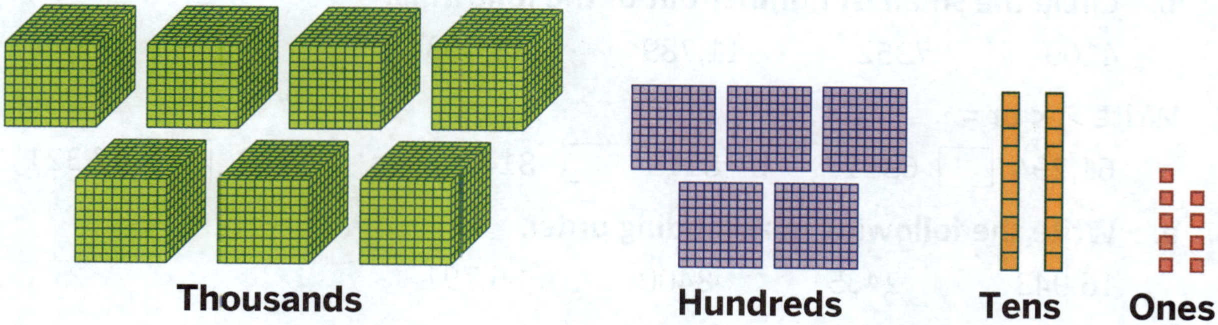

____

Show the same number on the abacus given alongside.

For the same number, write the following.

Number name: ____________________________________

Expanded form: ____ thousands ____ hundreds ____ tens ____ ones

or

__________ + __________ + __________ + __________

2. Represent the following number on the abacus.

56,785

3. Write the next four numbers.

a. 7234, __________, __________, __________, __________

b. 2309, __________, __________, __________, __________

c. 8798, __________, __________, __________, __________

d. 45,675, __________, __________, __________, __________

4. Write the number names for the following.

a. 6324 ____.

b. 18,109 ____.

5. Write the numerals for the following number names.

a. Eight thousand twelve __________

b. Fifty thousand three __________

6. a. **Circle the greatest number out of the following.**

13,219 7304 9012 5798

b. **Circle the smallest number out of the following.**

4109 7352 11,789 48,003

7. **Write >, < or =.**

a. 61,294 ☐ 6351 b. 8113 ☐ 8142 c. 17,320 ☐ 17,321

8. a. **Write the following in ascending order.**

16,943 2435 8400 65,791

__________, __________, __________, __________

b. **Write the following in descending order.**

11,059 9213 8340 11,269

__________, __________, __________, __________

9. **In 15,297,**

a. the place value of 5 is __________.

b. the face value of 9 is __________.

10. **Fill in the blanks.**

a. The successor of 2358 is __________.

b. The predecessor of 15,967 is __________.

c. The largest even 3-digit number is __________.

11. **Write the next four numbers counting in 10s.**

5440, __________, __________, __________, __________

12. **Write the next four numbers counting in 100s.**

2594, __________, __________, __________, __________

13. **Write the next four numbers counting in 1000s.**

2242, __________, __________, __________, __________

14. **Circle the even numbers and tick the odd numbers.**

22 2 516 12,489

2049 39 9370 9387 9999

14

340 1093 875

5522 1078

2 Addition

Prior Knowledge

- Properties of addition
- Adding 2-digit numbers with and without regrouping
- Adding 1-, 2- or 3-digit numbers with 3-digit numbers without regrouping
- Solving daily-life problems on addition
- Estimating the sum of given numbers

Learning Objectives

- Addition of 3-digit numbers with regrouping
- Addition of 4-digit numbers without and with regrouping
- Addition of 5-digit numbers without and with regrouping
- Word problems on addition
- Estimation of the sum

Let's Get Started

Look at the flowers and the number each represents. Replace the flowers with numbers and solve the sums given below.

 = 54  = 16  = 11

a.  +  =

b.  +  =

c.  +  =

d.  +  =

e.  +  +  =

f.  +  +  =

ADDITION OF 3-DIGIT NUMBERS WITHOUT REGROUPING

Addition of 3-digit numbers is done in the same way as addition of 2-digit numbers.

Example 1: Add 326 and 431.

Solution:

	H	T	O
	3	2	6
+	4	3	1
	7	5	7

Thus, 326 + 431 = 757.

Example 2: Add 213, 504 and 182.

Solution:

	H	T	O
	2	1	3
	5	0	4
+	1	8	2
	8	9	9

REMEMBER

- When we add 0 to a number, the value of the number does not change.
  For example:
  381 + 0 = 381
- When we add 1 to a number, the answer is 1 more than the number.
  For example:
  234 + 1 = 235
- In addition, we can add the numbers in any order. The order does not affect the answer.
  For example:
  496 + 5 = 5 + 496

EXERCISE 2.1

Add the following numbers.

1.

	H	T	O
	8	5	4
+	1	4	3

2.

	H	T	O
	7	2	3
+	1	6	4

3.

	H	T	O
	3	6	2
+	2	1	5

4.

	H	T	O
	2	4	9
+	4	5	0

5.

	H	T	O
	6	1	3
+	3	8	6

6.

	H	T	O
	5	5	5
+	4	0	4

7.

	H	T	O
	1	2	3
	3	0	4
+	1	5	1

8.

	H	T	O
	6	3	5
	1	4	2
+	2	1	0

9.

	H	T	O
	2	5	7
	3	0	0
+	1	2	1

10.

	H	T	O
	3	4	6
	2	1	2
+	3	1	0

11.

	H	T	O
	5	0	2
	1	7	3
+	1	2	4

12.

	H	T	O
	3	6	9
	1	0	0
+	2	0	0

13.

	H	T	O
	2	1	2
	1	3	3
+	3	0	3

14.

	H	T	O
	6	0	2
	1	1	2
+	2	1	2

15.

	H	T	O
	5	5	5
	1	2	3
+	3	2	1

16.

	H	T	O
	3	4	5
	4	2	1
+	2	1	2

17.

	H	T	O
	6	7	2
	1	0	3
+	1	2	1

18.

	H	T	O
	5	1	4
	1	2	1
+	2	3	0

ADDITION OF 3-DIGIT NUMBERS WITH REGROUPING FROM ONES TO TENS

Let us now learn how to add 3-digit numbers with carrying from ones to tens to hundreds.

Example 3: Add 657 and 128.

Solution:

	H	T	O
	6	[1]5	7
+	1	2	8
	7	8	5

Step 1: Add the digits in the ones column.

7 + 8 = 15.

Write '5' of 15 in the ones column and carry forward 1. Place this 1 above 5 in the tens column.

Step 2: Now, add the digits in the tens column.

5 + 2 + 1 = 8.

Place this 8 under 2 in the tens column.

Step 3: Next, add the digits in the hundreds column.

6 + 1 = 7.

Write 7 under 1 in the hundreds column.

Thus, 657 + 128 = 785.

Example 4: Add 356, 123 and 215.

Solution:

	H	T	O
	3	[1]5	6
	1	2	3
+	2	1	5
	6	9	4

Step 1: Add all the digits in the ones column.

6 + 3 + 5 = 14.

Write '4' of 14 under 5 in the ones column and carry forward 1. Place this 1 above 5 in the tens column.

Step 2: Now, add all the digits in the tens column.

1 + 5 + 2 + 1 = 9.

Place this 9 under 1 in the tens column.

Step 3: Next, add all the digits in the hundreds column.

3 + 1 + 2 = 6.

Write 6 under 2 in the hundreds column.

Thus, 356 + 123 + 215 = 694.

Exercise 2.2

Add the following.

1.

	H	T	O
	2	4	3
+	1	2	7

2.

	H	T	O
	4	3	5
+	2	1	9

3.

	H	T	O
	5	4	6
+	1	0	5

4.

	H	T	O
	6	2	7
+	1	3	5

5.

	H	T	O
	7	1	3
+	1	3	9

6.

	H	T	O
	2	3	9
+	1	0	6

7.

	H	T	O
	1	4	6
	2	3	2
+	4	1	7

8.

	H	T	O
	5	1	4
	1	3	8
+	2	4	1

9.

	H	T	O
	3	6	8
	2	0	8
+	1	1	2

10.

	H	T	O
	4	5	3
	1	2	6
+		1	5

11.

	H	T	O
	3	2	7
	2	4	3
+		1	6

12.

	H	T	O
	6	2	8
	2	5	4
+		1	2

ADDITION OF 3-DIGIT NUMBERS WITH REGROUPING FROM ONES TO TENS TO HUNDREDS

Let us now learn how to add 3-digit numbers with carrying from ones to tens.

Example 5: Add 657 and 168.

Solution:

	H	T	O
	$^{1}6$	$^{1}5$	7
+	1	6	8
	8	2	5

Step 1: Add the digits in the ones column.

7 + 8 = 15.

Write '5' of 15 in the ones column and carry forward 1 to tens column.

Step 2: Add the digits in the tens column.

5 + 6 + 1 = 12.

Write '2' of 12 in the tens column and carry forward 1 to hundreds column.

Step 3: Add the digits in the hundreds column.

6 + 1 + 1 = 8

Thus, 657 + 168 = 825.

Example 6: Add 346, 175 and 324.

Solution:

	H	T	O
	$^{1}3$	$^{1}4$	6
	1	7	5
+	3	2	4
	8	4	5

Step 1: Add all the digits in the ones column.

6 + 5 + 4 = 15.

Write '5' of 15 in the ones column and carry forward the '1' of 15. Place this 1 on top of 4 in the tens column.

Step 2: Now, add all the digits in the tens column.

1 + 4 + 7 + 2 = 14.

Write '4' of 14 in the tens column below 2 and carry forward the '1' of 14 on to the hundreds column.

Step 3: Now, add all the digits in the hundreds column.

1 + 3 + 1 + 3 = 8.

Write 8 in the hundreds column under 3.

Thus, 346 + 175 + 324 = 845.

Example 7: Add 246, 153 and 375.

Solution:

	H	T	O
	[1]2	[1]4	6
	1	5	3
+	3	7	5
	7	7	4

Thus, 246 + 153 + 375 = 774.

Example 8: Add 458, 263 and 158.

Solution:

	H	T	O
	[1]4	[1]5	8
	2	6	3
+	1	5	8
	8	7	9

Thus, 458 + 263 + 158 = 879.

EXERCISE 2.3

Add the following.

1.

	H	T	O
	3	4	5
+	2	7	6

2.

	H	T	O
	4	8	7
+	2	8	5

3.

	H	T	O
	1	8	7
+	2	4	7

4.

	H	T	O
	3	8	9
+	1	5	3

5.

	H	T	O
	5	6	8
+	2	4	5

6.

	H	T	O
	4	6	7
+	1	5	3

7.

	H	T	O
	7	8	4
	1	2	6
+		5	3

8.

	H	T	O
	3	7	5
	4	1	6
+		3	2

9.

	H	T	O
	2	6	8
	5	1	2
+		3	7

10.

	H	T	O
	4	7	6
	1	2	3
+	2	5	4

11.

	H	T	O
	3	6	7
	2	4	3
+	1	8	7

12.

	H	T	O
	5	4	6
	2	7	5
+	1	3	2

13.

	H	T	O
	4	7	3
	2	3	2
+	1	5	1

14.

	H	T	O
	2	6	4
	3	5	0
+	1	3	5

15.

	H	T	O
	1	7	2
	3	5	4
+	2	3	1

ADDING 4-DIGIT NUMBERS WITHOUT REGROUPING

4-digit numbers are added in the same way as 3-digit numbers.

We put one more column, that is the thousands (Th) column on the left of the hundreds (H) column.

Example 9: Find the following sums.

a. 4568 + 321

Solution:

	Th	H	T	O
	4	5	6	8
+		3	2	1
	4	8	8	9

Answer: 4889

b. 6234 + 2523

Solution:

	Th	H	T	O
	6	2	3	4
+	2	5	2	3
	8	7	5	7

Answer: 8757

c. 1324 + 2150 + 6423

Solution:

	Th	H	T	O
	1	3	2	4
	2	1	5	0
+	6	4	2	3
	9	8	9	7

Answer: 9897

ADDING 4-DIGIT NUMBERS WITH REGROUPING

We have already learnt to add 2-digit and 3-digit numbers with regrouping. We use the same method to add 4-digit numbers.

Example 10: 2563 + 1758 + 3916

Solution:

	Th	H	T	O
	2	1	1	
	2	5	6	3
	1	7	8	5
+	3	9	1	6
	8	2	6	4

Write the numbers vertically and add the digits.

Ones column: 3 + 5 + 6 = 14

Carry forward 1 to the tens column.

Tens column: 6 + 8 + 1 + 1 (carried forward) = 16

Carry forward 1 to the hundreds column.

Hundreds column: 5 + 7 + 9 + 1 (carried forward) = 22

Carry forward 2 to the thousands column.

Thousands column:

2 + 1 + 3 + 2 (carried forward) = 8

Thus, 2563 + 1785 + 3916 = 8264.

EXERCISE 2.4

Add the following.

1.

	Th	H	T	O
	2	1	0	3
+	3	5	7	2

2.

	Th	H	T	O
	6	7	4	5
+	1	1	2	3

3.

	Th	H	T	O
	4	7	8	0
+		2	1	9

4.

	Th	H	T	O
	1	5	3	0
	3	1	4	2
+	2	0	1	7

5.

	Th	H	T	O
	2	2	9	4
	1	3	0	1
+		2	0	4

6.

	Th	H	T	O
	2	8	3	4
	1	0	6	1
+	1	1	0	3

7.

	Th	H	T	O
	2	5	8	4
+	6	0	1	4

8.

	Th	H	T	O
	3	7	5	6
+	2	2	9	8

9.

	Th	H	T	O
	1	5	7	9
	2	4	8	6
+	1	3	6	5

10.

	Th	H	T	O
	1	9	3	6
	2	0	5	4
+	3	7	2	8

ADDITION OF TWO 5-DIGIT NUMBERS WITHOUT REGROUPING

Let us add two 5-digit numbers, 54435 and 12462, without carry forward.

		TTh	Th	H	T	O
Addend →		5	4	4	3	5
Addend →	+	1	2	4	6	2
Sum →		6	6	8	9	7

The number obtained after the addition of these two numbers, that is the sum is 66897.

ADDITION OF TWO 5-DIGIT NUMBERS WITH REGROUPING

Here, we use the same method as above. However, in this case, we carry forward numbers to the next higher place value, wherever required.

Let us add two 5-digit numbers, 64935 and 18462, with carry forward. Add the digits at each place value (O/T/H/Th/TTh) and regroup, if required. Carry forward to the next higher place value.

	TTh	Th	H	T	O
	1	1			
Addend →	6	4	9	3	5
Addend → +	1	8	4	6	2
Sum →	8	3	3	9	7

The number obtained after the addition of these two numbers, that is the sum is 83397.

EXERCISE 2.5

Add the following.

1.

	TTh	Th	H	T	O
	5	3	4	2	9
+	2	9	8	7	6

2.

	TTh	Th	H	T	O
	5	4	1	7	6
+	2	3	5	2	3

3.

	TTh	Th	H	T	O
	2	4	6	0	1
+	5	1	2	4	5

4.

	TTh	Th	H	T	O
	4	4	9	3	5
+	2	3	5	2	3

5. 32107 + 29416 + 3852 = ____________________
6. 63152 + 25103 + 4318 + 294 = ____________________
7. 97813 + 15347 + 37425 + 1820 = ____________________

WORD PROBLEMS ON ADDITION

In word problems, when a number is to increase by another given number, we add. We also add when we have to find the sum or the total of the given quantities.

Example 11: Amit has 256 red marbles and 135 blue marbles. What is the total number of marbles that Amit has?

Solution:

		H	T	O
Red marbles =		2	$^{1}5$	6
Blue marbles =	+	1	3	5
		3	9	1

Thus, Amit has 391 marbles in total.

REMEMBER

Look out for addition words in any problems. The keywords can give a clue for how to solve the problem.
Addition Words:
Add, total, altogether, sum, plus, more than, increase

Example 12: In a town, there are 357 red cars and 164 blue cars. How many red and blue cars are there in the town?

Solution:

		H	T	O
Red cars =		$^{1}3$	$^{1}5$	7
Blue cars =	+	1	6	4
		5	2	1

Thus, there are 521 red and blue cars in the town.

Example 13: An ice cream vendor sold 165 ice creams on Friday, 287 ice creams on Saturday and 345 ice creams on Sunday. How many ice creams did he sell in these three days?

Solution:

		H	T	O
Friday =		$^{1}1$	$^{1}6$	5
Saturday =	+	2	8	7
Sunday =		3	4	5
		7	9	7

Thus, the vendor sold 797 ice creams in three days.

Example 14: A poultry farm had 173 ducks and 614 hens. How many total birds are there in the farm?

Solution:

		H	T	O
Number of ducks =		1	7	3
Number of hens =	+	6	1	4
		7	8	7

Thus, there are a total of 787 birds in the farm.

Example 15: Sumit saved ₹5400 in January, ₹2900 in February and ₹6750 in March. What was the total amount of money he saved?

Solution:

			TTh	Th	H	T	O
In January, he saved = 5400		₹		$^{2}5$	4	0	0
In February, he saved = 2900		₹		2	9	0	0
In March, he saved = 6750	+	₹		6	7	5	0
		₹	1	5	0	5	0

The total amount saved by Sumit was ₹15,050.

EXERCISE 2.6

1. **163 people went to a movie hall on Saturday and 425 people went to the movie hall on Sunday. How many people went to the movie hall on Saturday and Sunday?**

		H	T	O
Saturday =				
Sunday =	+			

Thus, ______ people went to the movie hall on Saturday and Sunday.

2. **Priyanka has ₹578. Her mother gives her ₹152 more. How much money does Priyanka have now?**

Money Priyanka had = ₹

Money her mother gave = + ₹

H	T	O

Thus, Priyanka has ₹ ______ now.

3. **In a school, the number of students in Class 1 is 140, in Class 2 is 130 and in Class 3 is 120. What is the total number of students in the three classes?**

Class 1 =

Class 2 =

Class 3 =

+

H	T	O

Thus, there are ______ students in the three classes.

4. **An ice cream vendor sold 276 ice creams on Friday, 235 ice creams on Saturday and 324 ice creams on Sunday. What is the total number of ice creams he sold in these three days?**

Friday =

Saturday =

Sunday =

+

H	T	O

Thus, he sold ______ ice creams in these three days.

5. **629 children come to a school in school bus. 258 children come by car. What is the total number of children who come to school by school bus and car?**

School bus =

Car = +

H	T	O

Thus, ______ children come to the school by school bus and car.

6. **325 children went for a picnic on Monday and 243 children went on Tuesday. How many children went for the picnic in these two days?**

Monday =

Tuesday = +

H	T	O

Thus, ______ children went for the picnic in these two days.

7. **A toy mobile phone costs ₹450 and another phone costs ₹540. How much money Nitin needs to pay in total to buy the two phones?**

Cost of one toy phone = ₹

Cost of another toy phone = + ₹

H	T	O

Thus, Nitin needs to pay ₹ __________ in total.

8. **In one day, a train carried 664 passengers in its first trip and 312 passengers in its second trip. How many total passengers did the train carry on that day?**

Number of passengers in the first trip =

Number of passengers in the second trip =

	H	T	O
+			

Thus, the train carried ____________ passengers in all on that day.

9. **Sanjay put 139 red balloons and 220 blue balloons for his birthday party. What is the total number of balloons he put?**

Red balloons ________ Blue balloons ________

The total number of balloons he put is ________.

10. **A mother elephant weighs 4365 kg and her baby elephant weighs 1012 kg. How much do they weigh together?**

Mother elephant weighs =

Baby elephant weighs =

	Th	H	T	O
+				

Thus, they weigh ______ kg together.

ESTIMATION OF SUM

We do estimation when we do not give an actual value but guess a value close to the actual value. Estimation makes our calculations faster and easier. For example, if a T-shirt costs ₹395, we can say that it costs about ₹400.

We can round off the value of an item to the nearest 100 or 1000. Rounding off is a kind of estimation.

Rounding Off to the Nearest 10

For rounding off a number to the nearest 10, look at the **ones** digit.

- If the ones digit is **0, 1, 2, 3** or **4**—keep the tens digit as it is and replace the ones digit by 0.
- If the ones digit is **5, 6, 7, 8** or **9**—increase the tens digit by 1 and replace the ones digit by 0.

Rounding Off to the Nearest 100

For rounding off a number to the nearest 100, look at the **tens** digit.

- If the tens digit is **0, 1, 2, 3** or **4**—keep the hundreds digit as it is and replace the tens and ones digits with 0.
- If the tens digit is **5, 6, 7, 8** or **9**—increase the hundreds digit by 1 and replace the tens and ones digits with 0.

Rounding Off to the Nearest 1000

For rounding off a number to the nearest 1000, look at the **hundreds** digit.

- If the hundreds digit is **0, 1, 2, 3** or **4**—keep the thousands digit as it is and replace the hundreds, tens and ones digits with 0.
- If the hundreds digit is **5, 6, 7, 8** or **9**—increase the thousands digit by 1 and replace the hundreds, tens and ones digits with 0.

Example 16: Round off the following numbers as indicated.

To the nearest 10:

a. 26 b. 126 c. 362 d. 1257

To the nearest 100:

e. 330 f. 790 g. 4266 h. 6679

To the nearest 1000:

i. 1440 j. 2590 k. 5600 l. 3821

Solution:

Rounding off to nearest 10: a. 26 is rounded off to 30. (6 in the ones place)

b. 126 is rounded off to 130. (6 in the ones place)

c. 362 is rounded off to 360. (2 in the ones place)

d. 1257 is rounded off to 1260. (7 in the ones place)

Rounding off to nearest 100: e. 330 is rounded off to 300. (3 in the tens place)

f. 790 is rounded off to 800. (9 in the tens place)

g. 4266 is rounded off to 4300. (6 in the tens place)

h. 6679 is rounded off to 6700. (7 in the tens place)

Rounding off to nearest 1000: i. 1440 is rounded off to 1000. (4 in the hundreds place)

j. 2590 is rounded off to 3000. (5 in the hundreds place)

k. 5600 is rounded off to 6000. (6 in the hundreds place)

l. 3821 is rounded off to 4000. (8 in the hundreds place)

Estimating the Sum of Two Numbers

Example 17: Estimate the sum of 281 and 111 to the nearest hundred.

Solution:

281 is rounded off to 300. 111 is rounded off to 100.

So, the estimated sum is 300 + 100 = 400.

Let us verify the sum by adding the two numbers. 281 + 111 = 392

So, the actual answer is 392 and our estimated answer is 400, which is very close.

Example 18: Estimate the following sum to the nearest 100 and then to the nearest 1000.

1440 + 2590 + 1225 + 3365

Solution:

Rounding off to the nearest 100, we get

1400 + 2600 + 1200 + 3400

Thus, the estimate of the sum = 8600

Rounding off to the nearest 1000, we get

1000 + 3000 + 1000 + 3000

Thus, the estimate of the sum = 8000

Exercise 2.7

1. **Round off the following numbers to the nearest 10.**
   a. 36 b. 226 c. 462 d. 5257
2. **Round off the following numbers to the nearest 100.**
   a. 430 b. 890 c. 3266 d. 7779
3. **Round off the following numbers to the nearest 1000.**
   a. 2740 b. 3490 c. 8600 d. 5801
4. **Find the estimated sum by rounding off the numbers to the nearest 100. Verify your answers by actual addition.**
   a. 191 + 208 b. 211 + 170 c. 490 + 157
   d. 625 + 397 e. 190 + 782 f. 242 + 170
5. **Estimate the following sum to the nearest 10.**
   a. 36 + 226 + 5250 b. 430 + 3256 + 7709 c. 592 + 106 + 9506
6. **Estimate the following sum to the nearest 100.**
   a. 1464 + 3966 + 2468 b. 8014 + 3555 + 1016 c. 3545 + 2550 + 6462
7. **Estimate the following sum to the nearest 1000.**
   a. 2740 + 8600 + 5801 b. 9593 + 2816 + 7532 c. 6734 + 3815 + 1620

Key Concepts

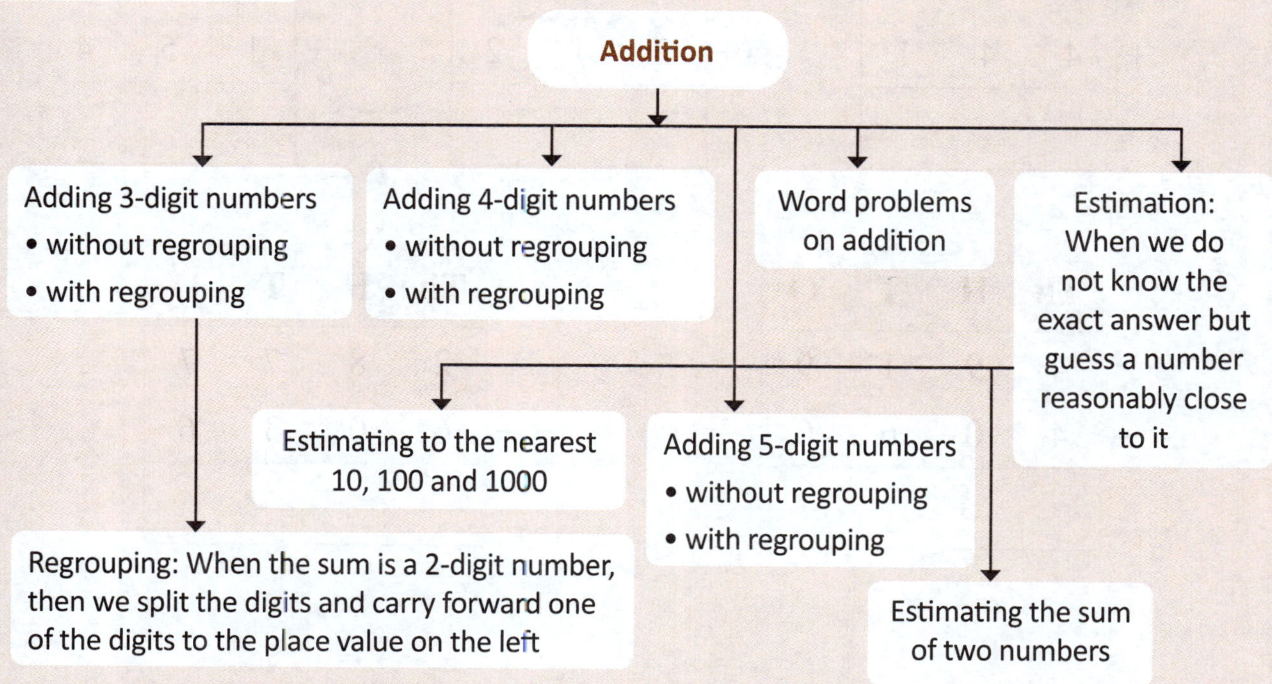

Revision Exercise

1. Add the following.

a.

	H	T	O
	5	4	1
+	2	1	7

b.

	H	T	O
	3	6	2
+	1	1	5

c.

	H	T	O
	6	1	1
+	1	2	0

d.

	H	T	O
	4	2	3
	3	0	4
+	1	5	1

e.

	H	T	O
	2	3	5
	5	4	2
+	1	2	1

f.

	H	T	O
	1	2	4
	2	4	5
+	2	2	6

g.

	H	T	O
	1	2	3
	3	0	7
+	4	4	1

h.

	H	T	O
	4	3	6
	2	7	5
+	2	1	2

i.

	H	T	O
	1	6	8
	5	3	2
+	1	5	4

j.

	Th	H	T	O
	4	9	1	9
+	4	0	6	0

k.

	Th	H	T	O
	2	8	7	7
+	6	0	3	6

l.

	TTh	Th	H	T	O
			8	8	8
			3	4	2
+			9	1	2

m.

	Th	H	T	O
	2	3	2	1
	3	0	8	7
+	3	7	7	0

n.

	TTh	Th	H	T	O
	2	0	1	2	2
+	2	0	0	6	7

o.

	TTh	Th	H	T	O
	3	4	5	2	2
+	4	5	8	6	1

2. The teacher bought 235 milk chocolates and 245 dark chocolates to distribute among students. What is the total number of chocolates the teacher bought?

3. In a school, there are 457 boys and 463 girls. What is the total number of students in the school?

4. A bookshop sold 256 English books, 228 Mathematics books and 126 History books in one month. How many books did the bookshop sell in that month?

5. Solve the following in your notebook.

a. 688 + 122 b. 302 + 158 + 471 c. 567 + 312

d. 543 + 47 + 10 e. 5678 + 2183 f. 2424 + 3980

g. 3030 + 3866 + 2079 h. 5958 + 2751 + 1039

i. 15867 + 48721 j. 46624 + 45155

6. Find the estimated sum by rounding off the numbers to the nearest 100. Verify your answers by actual addition.

a. 267 + 321 b. 605 + 122

3 Subtraction

Prior Knowledge

- Properties of subtraction
- Subtraction of 1- or 2-digit numbers from 3-digit numbers

Learning Objectives

- Subtraction of 3-digit numbers
- Subtraction of 4-digit numbers
- Subtraction of 5-digit numbers
- Word problems on subtraction
- Estimation of difference of two numbers

Let's Get Started

1. Subtract the following.

a.

	H	T	O
	7	3	6
–			9

b.

	H	T	O
	9	2	1
–			4

c.

	H	T	O
	8	6	4
–			5

d.

	H	T	O
	3	7	5
–			6

e.

	H	T	O
	6	6	4
–		3	7

f.

	H	T	O
	3	5	6
–		9	7

g.

	H	T	O
	5	9	2
–		4	8

h.

	H	T	O
	2	4	5
–		8	6

i.

	H	T	O
	3	4	2
–		7	8

j.

	H	T	O
	2	8	3
–		9	5

k.

	H	T	O
	4	5	3
–		1	6

l.

	H	T	O
	4	2	3
–		6	5

m.

	H	T	O
	5	7	4
–		9	6

n.

	H	T	O
	6	2	5
–		2	7

o.

	H	T	O
	8	2	2
–		3	9

p.

	H	T	O
	4	5	1
–		3	3

SUBTRACTION OF 3-DIGIT NUMBERS FROM 3-DIGIT NUMBERS WITHOUT REGROUPING

Let us learn to subtract a 3-digit number from a 3-digit number without regrouping with the help of an example.

Example 1: Subtract: 765 – 124

Solution: **Step 1:** Write the smaller number below the bigger number. Subtract 4 from 5 in the ones column, that is 5 – 4 = 1.

Write 1 under 4 in the ones column as the answer.

Step 2: Subtract 2 from 6 in the tens column, that is 6 – 2 = 4.

Write 4 under 2 in the tens column as the answer.

Step 3: Subtract 1 from 7 in the hundreds column, that is 7 – 1 = 6.

Write 6 under 1 in the hundreds column as the answer.

Thus, 765 – 124 = 641.

	H	T	O
	7	6	5
–	1	2	4
	6	4	1

Example 2: Subtract: 875 – 123

Solution:

	H	T	O
	8	7	5
–	1	2	3
	7	5	2

Thus, 875 – 123 = 752.

Example 3: Subtract: 964 – 521

Solution:

	H	T	O
	9	6	4
–	5	2	1
	4	4	3

Thus, 964 – 521 = 443.

EXERCISE 3.1

1. Subtract the following.

a.

	H	T	O
	5	4	3
–	2	1	2

b.

	H	T	O
	5	7	3
–	1	0	2

c.

	H	T	O
	9	8	6
–	2	1	4

d.

	H	T	O
	3	0	0
–	2	0	0

e.

	H	T	O
	6	7	9
−	1	3	8

f.

	H	T	O
	6	8	4
−	5	2	1

g.

	H	T	O
	5	3	7
−	2	1	6

h.

	H	T	O
	6	0	0
−	4	0	0

i.

	H	T	O
	4	8	2
−	3	5	1

j.

	H	T	O
	3	5	7
−	2	1	4

k.

	H	T	O
	4	2	9
−	1	0	8

l.

	H	T	O
	5	0	0
−	1	0	0

m.

	H	T	O
	3	7	6
−	1	2	5

n.

	H	T	O
	4	8	9
−	1	6	7

o.

	H	T	O
	5	4	2
−	3	0	1

p.

	H	T	O
	6	6	6
−	4	4	4

SUBTRACTION OF 3-DIGIT NUMBERS FROM 3-DIGIT NUMBERS WITH REGROUPING

Example 4: Subtract: 935 – 217

Solution: **Step 1:** Subtract 7 from 5 in the ones column. 7 is bigger than 5. So, borrow 1 from the '3' in the tens column. The '3' becomes '2' and the '5' in the ones column becomes '15'.

	H	T	O
	9	2 ~~3~~	15 ~~5~~
−	2	1	7
	7	1	8

Step 2: In the ones column, 15 – 7 = 8. In the tens column, 2 – 1 = 1. In the hundreds column, 9 – 2 = 7.

Thus, 935 – 217 = 718.

Example 5: Subtract: 846 – 359

Solution: **Step 1:** Subtract 9 from 6. Since 9 is bigger than 6, borrow 1 from 4 in the tens column.

The '4' in the tens place becomes '3' and the '6' in the ones column becomes '16'.

Step 2: In the ones column, 16 – 9 = 7. In the tens column, it is not possible to subtract 5 from 3 since 5 is greater than 3. So, borrow 1 from 8 in the hundreds column. The '8' in the hundreds column becomes '7' and the '3' in the tens column becomes '13'.

	H	T	O
		13	
	7	~~3~~	16
	~~8~~	~~4~~	~~6~~
–	3	5	9
	4	8	7

Step 3: In the tens column, 13 – 5 = 8.

Step 4: In the hundreds column, 7 – 3 = 4.

Thus, 846 – 359 = 487.

Example 6: Subtract: 653 – 124

Solution:

	H	T	O
		4	13
	6	~~5~~	~~3~~
–	1	2	4
	5	2	9

Thus, 653 – 124 = 529.

Example 7: Subtract: 742 – 365

Solution:

	H	T	O
		13	
	6	~~3~~	12
	~~7~~	~~4~~	~~2~~
–	3	6	5
	3	7	7

Thus, 742 – 365 = 377.

Subtraction With 1 in the Tens Place

Example 8: Subtract: 513 – 246

Solution: **Step 1:** Write the smaller number below the bigger number.

In the ones column, to subtract 6 from 3, we borrow 1 from '1' in the tens column. We are left with 0 in the tens column and the '3' in the ones column becomes '13'.

Step 2: In the ones column, 13 – 6 = 7. In the tens column, we cannot subtract 4 from 0. So, we borrow 1 from '5' in the hundreds column. In the tens place, we get 10 and in the hundreds column, we get 4.

	H	T	O
		10	
	4	~~0~~	13
	~~5~~	~~1~~	~~3~~
–	2	4	6
	2	6	7

Step 3: In the tens column, 10 – 4 = 6. In the hundreds column, 4 – 2 = 2.

Thus, 513 – 246 = 267.

More examples: (With 1 in the tens column)

a.

	H	T	O
	7	1	2
−	4	3	5

→

	H	T	O
	$^{6}\cancel{7}$	$\overset{10}{\overset{\cancel{0}}{\cancel{1}}}$	$^{12}\cancel{2}$
−	4	3	5
	2	7	7

b.

	H	T	O
	8	1	4
−	2	5	7

→

	H	T	O
	$^{7}\cancel{8}$	$\overset{10}{\overset{\cancel{0}}{\cancel{1}}}$	$^{14}\cancel{4}$
−	2	5	7
	5	5	7

Subtraction With 0 in the Tens Place

Example 9: Subtract: 402 – 136

Solution: **Step 1:** To subtract 6 from 2 in the ones column, we will have to borrow from the tens column. But the tens column has '0'. It has nothing to give us. So, we will first borrow 1 from '4' in the hundreds column. The hundreds column now becomes 3 and the tens column now becomes 10.

Step 2: Now, we can borrow 1 from the '10' in the tens column. The ones column now becomes 12 and the tens column becomes 9.

Step 3: In the ones column, 12 – 6 = 6. In the tens column, 9 – 3 = 6. In the hundreds column, 3 – 1 = 2.

Thus, 402 – 136 = 266.

	H	T	O
	$^{3}\cancel{4}$	$\overset{9}{\overset{\cancel{10}}{\cancel{0}}}$	$^{12}\cancel{2}$
−	1	3	6
	2	6	6

More examples: (With 0 in the tens column)

a.

	H	T	O
	9	0	3
−	5	1	6

→

	H	T	O
	$^{8}\cancel{9}$	$\overset{9}{\overset{\cancel{10}}{\cancel{0}}}$	$^{13}\cancel{3}$
−	5	1	6
	3	8	7

b.

	H	T	O
	7	0	2
−	1	3	5

→

	H	T	O
	$^{6}\cancel{7}$	$\overset{9}{\overset{\cancel{10}}{\cancel{0}}}$	$^{12}\cancel{2}$
−	1	3	5
	5	6	7

(With 0 in the ones and tens columns)

c.

	H	T	O
	5	0	0
−	2	4	7

→

	H	T	O
	$^{4}\cancel{5}$	$\overset{9}{\overset{\cancel{10}}{\cancel{0}}}$	$^{10}\cancel{0}$
−	2	4	7
	2	5	3

d.

	H	T	O
	8	0	0
−	3	6	5

→

	H	T	O
	$^{7}\cancel{8}$	$\overset{9}{\overset{\cancel{10}}{\cancel{0}}}$	$^{10}\cancel{0}$
−	3	6	5
	4	3	5

Exercise 3.2

1. **Subtract the following.**

a.

	H	T	O
	6	3	1
−	5	2	4

b.

	H	T	O
	7	5	2
−	3	4	8

c.

	H	T	O
	4	9	3
−	1	7	4

d.

	H	T	O
	2	3	5
−	1	4	7

e.

	H	T	O
	5	8	1
−	2	3	9

f.

	H	T	O
	6	2	8
−	4	0	9

g.

	H	T	O
	5	8	3
−	1	6	7

h.

	H	T	O
	7	6	6
−	2	3	8

i.

	H	T	O
	3	7	4
−	2	1	6

j.

	H	T	O
	7	5	4
−	3	2	6

k.

	H	T	O
	8	6	5
−	2	8	7

l.

	H	T	O
	5	1	8
−	3	4	9

2. **Subtract the following.**

a.

	H	T	O
	8	9	5
−	8	4	9

b.

	H	T	O
	5	0	3
−	2	7	9

c.

	H	T	O
	7	0	9
−	4	9	1

d.

	H	T	O
	5	6	3
−	1	5	6

e.

	H	T	O
	3	0	0
−	1	6	8

f.

	H	T	O
	6	0	0
−	2	7	4

g.

	H	T	O
	9	0	0
−	3	5	7

h.

	H	T	O
	7	7	7
−	6	9	9

i.

	H	T	O
	4	0	0
−	2	9	1

j.

	H	T	O
	8	0	0
−	6	3	2

k.

	H	T	O
	5	0	0
−	3	4	7

l.

	H	T	O
	5	7	0
−	3	9	9

3. **Subtract the following.**

a.

	H	T	O
	5	3	2
–	4	1	7

b.

	H	T	O
	4	9	7
–	1	3	8

c.

	H	T	O
	7	1	3
–	2	5	4

d.

	H	T	O
	3	0	8
–	1	2	9

e.

	H	T	O
	6	2	5
–	1	4	8

f.

	H	T	O
	9	2	3
–	1	8	5

g.

	H	T	O
	6	0	5
–	1	3	7

h.

	H	T	O
	9	1	4
–	6	5	7

i.

	H	T	O
	7	8	3
–	2	6	9

j.

	H	T	O
	8	6	2
–	3	9	6

k.

	H	T	O
	5	0	0
–	1	9	2

l.

	H	T	O
	2	0	0
–	1	3	5

MENTAL COMPUTATION OF SUM AND DIFFERENCE

Sometimes, we may use short-cut methods to add or subtract numbers. We split the numbers in ones and tens and do the operation.

Example 10: 35 + 52

Solution:

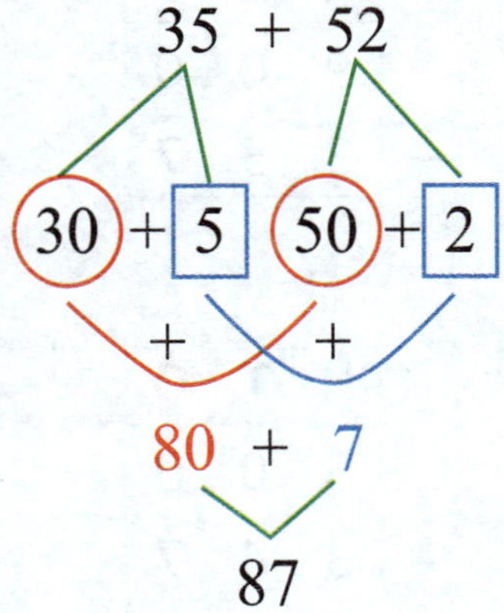

Example 11: 68 – 46

Solution:

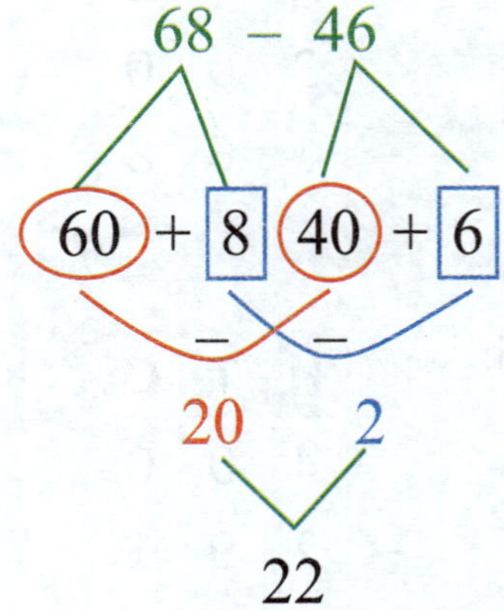

SUBTRACTION FROM 4-DIGIT NUMBERS WITHOUT REGROUPING

Let us now subtract 2-, 3- and 4-digit numbers from 4-digit numbers without regrouping.

Example 12: Subtract 36 from 3666.

Solution:

	Th	H	T	O
	3	6	6	6
–			3	6
	3	6	3	0

Thus, 3666 – 36 = 3630.

Example 13: Subtract 254 from 6389.

Solution:

	Th	H	T	O
	6	3	8	9
–		2	5	4
	6	1	3	5

Thus, 6389 – 254 = 6135.

Example 14: Subtract 2415 from 9837.

Solution:

	Th	H	T	O
	9	8	3	7
–	2	4	1	5
	7	4	2	2

First, subtract the ones. 7 – 5 = 2

Then, subtract the tens. 3 – 1 = 2

Then, subtract the hundreds. 8 – 4 = 4

Then, subtract the thousands. 9 – 2 = 7

Thus, 9837 – 2415 = 7422.

EXERCISE 3.3

1. Solve the following.

a.

	Th	H	T	O
	8	7	9	5
–			6	4

b.

	Th	H	T	O
	4	9	7	8
–		3	2	1

c.

	Th	H	T	O
	8	3	9	7
–	3	2	1	0

d.

	Th	H	T	O
	7	8	5	4
–	1	2	3	1

2. **Solve the following in your notebook.**

a. 4653 − 2241 b. 5022 − 1211 c. 9744 − 4213

d. 7652 − 4140 e. 8686 − 3143 f. 9153 − 3122

Regrouping From Tens to Ones

Example 15: Subtract 436 from 6954.

Solution: Write the two numbers vertically, with the greater number above the smaller number. Subtract the digits.

	Th	H	T	O
			4	14
	6	9	~~5~~	~~4~~
−		4	3	6
	6	5	1	8

Ones column: 4 < 6; borrow 1 ten from 5 tens. 5 becomes 4 in the tens place and 4 becomes 14 in the ones place. So, 14 – 6 = 8.

Tens column: 4 – 3 = 1

Hundreds column: 9 – 4 = 5

Thousands column: There is no digit to be subtracted from 6. Write 6 in the thousands place of the answer.

Thus, 6954 – 436 = 6518.

Regrouping From Hundreds to Tens

Example 16: Subtract 1393 from 2573.

Solution: Write the two numbers vertically, with the greater number above the smaller number. Subtract the digits.

	Th	H	T	O
		4	17	
	2	~~5~~	~~7~~	3
−	1	3	9	3
	1	1	8	0

Ones column: 3 – 3 = 0

Tens column: 7 < 9; borrow 1 hundred from 5 hundreds. 5 becomes 4 in the hundreds place and 7 becomes 17 in the tens place. So, 17 – 9 = 8.

Hundreds column: 4 – 3 = 1

Thousands column: 2 – 1 = 1

Thus, 2573 − 1393 = 1180.

Regrouping From Thousands to Hundreds

Example 17: Subtract 4911 from 5445.

Solution: Write the two numbers vertically, with the greater number above the smaller number. Subtract the digits.

	Th	H	T	O
	4	14		
	~~5~~	~~4~~	4	5
–	4	9	1	1
	0	5	3	4

Ones column: 5 – 1 = 4

Tens column: 4 – 1 = 3

Hundreds column: 4 < 9; borrow 1 thousand from 5 thousands. 5 becomes 4 in the thousands place and 4 becomes 14 in the hundreds place. So, 14 – 9 = 5.

Thousands column: 4 – 4 = 0

Thus, 5445 – 4911 = 534.

Regrouping From Tens, Hundreds and Thousands (Thrice)

Example 18: Subtract 1957 from 8326.

Solution: Write the two numbers vertically, with the greater number above the smaller number. Subtract the digits.

	Th	H	T	O
		12	11	
	7	~~2~~	~~1~~	16
	~~8~~	~~3~~	~~2~~	~~6~~
–	1	9	5	7
	6	3	6	9

Ones column: 6 < 7; borrow 1 ten from 2 tens. 2 becomes 1 in the tens place and 6 becomes 16 in the ones place. So, 16 – 7 = 9.

Tens column: 1 < 5; borrow 1 hundred from 3 hundreds. 3 becomes 2 in the hundreds place and 1 becomes 11 in the tens place. So, 11 – 5 = 6.

Hundreds column: 2 < 9; borrow 1 thousand from 8 thousands. 8 becomes 7 in the thousands place and 2 becomes 12 in the hundreds place.

So, 12 – 9 = 3.

Thousands column: 7 – 1 = 6

Thus, 8326 – 1957 = 6369.

EXERCISE 3.4

1. Solve the following.

a.

Th	H	T	O
5	7	7	2
– 3	6	4	1

b.

Th	H	T	O
7	2	3	4
– 2	6	4	2

c.

Th	H	T	O
6	0	3	0
– 3	5	4	2

d.

Th	H	T	O
4	4	3	2
– 2	5	4	4

e.

Th	H	T	O
8	3	1	6
– 6	5	4	7

f.

Th	H	T	O
9	7	8	3
– 4	5	4	5

2. Solve the following in your notebook.

a. 4653 – 244 b. 7121 – 576 c. 9144 – 435

d. 3652 – 1782 e. 9482 – 3743 f. 9243 – 4751

WORD PROBLEMS ON SUBTRACTION

Word problems on subtraction with 3-digit numbers are done just as subtraction with 2-digit numbers.

REMEMBER

We subtract

- when a quantity decreases by the amount given, that is to find how much is left.
- when a quantity is lesser than another quantity by a given amount.
- to find out how much lesser or more one quantity is than another.
- to find out the difference between two quantities.

Example 19: 450 people came to watch a cricket match on Monday. On Tuesday, 128 fewer people came to watch the match. How many people came to watch the match on Tuesday?

Solution: Number of people on Monday = 450

Number of fewer people on Tuesday = 128

Number of people on Tuesday = 450 – 128

	H	T	O
	4	$\overset{4}{\cancel{5}}$	$\overset{10}{\cancel{0}}$
–	1	2	8
	3	2	2

Thus, 322 people came to watch the match on Tuesday.

Example 20: Out of 520 people travelling in a train, 165 were children. How many were adults?

Solution: Total number of people = 520

Number of children = 165

Number of adults = Total number of people – Number of children

Thus, there were 355 adults.

	H	T	O
	$\overset{4}{\cancel{5}}$	$\overset{11}{\overset{1}{\cancel{2}}}$	$\overset{10}{\cancel{0}}$
–	1	6	5
	3	5	5

Example 21: Reema has ₹680. Seema has ₹570. Who has more money and by how much?

Solution: As 680 > 570, Reema has more money.

Reema has = ₹680

Seema has = ₹570

Difference = ₹680 – ₹570

Thus, Reema has ₹110 more than Seema.

	H	T	O
	6	8	0
–	5	7	0
	1	1	0

Example 22: Ramesh has ₹6295. Zehra has 2595 lesser than Ramesh. How much money does Zehra have?

Solution:

Amount with Ramesh = 6295

Amount less than Ramesh = 2595

Amount with Zehra

= Amount with Ramesh – Less amount

= 6295 – 2595 = 3700

Thus, Zehra has ₹3700.

	Th	H	T	O
	$\overset{5}{\cancel{6}}$	$\overset{12}{\cancel{2}}$	9	5
–	2	5	9	5
	3	7	0	0

Example 23: An ice cream vendor sold 5700 ice creams in June and 2850 ice creams in July. How many less ice creams did he sell in July than in June?

Solution:

		Th	H	T	O
		4 ~~5~~	16 ~~6~~ ~~7~~	10 ~~0~~	0
Ice creams sold in June	−	2	8	5	0
Ice creams sold in July		2	8	5	0

Thus, he sold 2850 less ice creams in July than in June.

EXERCISE 3.5

1. **An ice cream vendor had 215 ice creams. He sold 78 ice creams in one day. How many ice creams were left with him?**

		H	T	O
Total number of ice creams				
Number of ice creams sold	−			

Thus, ________ ice creams were left with him.

2. **A movie hall had 450 seats. 429 seats were occupied. How many seats were not occupied?**

		H	T	O
Total number of seats				
Number of seats occupied	−			

Thus, ________ seats were not occupied.

3. **Reena had 300 marbles. Rajan had 179 marbles. How many more marbles did Reena have than Rajan?**

		H	T	O
Number of marbles with Reena				
Number of marbles with Rajan	−			

Thus, Reena had ________ more marbles than Rajan.

4. **354 children sat for an examination. 328 children passed in the examination. How many children did not pass?**

Total number of children

Number of children passed −

H	T	O

Thus, ________ children did not pass.

5. **A bookshop had 285 books. 110 books got sold in 1 week. How many books were left in the shop?**

Total number of books

Books sold −

H	T	O

Thus, ________ books were left in the shop.

6. **The total number of students in a school is 825. On Monday, 95 students were absent. How many were present?**

Total number of students

Number of students absent −

H	T	O

Thus, ________ students were present.

7. **Out of 768 students in a club, 470 like to play cricket. How many do not like to play cricket?**

Total number of students

Number of students who like to play cricket −

H	T	O

Thus, ________ students do not like to play cricket.

8. **A shop had 557 chocolates. It sold 488 chocolates during the day. How many chocolates were left at the shop?**

Total chocolates

Chocolates sold −

H	T	O

Thus, ________ chocolates were left at the shop.

9. **There were 8675 apple trees in an orchard. 2134 trees were cut down. How many trees were left in the orchard?**

Total number of trees

Trees cut down −

Th	H	T	O

________ trees were left in the orchard.

10. **Anil earned ₹5780 in one week. He spent ₹2550. How much money was left with him?**

Money earned

Money spent −

Thus, ₹________ was left with Anil.

Th	H	T	O

WORD PROBLEMS INVOLVING ADDITION AND SUBTRACTION

The problems we just did involved only subtraction. Now, we will understand problems that involve both addition and subtraction.

Example 24: Rajat had 125 marbles. His mother bought him 150 more marbles. Then he lost 36 marbles. How many marbles does he have now?

Solution: Number of marbles Rajat had = 125

Number of marbles bought by his mother = 150

Total marbles = 125 + 150

= 275

	H	T	O
	1	2	5
+	1	5	0
	2	7	5

Number of marbles Rajat lost = 36

Marbles left with him = 275 – 36

Thus, Rajat has 239 marbles now.

	H	T	O
		6	15
	2	~~7~~	~~5~~
–		3	6
	2	3	9

Example 25: There were 256 cars parked in the parking lot. 128 cars drove away. 35 more cars came and parked. How many cars are there in the parking lot now?

Solution: Number of cars parked = 256

Number of cars that drove away = 128

Number of cars left = 256 – 128

	H	T	O
		4	16
	2	~~5~~	~~6~~
–	1	2	8
	1	2	8

Number of cars that came = 35

Total number of cars = 128 + 35

	H	T	O
		1	
	1	2	8
+		3	5
	1	6	3

Thus, total number of cars is 163.

Exercise 3.6

1. **There were 352 trees in a forest. 123 more trees were planted. Then, 46 trees were cut. How many trees were left in the forest?**

   Thus, ________ trees were left in the forest.

2. **In a garden, there were 125 flowers. 36 flowers died. 75 flowers grew. Now, how many flowers are there in the garden?**

   Thus, there are ________ flowers in the garden.

3. **Seema had ₹500. Her mother gave her ₹220 more. She spent ₹130 to buy a doll. How much money does Seema have now?**

   Thus, Seema has ₹ ________ now.

4. **A bakery baked 132 cakes in the morning and 120 cakes in the afternoon. In the evening, it sold 250 cakes. How many cakes were left?**

   Thus, ________ cakes were left.

5. **There were 102 children in a park. 56 children went back home. 94 more children came to the park. How many children are there in the park now?**

   Thus, there are ________ children in the park now.

ESTIMATION OF DIFFERENCE OF TWO NUMBERS

To estimate the difference between two numbers, we will first round off the two numbers to their estimated values and then subtract.

Example 26: Estimate the difference between 187 and 99.

Solution: 187 is rounded off to 200.

99 is rounded off to 100.

	H	T	O
	2	0	0
–	1	0	0
	1	0	0

To verify our answer, let us actually subtract 99 from 187.

	H	T	O
	$^{0}\not{1}$	$\overset{17}{\not{7}}\ \not{8}$	$^{17}\not{7}$
–		9	9
		8	8

The actual answer is 88, and our estimated answer was 100, which is very close.

Example 27: Estimate the following to the nearest 1000.

a. 7444 – 5988   b. 9862 – 6288

Solution:

a. Rounding off to nearest 1000, we get

   7000 – 6000 = 1000

   Actual difference = 7444 – 5988 = 1456

b. Rounding off to nearest 1000, we get

   10000 – 6000 = 4000

   Actual difference = 9862 – 6288 = 3574

Exercise 3.7

1. **Find the estimated difference by rounding off the numbers to the nearest 100. Verify your answers by actual subtraction.**

   a. 420 – 160 b. 790 – 480 c. 826 – 275

   d. 398 – 134 e. 349 – 223 f. 820 – 689

2. **Estimate the following to the nearest 1000.**

   a. 6443 – 4844 b. 8861 – 6282 c. 3677 – 2676

   d. 7344 – 4600 e. 5942 – 4900 f. 9201 – 8400

SUBTRACTION OF 5-DIGIT NUMBERS WITH BORROWING

Let us subtract 31,869 from 87,352. We first subtract the digits in the ones place, then the digits in the tens place, followed by those in the hundreds, the thousands and the ten thousands places.

Wherever required, we borrow numbers from the next higher place. The difference between the two numbers is 55,483.

		TTh	Th	H	T	O
Minuend		8	~~7~~ 6	~~3~~ 12	~~5~~ 14	~~2~~ 12
Subtrahend	–	3	1	8	6	9
Difference		5	5	4	8	3

Exercise 3.8

1. **Solve the following.**

a.

	TTh	Th	H	T	O
	4	2	3	4	1
–	2	6	4	5	1

b.

	TTh	Th	H	T	O
	5	5	3	4	2
–	2	6	4	3	1

c.

	TTh	Th	H	T	O
	6	5	3	4	3
–	3	6	4	5	2

d.

	TTh	Th	H	T	O
	7	6	3	4	6
–	5	7	4	5	7

e.

	TTh	Th	H	T	O
	8	5	4	4	3
–	4	6	4	5	5

f.

	TTh	Th	H	T	O
	9	1	3	4	5
–	7	6	5	5	6

2. Solve the following in your notebook.

a. 24653 – 17244 b. 36121 – 22576 c. 48144 – 32435

d. 54651 – 31682 e. 78481 – 43743 f. 96243 – 44751

Key Concepts

Subtraction

Subtracting 3-digit numbers

Step 1: Write the smaller number below the bigger number. Subtract digits in the ones column.

Write the difference in the ones column as the answer.

Step 2: Subtract digits in the tens column. Write the difference in the tens column as the answer.

Step 3: Subtract digits in the hundreds column. Write the difference in the hundreds column as the answer.

Subtraction with regrouping

	H	T	O
	9	[2] ~~3~~	[15] ~~5~~
–	2	1	7
	7	1	8

Mental computation:

Split the numbers in ones and tens and do the operation

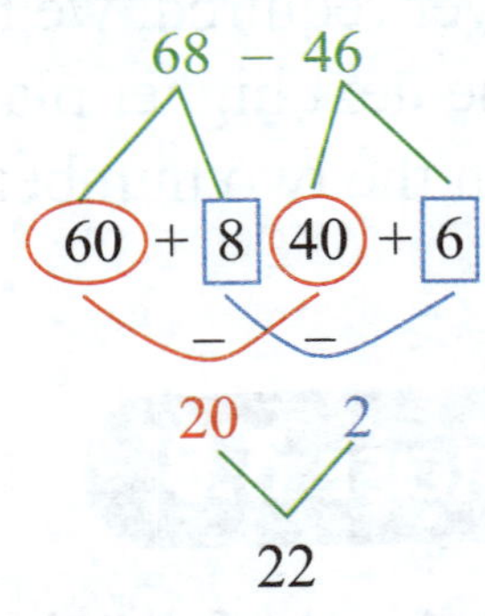

Word Problems

Look out for words related to subtraction:

• Change	• Difference	• Have left	• How many did not have
• How much more	• Remain	• Decreased by	• Fewer
• Take away	• How many more	• Less than	• Taller/Shorter

REVISION EXERCISE

1. Solve the following.

a.

	H	T	O
	8	9	4
–	2	1	3

b.

	H	T	O
	5	9	3
–	2	8	1

c.

	H	T	O
	7	6	3
–	3	1	2

d.

	H	T	O
	4	8	7
–	1	2	1

e.

	H	T	O
	8	4	2
–	4	1	5

f.

	H	T	O
	9	4	3
–	6	7	1

g.

	H	T	O
	4	0	3
–	1	2	7

h.

	H	T	O
	9	0	0
–	3	4	8

i.

	H	T	O
	8	0	9
–	5	2	3

2. Solve the following in your notebook.

a. 786 – 84 b. 909 – 210 c. 850 – 245 d. 680 – 290

e. 700 – 655 f. 732 – 67 g. 480 – 440 h. 348 – 123

i. 2651 – 2244 j. 3121 – 1575 k. 4166 – 2431 l. 7352 – 4784

m. 19482 – 13753 n. 49243 – 24750 o. 58443 – 44854 p. 91243 – 72756

3. A bookseller sold 238 books out of 525 books. How many books were left with him?

__________ books were left with the book bookseller.

4. An ice cream vendor sold 790 ice creams in June. He sold 186 fewer ice creams in July. How many ice creams did he sell in July?

The ice cream vendor sold __________ ice creams in July.

5. What is the difference between 800 and 205?

The difference is __________.

6. **There were 760 students in a school. When the year got over, 125 students left the school. However, 185 more students joined the school. How many students were there in the school?**

There were __________ students in the school.

7. **Nancy bought a desk for ₹5690, a chair for ₹2000 and a stool for ₹1000. What is the total amount she spent?**

8. **A school had 7180 students. At the end of the session, 1200 students left the school. In the next session, 2572 students took admission. How many students are there in the school now?**

9. **There are ₹9500 in Manjari's account. She spent ₹4250 on books. How much money is left with Manjari?**

10. **A dairy farm produces 8545 litres of milk every day. It supplies 5625 litres of milk to a milk depot and the rest to a market. How much milk is supplied to the market?**

11. **A football stadium has 10,000 seats. One day, 2461 people came to see the match. Estimate the number of vacant seats to the nearest 100. How many seats are actually vacant?**

12. **There are 58,640 people in a village. The number of women in this village is 30,560. Estimate the number of men to the nearest 1000. Find the actual number of men in this village.**

4 Multiplication

Prior Knowledge

- Multiplication as repeated addition
- Multiplication facts
- Multiplication tables of 1, 2, 3, 4, 5 and 10
- Multiplication of 2-digit numbers with 1-digit numbers
- Word problems on multiplication

Learning Objectives

- Multiplying by numbers ending with zeros
- Multiplication of 3-digit numbers by 1- and 2-digit numbers
- Multiplication of two 2-digit numbers
- Multiplication of 4-digit numbers by 1-digit numbers
- Estimation of product of two numbers
- Multiplication by Lattice method

Let's Get Started

Help the birds find their way to the birdhouse. Make a path by drawing a line through the boxes that have products less than 50.

				11 × 3 = 33	7 × 3	8 × 5	8 × 5	8 × 4	2 × 7
8 × 9	7 × 8	9 × 9	7 × 9	8 × 10	9 × 7	10 × 7	9 × 5	10 × 6	9 × 10
8 × 7	9 × 9	10 × 3				5 × 2	3 × 4	5 × 6	4 × 2
10 × 9	9 × 2	6 × 10				4 × 8	5 × 12	7 × 8	5 × 11
9 × 9	9 × 8	6 × 8	4 × 6	3 × 3	20 × 3	2 × 2	7 × 2	5 × 5	5 × 13
7 × 10	7 × 7	5 × 9	7 × 2	5 × 8	8 × 10	4 × 3	6 × 6	6 × 5	7 × 4

MULTIPLICATION TABLES

You have learnt multiplication tables of 1, 2, 3, 4, 5 and 10 in the previous class. Let us learn a few more multiplication tables.

Table of 7	Table of 8	Table of 9	Table of 11	Table of 12
$1 \times 7 = 7$	$1 \times 8 = 8$	$1 \times 9 = 9$	$1 \times 11 = 11$	$1 \times 12 = 12$
$2 \times 7 = 14$	$2 \times 8 = 16$	$2 \times 9 = 18$	$2 \times 11 = 22$	$2 \times 12 = 24$
$3 \times 7 = 21$	$3 \times 8 = 24$	$3 \times 9 = 27$	$3 \times 11 = 33$	$3 \times 12 = 36$
$4 \times 7 = 28$	$4 \times 8 = 32$	$4 \times 9 = 36$	$4 \times 11 = 44$	$4 \times 12 = 48$
$5 \times 7 = 35$	$5 \times 8 = 40$	$5 \times 9 = 45$	$5 \times 11 = 55$	$5 \times 12 = 60$
$6 \times 7 = 42$	$6 \times 8 = 48$	$6 \times 9 = 54$	$6 \times 11 = 66$	$6 \times 12 = 72$
$7 \times 7 = 49$	$7 \times 8 = 56$	$7 \times 9 = 63$	$7 \times 11 = 77$	$7 \times 12 = 84$
$8 \times 7 = 56$	$8 \times 8 = 64$	$8 \times 9 = 72$	$8 \times 11 = 88$	$8 \times 12 = 96$
$9 \times 7 = 63$	$9 \times 8 = 72$	$9 \times 9 = 81$	$9 \times 11 = 99$	$9 \times 12 = 108$
$10 \times 7 = 70$	$10 \times 8 = 80$	$10 \times 9 = 90$	$10 \times 11 = 110$	$10 \times 12 = 120$

Table of 13	Table of 14	Table of 15	Table of 18	Table of 20
$1 \times 13 = 13$	$1 \times 14 = 14$	$1 \times 15 = 15$	$1 \times 18 = 18$	$1 \times 20 = 20$
$2 \times 13 = 26$	$2 \times 14 = 28$	$2 \times 15 = 30$	$2 \times 18 = 36$	$2 \times 20 = 40$
$3 \times 13 = 39$	$3 \times 14 = 42$	$3 \times 15 = 45$	$3 \times 18 = 54$	$3 \times 20 = 60$
$4 \times 13 = 52$	$4 \times 14 = 56$	$4 \times 15 = 60$	$4 \times 18 = 72$	$4 \times 20 = 80$
$5 \times 13 = 65$	$5 \times 14 = 70$	$5 \times 15 = 75$	$5 \times 18 = 90$	$5 \times 20 = 100$
$6 \times 13 = 78$	$6 \times 14 = 84$	$6 \times 15 = 90$	$6 \times 18 = 108$	$6 \times 20 = 120$
$7 \times 13 = 91$	$7 \times 14 = 98$	$7 \times 15 = 105$	$7 \times 18 = 126$	$7 \times 20 = 140$
$8 \times 13 = 104$	$8 \times 14 = 112$	$8 \times 15 = 120$	$8 \times 18 = 144$	$8 \times 20 = 160$
$9 \times 13 = 117$	$9 \times 14 = 126$	$9 \times 15 = 135$	$9 \times 18 = 162$	$9 \times 20 = 180$
$10 \times 13 = 130$	$10 \times 14 = 140$	$10 \times 15 = 150$	$10 \times 18 = 180$	$10 \times 20 = 200$

MULTIPLYING BY NUMBERS ENDING WITH ZEROS

Multiplying by 10 and 100

Look at the following.

$2 \times 10 = 20$	$15 \times 10 = 150$	$72 \times 10 = 720$
$5 \times 100 = 500$	$29 \times 100 = 2900$	$83 \times 100 = 8300$

We see that

- when we **multiply a number by 10**, we get the answer by **putting a zero** at the end of the factor other than 10.
- when we **multiply a number by 100**, we get the answer by **putting two zeros** at the end of the factor other than 100.

Multiplying by Numbers Ending With One Zero

While multiplying numbers by 10, 20, 30, …, 90, we need not use the long multiplication method. Instead, we can use the following method.

Multiplying by 1-digit Numbers

Example 1: Multiply: 3×20

$3 \times 20 = \underline{\ \ 0}$ While multiplying 20 by a 1-digit number, first write 0 on the right end of the answer because 20 has one zero.

$3 \times 20 = \underline{60}$ Now, multiply 2 by 3. We get 6, which we write before 0.

	T	O
	2	0
×		3
	6	0

The same multiplication can be done vertically.

Multiplying by 2-digit Numbers

Example 2: Multiply: 32×20

$32 \times 20 = \underline{0}$ First, write 0 at the right end of the answer because 20 has one zero.

$32 \times 20 = \underline{40}$ Now, multiply 2 by 2. We get 4, which we write before 0 in the answer.

32 × 20 = <u>640</u> Finally, multiply 3 by 2. We get 6. Write it before 4 in the answer.

The same multiplication can be done vertically as follows.

	T	O
	3	2
×	2	0
		0

Since 20 has one 0, write 0 on the extreme right.

	H	T	O
		3	2
×		2	0
	6	4	0

Thus, 32 × 20 = 640.

Example 3: Multiply: 25 × 30

25 × 30 = 0 Write 0 at the right end of the answer because 30 has one 0.

[1]25 × 30 = 50 Now, multiply 5 by 3. We get 15.

Write the 5 of 15 just before 0 in the answer and write the 1 of 15 above 2.

[1]25 × 30 = 750 Now, multiply 2 by 3. We get 6. Add 6 and 1 to get 7.

Write 7 just before 5 in the answer.

The same multiplication can be done vertically as follows.

	T	O
	2	5
×	3	0
		0

Since 30 has one zero, write 0 on the extreme right.

	H	T	O
		[1]2	5
×		3	0
	7	5	0

Now, multiply 25 with 3 to get 75.

Thus, 25 × 30 = 750.

Multiplying by Numbers Ending With Two Zeros

Multiplying by 1-digit Numbers

Example 4: Multiply: 6 × 200

6 × 200 = __00__ Since 200 has two zeros, write 00 at the right end of the answer.

6 × 200 = __1200__ Now, multiply 6 by 2. We get 12, which we write before 00.

Thus, 6 × 200 = 1200.

EXERCISE 4.1

1. **Solve the following.**

a. 3 × 10 = ____ b. 78 × 10 = ____ c. 94 × 10 = ____

d. 5 × 100 = ____ e. 63 × 100 = ____ f. 48 × 100 = ____

2. **Multiply the following without carrying.**

a. 3 × 20 = _____

	T	O
		3
×	2	0

b. 43 × 20 = _____

	T	O
	4	3
×	2	0

c. 14 × 20 = _____

	T	O
	1	4
×	2	0

d. 21 × 30 = _____

	T	O
	2	1
×	3	0

e. 20 × 40 = _____

	T	O
	2	0
×	4	0

f. 3 × 200 = _____

	H	T	O
			3
×	2	0	0

g. 5 × 300 = ______

	Th	H	T	O
				5
×		3	0	0

h. 5 × 200 = ______

	Th	H	T	O
				5
×		2	0	0

i. 6 × 300 = ______

	Th	H	T	O
				6
×		3	0	0

3. Multiply the following with carrying.

a. 8 × 50 = ______

	H	T	O
			8
×		5	0

b. 47 × 30 = ______

	Th	H	T	O
			4	7
×			3	0

c. 28 × 50 = ______

	Th	H	T	O
			2	8
×			5	0

d. 76 × 40 = ______

	Th	H	T	O
			7	6
×			4	0

e. 25 × 60 = ______

	Th	H	T	O
			2	5
×			6	0

f. 25 × 70 = ______

	Th	H	T	O
			2	5
×			7	0

g. 45 × 30 = ______

	Th	H	T	O
			4	5
×			3	0

h. 35 × 60 = ______

	Th	H	T	O
			3	5
×			6	0

i. 84 × 20 = ______

	Th	H	T	O
			8	4
×			2	0

MULTIPLICATION OF 3-DIGIT NUMBERS

Let us learn how to multiply 3-digit numbers by 1-digit numbers.

Without Carrying

Example 5: 123 × 3

Solution: Step 1: Multiply the ones.

	H	T	O
	1	2	3
×			3
			9

$3 \times 3 = 9$

Step 2: Multiply the tens.

	H	T	O
	1	2	3
×			3
		6	9

$2 \times 3 = 6$

Step 3: Multiply the hundreds.

	H	T	O
	1	2	3
×			3
	3	6	9

$1 \times 3 = 3$

So, 123 × 3 = 369.

With Carrying (Regrouping)

Regrouping Ones

Example 6: 116 × 4

Solution: Step 1: Multiply the ones and regroup the ones into tens.

	H	T	O
	1	$^{2}1$	6
×			4
			4

$6 \times 4 = 24$ ones (= 2 tens and 4 ones)

Write **4** of **24** in the ones column below 4.

Carry forward **2** of **24** to the tens column and write it above 1.

Step 2: Multiply the tens and then the hundreds.

	H	T	O
	1	[2]1	6
×			4
	4	6	4

Tens: 1 × 4 = 4; now add 2 (carried forward). 4 + 2 = 6

Write this 6 in the tens column, before 4.

Hundreds: 1 × 4 = 4

Write this 4 in the hundreds column, before 6.

So, 116 × 4 = 464.

Regrouping Tens

Example 7: 361 × 2

Solution:

	H	T	O
	[1]3	6	1
×			2
	7	2	2

So, 361 × 2 = 722.

Step 1: Multiply the ones. 2 × 1 = 2.

Step 2: Multiply the tens and regroup the tens into hundreds.

6 × 2 = 12 tens (= 1 hundred and 2 tens)

Carry forward 1 of 12 to the hundreds column and write 2 in the tens column.

Step 3: Multiply the hundreds.

3 × 2 = 6; now add 1 (carried forward). Thus, 6 + 1 = 7.

Write 7 in the hundreds column.

So, 361 × 2 = 722.

Regrouping Hundreds

Example 8: 412 × 4

Solution:

	Th	H	T	O
		4	1	2
×				4
	1	6	4	8

Thus, 412 × 4 = 1648.

Step 1: Multiply the ones first and then the tens.

Ones: 2 × 4 = 8; **Tens:** 1 × 4 = 4

Step 2: Multiply the hundreds and regroup.

4 × 4 = 16 hundreds (= 1 thousand and 6 hundreds)

Write 6 in the hundreds column and 1 in the thousands column.

Regrouping Ones, Tens and Hundreds

Example 9: 356 × 3

Solution:

	Th	H	T	O
		[1]3	[1]5	6
×				3
	1	0	6	8

Thus, 356 × 3 = 1068.

Step 1: Multiply the ones and regroup.

6 × 3 = 18 ones (= 1 ten and 8 ones); carry forward **1** of **18** to the tens column. Write 8 in the ones column.

Step 2: Multiply the tens and regroup.

5 × 3 = 15; now add 1 (carried forward). Thus, 15 + 1 = 16 tens (= 1 hundred and 6 tens); carry forward **1** of **16** to the hundreds column and write 6 in the tens column.

Step 3: Multiply the hundreds and regroup.

3 × 3 = 9; now add 1 (carried forward).
Thus, 9 + 1 = 10 hundreds (= 1 thousand).

Write 0 in the hundreds column and 1 in the thousands column.

Exercise 4.2

1. **Multiply the following.**

a.

	H	T	O
	1	3	2
×			3

b.

	H	T	O
	1	2	9
×			4

c.

	H	T	O
	2	3	2
×			3

d.

	H	T	O
	1	6	4
×			5

2. **Fill in the missing digits.**

a. 115 × 6 = 6__0 b. 349 × 2 = 69__ c. 507 × 3 = 1____1

d. 232 × 3 = 69__ e. 134 × 5 = __7__ f. 423 × 4 = __6__2

MULTIPLICATION OF TWO 2-DIGIT NUMBERS

Let us now learn to multiply a 2-digit number by a 2-digit number.

Without Carrying

Example 10: 12 × 23

Solution:

Step 1: Multiply the ones.

	H	T	O
		1	2
×		2	3
		3	6

First, 2 × 3 = 6.
Write 6 below 3.
Next, 1 × 3 = 3.
Write 3 below 2.

Step 2: Multiply the tens.

	H	T	O
		1	2
×		2	3
		3	6
	2	4	0

Write 0 below 6 in the ones column.
Then, 2 × 2 = 4; write 4 below 3.
Now, 1 × 2 = 2; write 2 before 4.

Step 3: Add both the products.

	H	T	O
		1	2
×		2	3
		3	6
+	2	4	0
	2	7	6

Draw a line below 240 and add.
Ones column: 6 + 0 = 6
Tens column: 3 + 4 = 7
Hundreds column: We have only 2.

So, 12 × 23 = 276.

With Carrying

Example 11: 26 × 15

Solution: Step 1: Multiply the ones and regroup.

	H	T	O
		[3]2	6
×		1	5
	1	3	0

First, 6 × 5 = 30.
Write 0 below 5 in the ones column.
Carry forward **3** of **30** to the tens column.
2 × 5 = 10; now add 3 (carried forward). Thus, 10 + 3 = 13.
Write 13 before 0.

Step 2: Multiply the tens.

	H	T	O
		[3]2	6
×		1	5
	1	3	0
	2	6	0

Write 0 below 0 in the ones column. Then,
6 × 1 = 6
2 × 1 = 2

Step 3: Add both the products.

	H	T	O
		[3]2	6
×		1	5
	1	3	0
+	2	6	0
	3	9	0

So, 26 × 15 = 390.

Regrouping Ones and Tens

Example 12: 86 × 32

Solution:

	Th	H	T	O
			①[1]8	6
×			3	2
		1	7	2
+	2	5	8	0
	2	7	5	2

We have circled 1 to distinguish it from the earlier carried forward number 1.

So, 86 × 32 = 2752.

ALERT !

- If we write the number carried forward, one on top of the other, then we will not make mistakes.
- When multiplying the tens, first write 0 in the ones column and then multiply the digits.

	H	T	O
		①[2]2	5
×		3	4
	1	0	0
		7	5
	1	7	5

	H	T	O
		①[2]2	5
×		3	4
	1	0	0
+	7	5	0
	8	5	0

MULTIPLICATION OF 3-DIGIT NUMBERS BY 2-DIGIT NUMBERS

Without Carrying

Let us multiply a 3-digit number by a 2-digit number.

Example 13: 121 × 24

Solution:

	Th	H	T	O
		1	2	1
×			2	4
		$^{1}4$	8	4
+	2	4	2	0
	2	9	0	4

So, 121 × 24 = 2904.

With Carrying

Example 14: 252 × 36

Solution:

	Th	H	T	O
		(1) $^{3}2$	$^{1}5$	2
×			3	6
	$^{1}1$	5	1	2
+	7	5	6	0
	9	0	7	2

So, 252 × 36 = 9072.

MULTIPLICATION OF 4-DIGIT NUMBERS BY 1-DIGIT NUMBERS

Without Carrying

Example 15: 2313 × 2

Solution:

	Th	H	T	O
	2	3	1	3
×				2
	4	6	2	6

So, 2313 × 2 = 4626.

With Carrying

Example 16: 1516 × 4

Solution:

	Th	H	T	O
	$^{2}1$	5	$^{2}1$	6
×				4
	6	0	6	4

So, 1516 × 4 = 6064.

Exercise 4.3

1. **Solve the following.**

a.

	H	T	O
		2	5
×		1	3

b.

	H	T	O
		1	6
×		2	3

c.

	Th	H	T	O
		2	1	1
×			2	6

d.

	Th	H	T	O
		1	1	3
×			2	6

e.

	Th	H	T	O
	1	9	6	5
×				8

f.

	Th	H	T	O
	2	5	4	2
×				4

g.

	Th	H	T	O
	3	1	6	4
×				3

h.

	Th	H	T	O
	1	7	6	5
×				7

2. **Find the product.**

a. 23 × 42　　b. 35 × 27　　c. 42 × 27

d. 26 × 15　　e. 447 × 18　　f. 2234 × 3

g. 1865 × 6　　h. 1142 × 5　　i. 1514 × 3

j. 2764 × 4　　k. 3102 × 2　　l. 1299 × 9

WORD PROBLEMS ON MULTIPLICATION

Example 17: There are 30 chairs in 1 classroom. How many chairs will be there in 5 classrooms?

Solution: Number of chairs in 1 classroom = 30

Number of chairs in 5 classrooms = 30 × 5

Thus, 5 classrooms will have 150 chairs.

	H	T	O
		3	0
×			5
	1	5	0

Example 18: A baker sells 25 cakes in 1 day. How many cakes does he sell in 2 days?

Solution: Number of cakes sold by the baker in 1 day = 25

Number of cakes sold by the baker in 2 days = 25 × 2

Thus, in 2 days, the baker sells 50 cakes.

	T	O
	$^{1}2$	5
×		2
	5	0

Example 19: If a fruit vendor sells 50 apples in 1 day, how many apples does he sell in 6 days?

Solution: Number of apples sold by the vendor in 1 day = 50

Number of apples sold by the vendor in 6 days = 50 × 6 = 300

Thus, the vendor sells 300 apples in 6 days.

	H	T	O
		5	0
×			6
	3	0	0

Example 20: A *kurti* costs ₹325. A saree costs four times the *kurti*. How much does the saree cost?

Solution: 1 *kurti* costs ₹325.

1 saree costs 4 × ₹325 = ₹1300.

So, the cost of the saree is ₹1300.

	Th	H	T	O
		$^{1}3$	$^{2}2$	5
×				4
	1	3	0	0

Example 21: In one box, I can keep 15 pens. How many pens can I keep in 12 boxes?

Solution: 1 box contains = 15 pens

12 boxes contain = 15 × 12 pens = 180 pens.

So, I can keep 180 pens in 12 boxes.

	H	T	O
		$^{1}1$	5
×		1	2
		3	0
+	1	5	0
	1	8	0

EXERCISE 4.4

1. 1 box has 12 chocolates. How many chocolates are there in 7 boxes?

	T	O
	☐	☐
×		☐

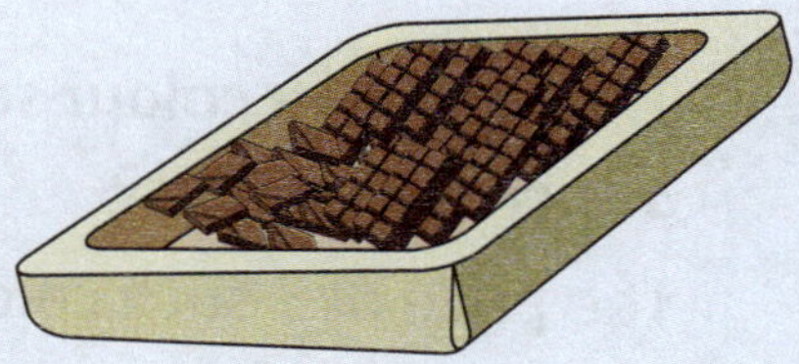

Answer: ☐ chocolates

2. On 1 sheet of paper, Sita painted 2 pictures. How many pictures did she paint on 10 sheets of paper?

☐ × ☐ = ☐

Answer: ☐ pictures

3. 53 people can sit in 1 bus. How many people can sit in 3 buses?

Thus, ________ can sit in 3 buses.

4. Ram earns ₹90 in 1 day. How much money does he earn in 2 days?

Thus, Ram earns ₹________ in 2 days.

5. 95 people can sit in 1 aeroplane. How many people can sit in 3 aeroplanes?

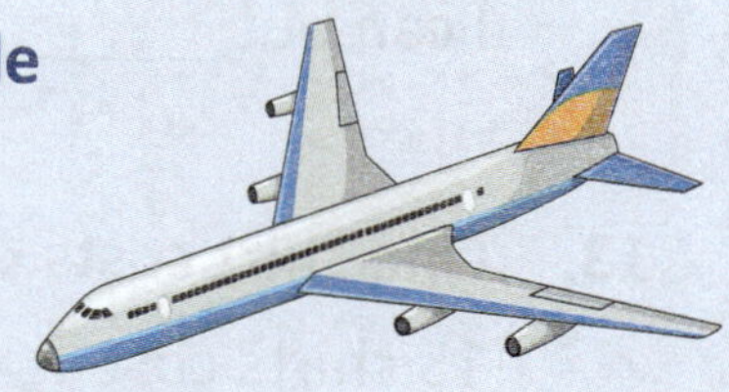

Thus, ________ people can sit in 3 aeroplanes.

6. There are 72 colour pencils in 1 packet. How many colour pencils are there in 5 packets?

Thus, ________ pencils are there in 5 packets.

7. **1 box has 26 pieces of chocolates. How many pieces of chocolates are there in 3 boxes?**

Thus, ________ pieces of chocolates are there in 3 boxes.

8. **The price of a colour set is ₹85. What will be the price of 3 such colour sets?**

The price of 3 such colour sets will be ₹________.

9. **Rajiv bought 9 packets of sweets. Each packet had 32 sweets. How many sweets did Rajiv buy?**

Thus, Rajiv bought ________ sweets.

10. **Sachin has 25 marbles. Kunal has 13 times the number of marbles that Sachin has. How many marbles does Kunal have?**

Kunal has ____________ marbles.

11. **One box of chocolate has 24 pieces in it. How many pieces of chocolates are there in 15 such boxes?**

There are ____________ pieces of chocolates in 15 such boxes.

12. **If I can put 35 books on one shelf, how many books can I put in 17 shelves?**

I can put ____________ books in 17 shelves.

13. **One shirt costs ₹250. How much do 15 shirts cost?**

15 shirts cost ₹____________.

ESTIMATION OF PRODUCT OF TWO NUMBERS

To estimate the product of two numbers, we will first round off the two numbers to their estimated values and then multiply.

Example 22: Estimate the product of 9 and 18.

Solution: 9 is rounded off to 10.

18 is rounded off to 20.

$20 \times 10 = 200$ (We multiply 2 by 1 and put two zeros)

So, the estimated product is 200.

To verify our answer, let us actually multiply 9 and 18.

	H	T	O
		$^{7}1$	8
×			9
	1	6	2

The actual answer is 162 and our estimated answer is 200 which is close to the actual answer.

EXERCISE 4.5

Write the estimated product and verify your answer by actual multiplication.

a. 9 × 12 b. 42 × 8 c. 92 × 9

d. 84 × 9 e. 22 × 8 f. 28 × 9

MULTIPLICATION BY LATTICE METHOD

To multiply numbers using Lattice method, follow the steps given below.

- Draw a box with a diagonal line.
- Write the numbers to be multiplied outside the box.
- Write the product inside the box.

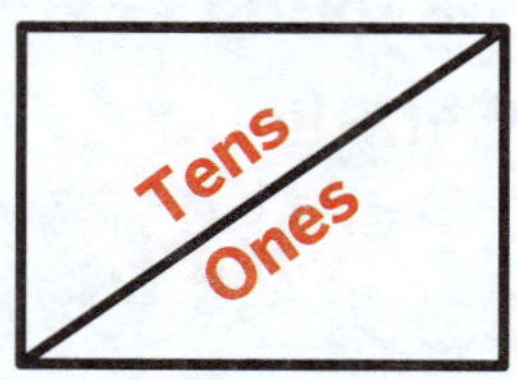

Example 23: Multiply 2 by 9.

Solution:

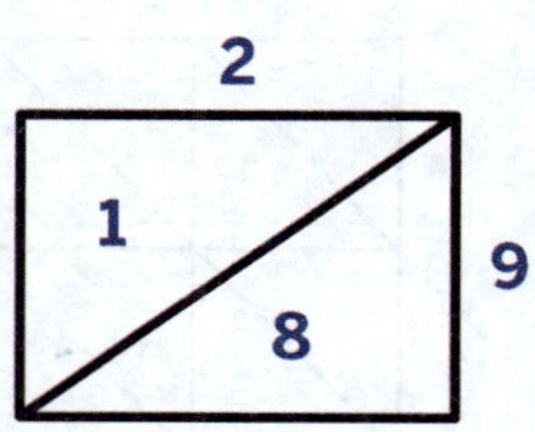

- Make a box with a diagonal line.
- Write 2 and 9 outside the box.
- $2 \times 9 = 18$. So, write 8 of 18 in the ones space and 1 in the tens space inside the box.

Example 24: Multiply 6182 and 4.

Solution:

Step 1: Make a lattice with 4 columns and 1 row as shown.

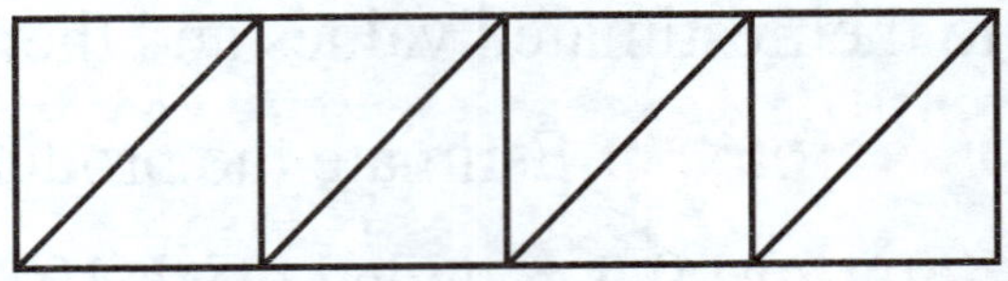

Step 2: Write the multiplicand on the top and the multiplier on the right.

Step 3: Multiply 2 by 4. $2 \times 4 = 8$. Write it as 08.

In the first column, write the tens digit above the diagonal line. Write the ones digit below the diagonal line.

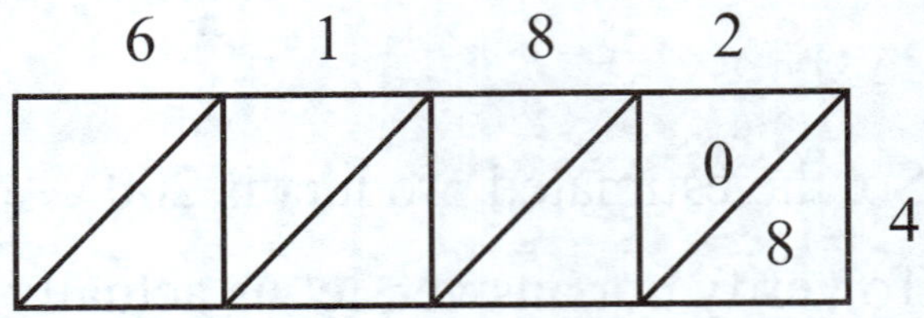

Similarly, multiply 8, 1 and 6 by 4. Write the products as shown.

$8 \times 4 = 32$

$1 \times 4 = 04$

$6 \times 4 = 24$

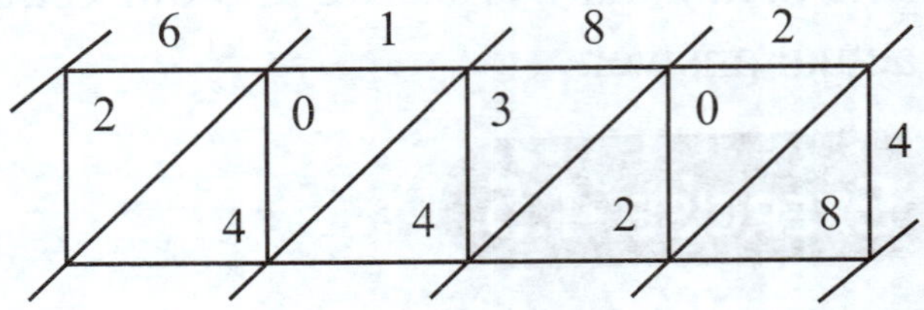

Step 4: Now, add the digits diagonally (only those numbers inside the rectangle).

Step 5: To get the answer, read down the left side and across the bottom.

On reading down the left side and then across bottom, we get 24728.

Thus, $6182 \times 4 = 24728$.

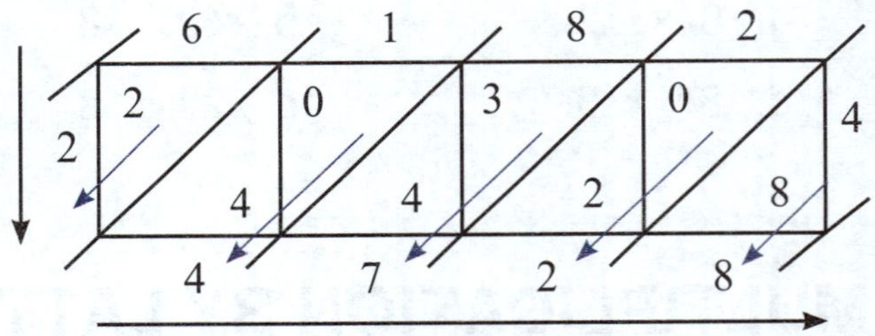

Example 25: Multiply 23 by 47.

Solution:

Step 1:

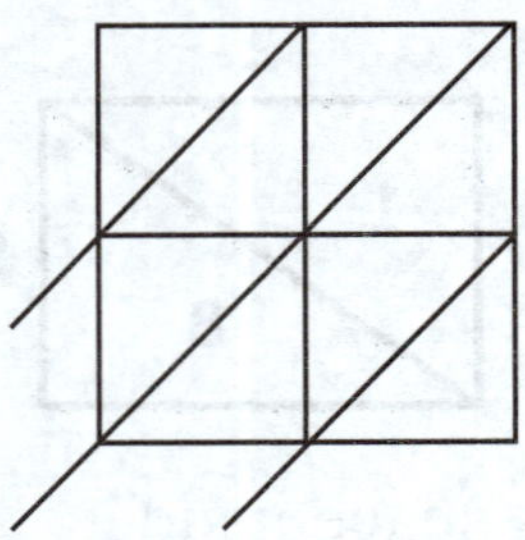

Step 2:

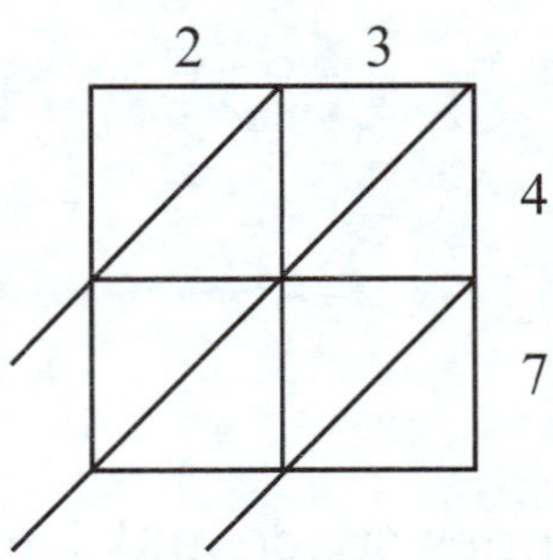

Step 3:

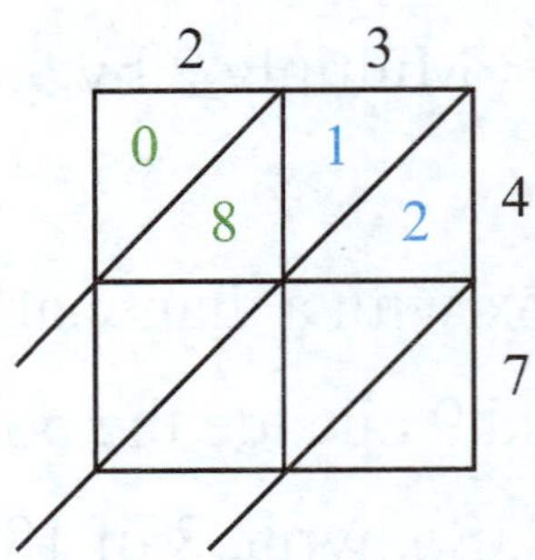

$3 \times 4 = 12$

$2 \times 4 = 8$

Step 4:

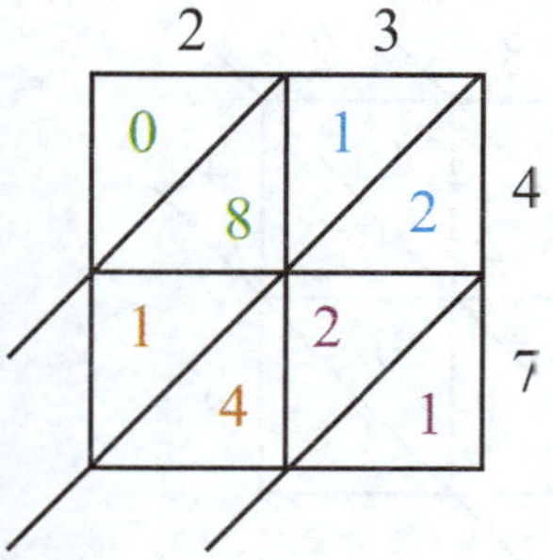

$3 \times 7 = 21$

$2 \times 7 = 14$

Step 5:

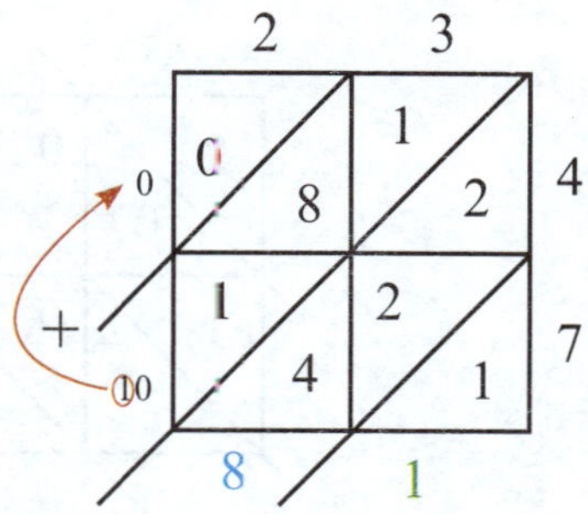

$1 = 1$ $\quad$ $1 + 8 + 1 = 10$

$2 + 2 + 4 = 8$ $\quad$ $0 + 1 = 1$

Step 6:

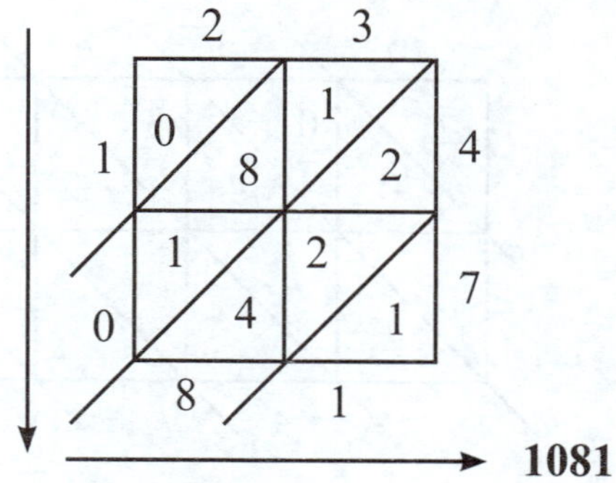

So, $23 \times 47 = 1081$.

Example 26: Multiply 213 by 45.

Solution:

Step 1:

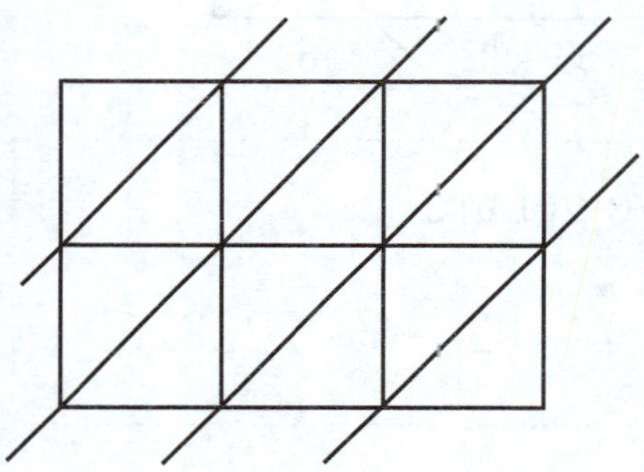

Step 2:

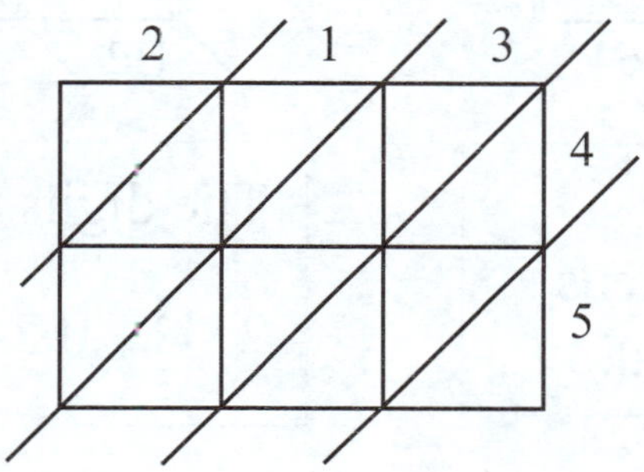

Step 3:

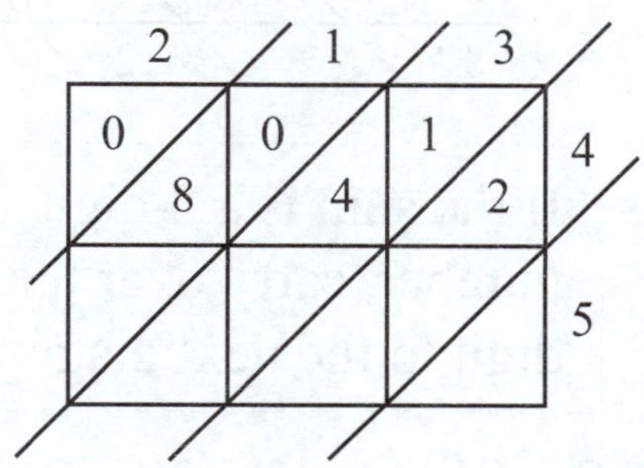

Step 4:

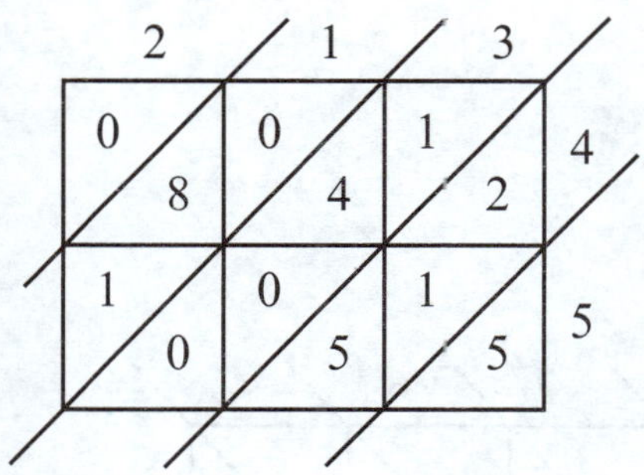

Step 5:

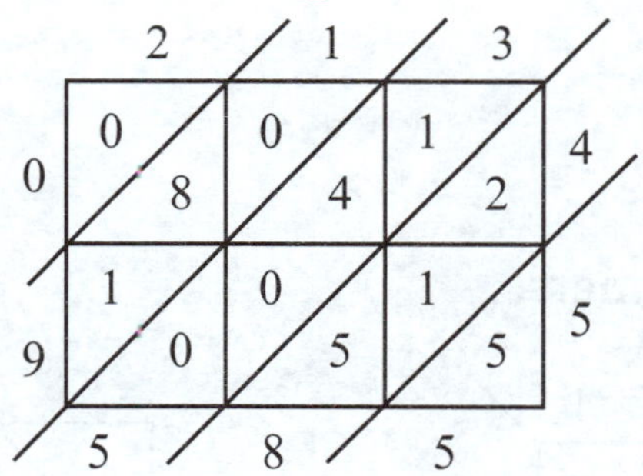

Step 6:

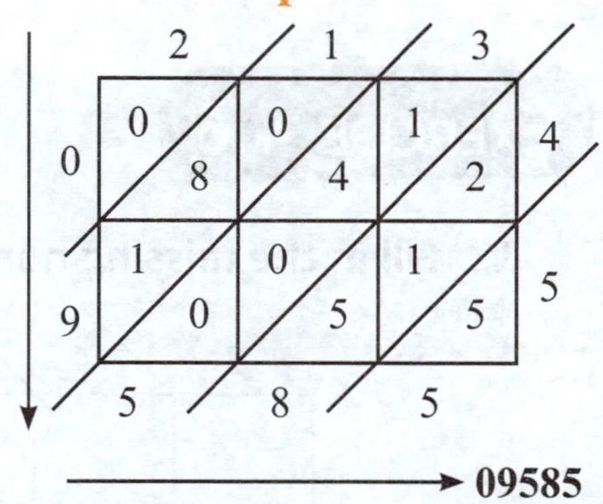

So, $213 \times 45 = 09585 = 9585$.

Example 27: Multiply 5182 by 43.

Solution:

Step 1:

Step 2:

Step 3:

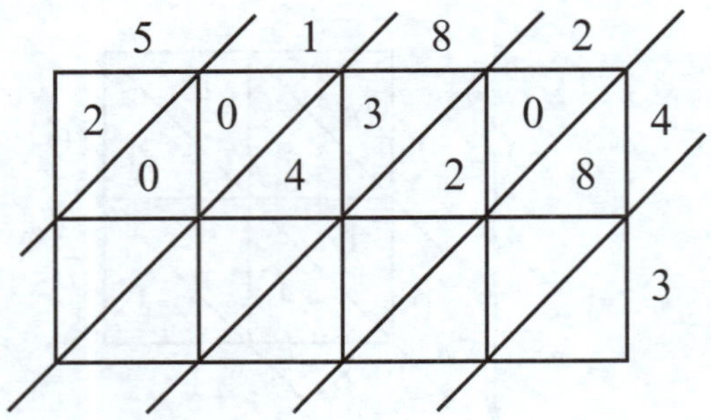

Step 4:

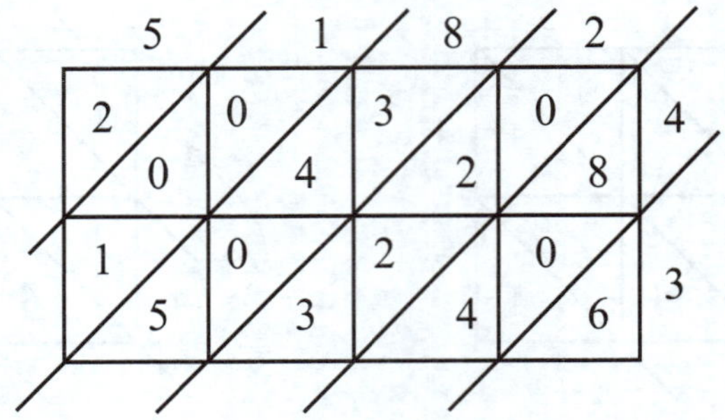

Step 5:

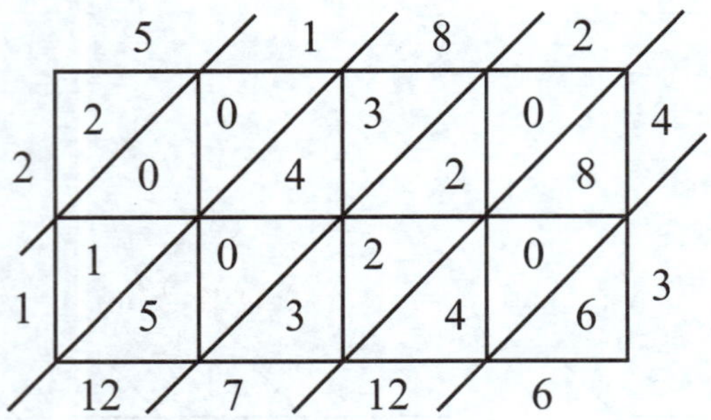

Step 6:

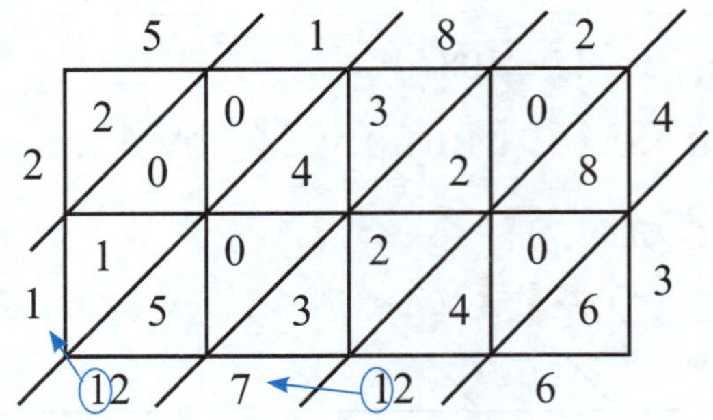

If the sum is a 2-digit number, carry over the tens digit to the next diagonal.

The digits we get are

2 1 12 7 12 6 = 222826.

So, 5182 × 43 = 222826.

EXERCISE 4.6

1. Fill in the missing numbers.

a.

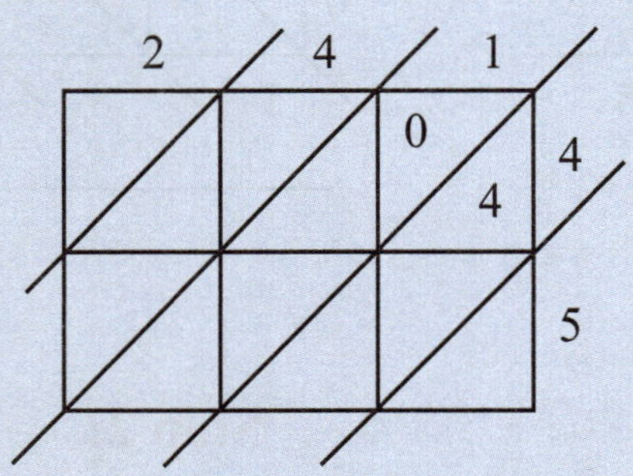

b.

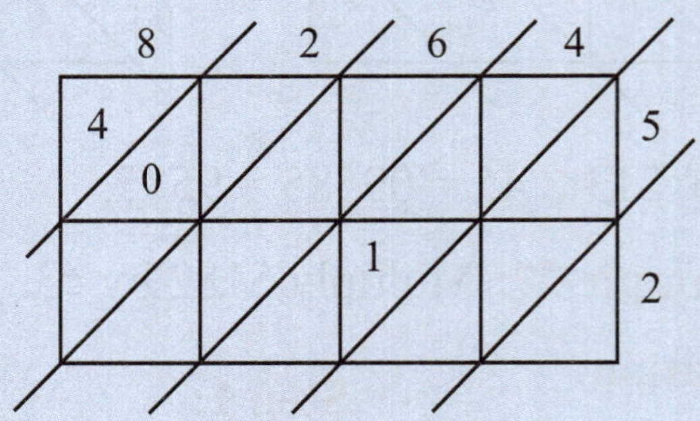

2. Solve the following using lattice method.

a. 422 × 2

b. 4326 × 69

c. 232 × 212

d. 1258 × 427

e. 926 × 341

Key Concepts

Multiplication

Numbers Ending with Zeros

$72 \times 10 = 720$

$83 \times 100 = 8300$

	T	O
	2	0
×		3
	6	0

Multiplication of 3-digit Numbers

	Th	H	T	O
		1	2	1
×			2	4
		^{1}4	8	4
+	2	4	2	0
	2	9	0	4

	Th	H	T	O
		(1) ^{3}2	5	2
×			3	6
	^{1}1	5	1	2
+	7	5	6	0
	9	0	7	2

Multiplication of 4-digit Numbers

	Th	H	T	O
	2	3	1	3
×				2
	4	6	2	6

	Th	H	T	O
	^{2}1	5	^{2}1	6
×				4
	6	0	6	4

Lattice Method

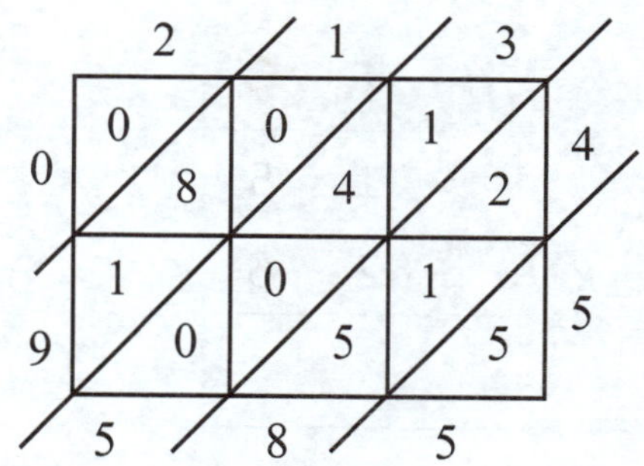

$213 \times 45 = 9585$

Revision Exercise

1. Solve the following.

a.

	T	O
	3	2
×	1	2

b.

	T	O
	5	6
×	2	3

c.

	T	O
	2	0
×	3	2

d.

	T	O
	2	4
×	2	3

e.

	T	O
	6	3
×	4	2

f.

	T	O
	5	7
×	1	3

g.

	H	T	O
	1	3	2
×			3

h.

	H	T	O
	2	0	3
×			2

i.

	H	T	O
	4	3	0
×			2

j.

	H	T	O
		1	5
×		2	6

k.

	H	T	O
	1	3	4
×			6

l.

	H	T	O
	1	2	5
×			6

m.

	Th	H	T	O
	2	2	4	3
×				4

n.

	Th	H	T	O
	1	5	9	6
×				6

o.

	TTh	Th	H	T	O
			7	6	2
×				9	1

p.

	TTh	Th	H	T	O
	1		1	6	5
×					9

q.

	H	T	O
	3	0	0
×			2

r.

	H	T	O
	8	0	0
×			3

2. **Use the short multiplication method to solve the following.**

a. 39 × 10 = _____ b. 72 × 10 = _____ c. 5 × 100 = _____

d. 27 × 100 = _____ e. 92 × 100 = _____ f. 29 × 100 = _____

3. **Solve the following in your notebook using lattice method.**

a. 35 × 2 b. 47 × 6 c. 94 × 4 d. 283 × 4

e. 24 × 35 f. 643 × 27 g. 347 × 23 h. 1985 × 11

4. **A box of chocolates has 36 pieces of chocolates in it. How many pieces of chocolates are there in 8 boxes?**

There are _______ pieces of chocolates in 8 boxes.

5. **A storybook has 24 pages. How many pages are there in 6 such storybooks?**

There are pages _______ in 6 such storybooks.

6. **If there are 25 students in a class, how many students are there in 13 classes?**

7. **How much money do 5 children collect, if each child brings ₹125?**

8. **Write the estimated product and verify your answer by actual multiplication.**

a. 61 × 9 b. 52 × 8

9. **If the cost of 1 book is ₹53, what is the cost of 15 books?**

10. **If 1 year is equal to 365 days, how many days are there in 11 such years?**

11. **If 750 children join a school every year, how many children join the school in 8 years?**

12. **A train ticket from New Delhi to Chandigarh costs ₹390. If there are 200 passengers, then find out the total fare collected from them.**

13. **Surenther purchased 24 chairs at the rate of ₹380 each. Find the amount he spent to purchase the chairs.**

14. **A gift store in a mall ordered 35 bracelets each worth ₹126. What is the amount to be paid by the store for the bracelets?**

15. **A book contains 722 pages. If a book seller purchased 14 such books, then how many pages are there in all?**

5 Division

Prior Knowledge

- Division as equal sharing and repeated subtraction
- Equal grouping
- Properties of division
- Division of 2-digit numbers by 1-digit numbers

Learning Objectives

- Division of 3-digit numbers by 1-digit number
- Division of 4-digit numbers by 1-digit number
- Division by 2-digit number
- Word problems

Let's Get Started

Share the following objects equally.

1. Share 12 mangoes equally among 3 children.

   a. Each child will get __________ mangoes.

   b. Write the division fact. ________________

2. Share 20 flowers equally among 4 baskets.

   a. Each basket will have __________ flowers.

   b. Write the division fact. ________________

TERMS USED IN DIVISION

Let us consider the following division fact.

$18 \div 2 = 9$

Dividend	Divisor	Quotient
The number we are dividing is the dividend.	The number by which we are dividing is the divisor.	The number we get as the answer is the quotient.

```
                  quotient
            1 8 ↙
divisor → 4 ) 7 5 ↖
          – 4 ↓   dividend
            3 5
          – 3 2
remainder → 3
```

DIVISION OF 2-DIGIT NUMBERS BY 1-DIGIT NUMBERS

Division Without Regrouping and No Remainder

Example 1: Divide 68 by 2.

Solution: Let us divide using the long division method. Write the division problem as given below.

```
2 ) 6 8

    3
2 ) 6 8
  – 6
    0

    3 4
2 ) 6 8
  – 6 ↓
    0 8
  –   8
      0
```

Step 1: Take the first digit of 68, which is 6. Divide it by 2. So, $6 \div 2 = 3$ (as $3 \times 2 = 6$).
Write 3 in the quotient's place, 6 below 6 and subtract.
Draw a line below 6 and write 0 below the line.

Step 2: Bring 8 down and write it next to 0.

Step 3: Now, divide 8 by 2.
$8 \div 2 = 4$ (as $4 \times 2 = 8$)
Write 4 in the quotient's place next to 3 and 8 under 8.
Draw a line below 8 and subtract.
We get 0 as the remainder and 34 as the quotient.

Therefore, $68 \div 2 = 34$, where quotient = 34 and remainder = 0.

Division With Regrouping and No Remainder

Example 2: Divide 74 by 2.

Solution:

```
    3 7
2 ) 7 4
  – 6 ↓
    1 4
  – 1 4
      0
```

Thus, $74 \div 2 = 37$.

Step 1: Divide 7 by 2. We get 3 as quotient and 1 as remainder.

Step 2: Bring down 4 of dividend and write it alongside 1 (remainder). The number we get is 14.

Step 3: Divide 14 by 2. Write 7 in the quotient next to 3 and 14 under 14. Draw a line below 14 and subtract, which gives 0 as the remainder.

Division With Regrouping and Remainder

Example 3: Divide 58 by 3.

Solution:

```
     19
 3 ) 58
   - 3↓
     28
   - 27
      1
```

Step 1: Divide 5 by 3. We get 1 as quotient and 2 as remainder.

Step 2: Bring down 8 of dividend and write it alongside 2. The number we get is 28.

Step 3: Divide 28 by 3. Write 9 in the quotient and 27 under 28. Draw a line below 27 and subtract, which gives 1 as the remainder.

So, the quotient is 19 and the remainder is 1.

Division Involving Zero in the Quotient

Example 4: Divide 40 by 2.

Solution: Write the division problem as shown below.

```
 2 ) 40
```

Step 1: Divide the first digit of 40 by 2, which is 4.

$4 \div 2 = 2$ (as $2 \times 2 = 4$)

```
      2
 2 ) 40
   - 4
     0
```

Step 2: Write 2 in the quotient and 4 below 4. Draw a line below 4 and subtract, $4 - 4 = 0$. Write 0 below the line.

```
     20
 2 ) 40
   - 4↓
     00
   - 00
      0
```

Step 3: Now, bring down the 0 of 40. Divide 0 by 2, that is $0 \div 2 = 0$. Write 0 in the quotient next to 2 and 0 below 0. Subtract 0 from 0, which gives 0 as the remainder.

REMEMBER

After bringing down a digit, if the number to be divided is still smaller than the divisor, or it is 0, then we put 0 in the quotient.

Thus, Quotient = 20, Remainder = 0.

EXERCISE 5.1

Divide the following 2-digit numbers using the long division method.

1. 24 ÷ 2	2. 39 ÷ 3	3. 68 ÷ 6	4. 72 ÷ 2
5. 55 ÷ 3	6. 72 ÷ 6	7. 85 ÷ 4	8 70 ÷ 7

DIVISION OF 3-DIGIT NUMBERS BY 1-DIGIT NUMBERS

Division Without Regrouping and No Remainder

Example 5: Solve: 864 ÷ 2

Solution:

```
     4 3 2
3 ) 8 6 4
  − 8↓  |
   0 6  |
  −   6 ↓
     0 4
  −    4
       0
```

Thus, Quotient = 432, Remainder = 0.

Division With Regrouping and No Remainder

Example 6: Solve: 784 ÷ 4

Solution:

```
     1
4 ) 7 8 4
  − 4↓
    3 8
```

Step 1: First divide 7 by 4.

4 × 1 = 4 4 × 2 = 8

As 8 is greater than 7, use 4.

Subtract 4 from 7 to get 3.

Bring down the next digit, that is 8.

```
     1 9
4 ) 7 8 4
  − 4↓  |
    3 8 |
  − 3 6 ↓
      2 4
```

Step 2: Next, divide 38 by 4.

4 × 9 = 36 4 × 10 = 40

As 40 is greater than 38, use 36.

Then, subtract 36 from 38, we get 2.

Now, bring down the last digit, that is 4.

```
     1 9 6
4 ) 7 8 4
  − 4↓  |
    3 8 |
  − 3 6 ↓
      2 4
  −   2 4
        0
```

Step 3: Now, divide 24 by 4.

4 × 6 = 24

Subtract 24 from 24, we get 0.

So, Quotient = 196, Remainder = 0.

Division with Regrouping and Remainder

Example 7: Solve: 597 ÷ 2

Solution:

```
     2 9 8
  2) 5 9 7
   - 4↓  |
   -----
     1 9 |
   - 1 8 ↓
   -------
       1 7
   -   1 6
   -------
         1
```

So, Quotient = 298, Remainder = 1.

Division Involving Zero in the Quotient

Case 1: When the Dividend Involves 0

Example 8: Solve: 340 ÷ 2

Solution:

```
     1 7 0
  2) 3 4 0
   - 2 ↓ |
   -------
     1 4 |
   - 1 4 ↓
   -------
       0 0
```

When the last digit is 0 and there is nothing left to divide, write a 0 in the quotient.

So, Quotient = 170, Remainder = 0.

Example 9: Solve: 502 ÷ 5

Solution:

```
     1 0
  5) 5 0 2
   - 5 ↓ ↓
   -------
     0 0 2
```

Step 1: Divide 5 by 5 to get 1. Next, bring down the 0. As 00 is smaller than the divisor 5, put a 0 in the quotient and bring down the next digit, which is 2.

```
     1 0 0
  2) 5 0 2
   - 5 ↓ ↓
   -------
     0 0 2
   -     0
   -------
         2
```

Step 2: 2 is also smaller than the divisor 5. Write another 0 in the quotient and write 0 below 2 (because 5 × 0 = 0). Now, subtract: 2 − 0 = 2.

REMEMBER

Whenever the number to be divided is smaller than the divisor, we write 0 in the quotient and bring down the next digit.

So, Quotient = 100, Remainder = 2.

Case 2: When the Dividend Does Not Involve 0

Example 10: Solve: 636 ÷ 6.

Solution:

```
     1 0
6 ) 6 3 6
  − 6 ↓ ↓
    0 3 6
```

Step 1: Divide 6 by 6 to get 1. Next, bring down 3. Here, 3 is smaller than the divisor 6. Write 0 in the quotient. Bring down the next digit, which is 6.

```
     1 0 6
6 ) 6 3 6
  − 6 ↓ ↓
    0 3 6
  −   3 6
      0 0
```

Step 2: Divide 36 by 6.
$6 \times 6 = 36$
So, $36 - 36 = 0$.

So, Quotient = 106,
Remainder = 0.

EXERCISE 5.2

Solve the following in your notebook using the long division method.

1. 284 ÷ 2	2. 936 ÷ 3	3. 648 ÷ 9	4. 625 ÷ 4
5. 435 ÷ 7	6. 514 ÷ 3	7. 960 ÷ 4	8. 600 ÷ 5

DIVISION OF 4-DIGIT NUMBERS BY 1-DIGIT NUMBERS

Example 11: Divide 8964 by 2

Solution:

```
      4 4 8 2
2 )  8 9 6 4
   − 8 ↓
     0 9
   −   8 ↓
       1 6
   −   1 6 ↓
         0 4
   −       4
           0
```

So, Quotient = 196, Remainder = 0.

Example 12: Divide 5938 by 7.

Solution:

```
      0 8 4 8
7 )  5 9 3 8
   − 0 ↓
     5 9
   − 5 6 ↓
       3 3
   −   2 8 ↓
         5 8
   −     5 6
           2
```

So, Quotient = 848, Remainder = 2.

DIVISION BY 2-DIGIT NUMBERS

Example 13: Divide 938 by 14.

Solution:

```
      0 6 7
 1 4) 9 3 8
    - 0
    -----
      9 3
    - 8 4
    -----
        9 8
    -   9 8
    -------
          0
```

So, Quotient = 67, Remainder = 0.

Example 14: Divide 425 by 15.

Solution:

```
      0 2 8
 1 5) 4 2 5
    - 0
    -------
      4 2
    - 3 0
    -------
      1 2 5
    - 1 2 0
    -------
          5
```

So, Quotient = 28, Remainder = 5.

Example 15: Divide 4212 by 18.

Solution:

```
      0 2 3 4
 1 8) 4 2 1 2
    - 0
    ---------
      4 2
    - 3 6
    ---------
        6 1
    -   5 4
    ---------
          7 2
    -     7 2
    ---------
            0
```

So, Quotient = 234, Remainder = 0.

Example 16: Divide 9364 by 24.

Solution:

```
      0 3 9 0
 2 4) 9 3 6 4
    - 0
    ---------
      9 3
    - 7 2
    ---------
      2 1 6
    - 2 1 6
    ---------
          0 4
    -       0
    ---------
            4
```

So, Quotient = 390, Remainder = 4.

EXERCISE 5.3

Solve the following in your notebook using the long division method.

1. 1284 ÷ 2	2. 2936 ÷ 3	3. 3648 ÷ 9	4. 5625 ÷ 4
5. 7435 ÷ 7	6. 8514 ÷ 3	7. 9960 ÷ 4	8. 9600 ÷ 5
9. 6679 ÷ 6	10. 8799 ÷ 8	11. 242 ÷ 11	12. 326 ÷ 12
13. 924 ÷ 18	14. 920 ÷ 15	15. 267 ÷ 19	16. 1922 ÷ 12
17. 3294 ÷ 16	18. 6684 ÷ 24	19. 9540 ÷ 25	20. 6465 ÷ 35

WORD PROBLEMS ON DIVISION

- In word problems, we divide
  a. when something is distributed or shared equally.
  b. when we know the value of many quantities and we have to find the value of one quantity.
- When we divide, the greater number is written inside the division sign and the smaller number is written outside the division sign as shown below.

  $\text{Smaller number}\overline{\smash{)}\text{Greater number}}$

Example 17: 8 sweets are to be divided among 2 friends. How many sweets will each friend get?

Solution: Number of sweets = 8

Number of friends = 2

Number of sweets with each friend
= 8 ÷ 2

$$\begin{array}{r} 4 \\ 2\overline{\smash{)}8} \\ -8 \\ \hline 0 \\ \hline \end{array}$$

Thus, each friend gets 4 sweets.

Example 18: For a picnic, Janet has to pack 18 sandwiches. She puts 3 sandwiches in one lunch box. How many boxes will she need?

Solution: Number of sandwiches = 18

Number of sandwiches in one lunch box = 3

$$\begin{array}{r} 6 \leftarrow \text{Number of lunch boxes needed} \\ 3\overline{\smash{)}18} \\ -18 \\ \hline 0 \\ \hline \end{array}$$

Thus, Janet will need 6 lunch boxes.

Example 19: 48 doughnuts were distributed among 3 groups. How many doughnuts did each group get?

Solution: Number of doughnuts = 48

Number of groups = 3

Doughnuts with each group = 48 ÷ 3

So, each group got 16 doughnuts.

$$\begin{array}{r} 16 \\ 3\overline{\smash{)}48} \\ -3\downarrow \\ \hline 18 \\ -18 \\ \hline 0 \end{array}$$

Example 20: 634 books were packed in cartons containing 20 books each.

How many cartons will be packed and how many books will be left?

Solution: Number of books = 634

Number of books in each carton = 20

Number of cartons packed = 634 ÷ 20

So, 31 cartons will be packed, and 14 books will be left unpacked.

```
Cartons ←——— 3 1
packed    20 ) 6 3 4
              − 6 0 ↓
                 3 4
               − 2 0
Books left ←——— 1 4
```

Exercise 5.4

1. **54 oranges are packed equally in 9 baskets. How many oranges does each basket contain?**
   Each basket contains ________ oranges.

2. **636 flower saplings are to be planted in rows. There should be 6 flower saplings in each row. How many rows will be made?**
3. **125 people are travelling to Delhi by cars. 5 people can sit in 1 car. How many cars will they need?**

4. **168 toffees have to be distributed among 8 children. How many toffees will each child get?**
5. **115 people were made to sit equally in 23 benches. How many people sat on 1 bench?**
6. **96 books were distributed among 8 children. How many books did each child get?**
7. **If 6 people have to collect ₹60, how much money should each person bring?**
8. **125 biscuits were packed in packets containing 20 biscuits each. How many packets were made and how many biscuits were left?**

Key Concepts

Division

Division Facts

$18 \div 2 = 9$

Dividend
The number we are dividing is the dividend.

Divisor
The number by which we are dividing is the divisor.

Quotient
The number we get as the answer is the quotient.

```
          18   ← quotient
divisor → 4 ) 75  ← dividend
            – 4↓
              35
            – 32
remainder →    3
```

Smaller number) Greater number

Word Problems

Divide when

- something is distributed
- shared equally.
- when we know the value of many quantities and we have to find the value of one quantity.

Examples

```
     4482
  2 )8964
  – 8
    09
  – 8
     16
   – 16
      04
    –  4
       0
```

```
      028
  15 )425
    –  0
      42
    –30
     125
   – 120
       5
```

```
      0390
  24 )9364
    –  0
      93
    – 72
      216
    – 216
       04
     –  0
        4
```

Revision Exercise

1. Fill in the blanks.

a. If 9 × 8 = 72,
then 72 ÷ 9 = _____
and 72 ÷ 8 = _____

b. If 7 × 8 = 56,
then 56 ÷ 7 = _____
and 56 ÷ 8 = _____

2. Fill in the blanks.

a. If 42 ÷ 7 = 6, then 7 × 6 = _____.

b. If 36 ÷ 4 = 9, then 9 × 4 = _____.

3. Solve the following by long division method.

a. 12 ÷ 2　　b. 25 ÷ 5　　c. 21 ÷ 7

e. 24 ÷ 8　　d. 36 ÷ 9　　f. 28 ÷ 4

4. Solve the following in your notebook.

a. $8\overline{)420}$　　b. $3\overline{)530}$　　c. $4\overline{)549}$　　d. $3\overline{)600}$

e. $7\overline{)918}$　　f. $40\overline{)746}$　　g. $60\overline{)980}$　　h. $20\overline{)150}$

5. Solve the following by long division method.

a. 2151 ÷ 2　　b. 4050 ÷ 3　　c. 4152 ÷ 4　　d. 4198 ÷ 5

e 4210 ÷ 6　　f. 234 ÷ 16　　g. 515 ÷ 13　　h. 237 ÷ 14

i. 692 ÷ 18　　j. 987 ÷ 19　　k. 2034 ÷ 17　　l. 6927 ÷ 28

m. 8503 ÷ 39　　n. 2069 ÷ 5　　o. 3795 ÷ 25

6. 64 people went for boating in a lake. If each boat can carry 8 people and all the people want to go boating at the same time, how many boats will be required?

7. An egg tray can hold 6 eggs. Samar has got 54 eggs. How many trays will he need to store all the eggs?

8. 480 students are made to stand in 3 queues. How many students will be there in 1 queue?

9. Nazia paints 3 flowers on one card. She makes 120 such flowers. How many cards does she make?

10. The teacher distributed 240 crayons equally among 20 students. How many crayons did each student get?

11. If a tailor needs 5 buttons for 1 shirt, how many shirts can he make with 35 buttons?

12. Radhika had 305 apples. She put 15 apples in one basket. How many baskets did she fill and how many apples were left?
13. 325 students went for a picnic in 13 buses. How many students sat in one bus, if each bus had the same number of students?
14. For a school picnic trip, ₹6300 was collected from 9 students. How much did each student pay?
15. The cost of 8 books is ₹4720. What is the cost of one book?
16. There are 5352 books to be distributed among 12 schools. How many books will each school get?
17. A total of 2640 people are made to sit in 12 buses. How many people will sit in 1 bus?
18. What is the least number of packets required if 6220 biscuits are to be packed with each packet containing 22 biscuits. How many biscuits will be left over?
19. Rakesh has to travel a distance of 1250 km in 5 days. What distance should he travel every day?
20. If 4125 trees are planted in 25 rows, how many trees would be there in each row?
21. If 9788 oranges are packed in 28 bags, how many oranges will be there in each bag? Are there any oranges left? How many are left?
22. A total of 576 chocolates were packed in 24 boxes. How many chocolates were there in each box?
23. A school has 4704 students. Groups were formed for an event. A group has 32 students. How many groups would be formed for the event?
24. ₹6435 was distributed among 39 people. How much money did each person get?
25. A total of 8976 books are arranged on 24 shelves. If a shelf can hold the same number of books, how many books are there on each shelf?

6 Money

Prior Knowledge

- Notes and coins
- Addition of money
- Subtraction of money
- Daily-life problems related to money

Learning Objectives

- Conversion of rupees to paise and vice versa
- Addition and subtraction of money
- Word problems

Let's Get Started

A. Ankit has ________________ rupees.

B. He gets __________ rupees for doing chores.

C. His grandma gives him ______ rupees.

D. He finds __________ rupees on the sofa.

How much money does he have in total?

RUPEE–PAISA CONVERSION

We know that we need money to buy food, clothes, medicines, etc. Every country has its own currency consisting of notes and coins. In India, the currency used is called 'rupee' and 'paisa'.

Look at some of the notes and coins used in India. Some of the notes shown here are not in use these days.

Notes

Coins

The plural of rupee is rupees, and the plural of paisa is paise. The symbol for rupees is ₹, and the symbol for paise is **p**.

₹1 = 100 p

₹2.50 = 2 rupees 50 paise

₹9.70 = 9 rupees 70 paise

A dot separates the rupees and paise. On the left of the dot are rupees and on the right of the dot are paise.

REMEMBER

Every country has its own currency. The Unites States uses the dollar, England uses the pound and Japan uses the yen.

Example 1: Write the following in symbolic form.

a. 6 rupees 68 paise

b. 74 rupees 65 paise

c. 214 rupees 80 paise

d. 890 rupees 5 paise

Solution:

a. 6 rupees 68 paise = ₹6.68

b. 74 rupees 65 paise = ₹74.65

c. 214 rupees 80 paise = ₹214.80

d. 890 rupees 5 paise = ₹890.05

Example 2: Write the following in words.

a. ₹9.50 b. ₹16.04 c. ₹84.68 d. ₹108.55

Solution:

a. ₹9.50 = 9 rupees 50 paise

b. ₹16.04 = 16 rupees 4 paise

c. ₹84.68 = 84 rupees 68 paise

d. ₹108.55 = 108 rupees 55 paise

Converting Rupees to Paise

₹1 = 100 p

While converting rupees to paise, we multiply by 100.

Example 3: Convert the following into paise.

a. ₹7 b. ₹18

Solution:

a. ₹7 = 7 × 100 = 700 paise

b. ₹18 = 18 × 100 = 1800 paise

Example 4: Convert 9 rupees 25 paise to paise.

Solution: To convert rupees and paise into paise, we multiply rupees by 100 and then add the existing paise to the product. We first convert 9 rupees to paise and then add 25 paise to the answer.

9 rupees = 9 × 100 = 900 paise

9 rupees 25 paise = 900 paise + 25 paise

= 925 paise

So, 9 rupees 25 paise = 925 paise.

Example 5: Convert 5 rupees 40 paise to paise.

Solution: 5 rupees = 5 × 100 = 500 paise

5 rupees 40 paise = 500 paise + 40 paise

= 540 paise

So, 5 rupees 40 paise = 540 paise.

A shorter method for converting rupees and paise to paise is to just remove the dot. Remove the rupee symbol and write p at the end.

₹13.25 = 1325 p ₹42.70 = 4270 p

Converting Paise to Rupees

100 p = ₹1

While converting paise to rupees, we divide by 100. To convert paise to rupees, leave two digits from the right and put the dot. Put the symbol of rupee at the beginning. Remember that there are always 2 digits for paise.

Example 6: Convert 500 paise to rupees.

Solution: To convert 500 paise to rupees, we divide by 100.

Leave two digits from the right and put a dot. We get ₹5.

So, 500 p = ₹5.

Example 7: Convert 523 paise to rupees.

Solution: Leave two digits from the right and put a dot. We get ₹5.23

So, 523 p = ₹5.23.

Example 8: Convert 59 paise to rupees.

Solution: Keeping last two digits for paise and putting the dot, we get ₹0.59

So, 59 p = ₹0.59.

Example 9: Convert 7 paise to rupees.

Solution: Two digits have to be kept for paise. So, we add a zero before 7 and put the dot.

So, we get = ₹0.07

So, 7 p = ₹0.07.

Example 10: Convert 5 rupees 25 paise to rupees.

Solution: 5 rupees = 500 paise

5 rupees 25 paise = 500 paise + 25 paise

= 525 paise

So, moving the dot two places from the right,
525 paise = ₹5.25

So, 5 rupees 25 paise = ₹5.25.

EXERCISE 6.1

1. **Write the following in symbolic form.**
   a. 7 rupees 78 paise
   b. 64 rupees 6 paise
   c. 409 rupees 8 paise
   d. 790 rupees 50 paise
2. **Write the following in words.**
   a. ₹7.25
   b. ₹60.04
   c. ₹63.08
   d. ₹327.75
3. **Convert the following to paise.**
   a. ₹7
   b. ₹12
   c. ₹9
   d. ₹56
   e. ₹90
   f. ₹62
   g. ₹22
   h. ₹38
4. **Convert the following to rupees.**
   a. 800 paise
   b. 1600 paise
   c. 725 paise
   d. 950 paise
   e. 550 paise
   f. 1230 paise
   g. 1505 paise
   h. 4535 paise
5. **Convert the following to paise.**
   a. ₹5.30
   b. ₹15.45
   c. ₹23.09
   d. 12 rupees and 50 paise
   e. 15 rupees and 12 paise
   f. 38 rupees and 9 paise
6. **Convert the following to rupees.**
   a. 3 rupees 12 paise
   b. 12 rupees 35 paise
   c. 17 rupees 3 paise
   d. 33 rupees 2 paise

ADDITION AND SUBTRACTION OF RUPEES AND PAISE

Rupees and paise are added and subtracted just like numbers.

After adding or subtracting, remember to place the dot just before two places from the right. The dot separates the rupees part from the paise part. On the left side of the dot, we write rupees and on the right side of the dot, we write paise.

Example 11: Solve the following.

a. ₹400 + ₹500 + ₹5

b. ₹2.50 + ₹13.25

c. ₹39.87 + ₹169.07

d. ₹12.69 + ₹3.95 + 16 p

Solution:

a.
```
    ₹
  4 0 0
  5 0 0
+     5
-------
  9 0 5
```
Answer = ₹905

b.
```
    ₹  p
   2.50
+ 13.25
-------
  15.75
```
Answer = ₹15.75

c.
```
    ₹  p
   1 1
   39.87
+ 1
  169.07
--------
  208.94
```
Answer = ₹208.94

d.
```
    ₹  p
   1 2
   12.69
    3.95
+   0.16
--------
   16.80
```
Answer = ₹16.80

Example 12: Solve the following.

a. ₹495 – ₹13 b. ₹93.12 – ₹12.35

Solution:

a.
```
    ₹
  4 9 5
–   1 3
-------
  4 8 2
```
Answer = ₹482

b.
```
     ₹  p
   2 10 0 12
   9 3 .1 2
– 1 2 .3 5
----------
  8 0 .7 7
```
Answer = ₹80.77

Example 13: Subtract ₹13. 25 from ₹19.

Solution:

```
     ₹  p
       9
    8 10 10
  1 9 .0 0
– 1 3 .2 5
----------
  0 5 .7 5
```
Answer = ₹5.75

REMEMBER

1. If there is no paisa, write 00 after the dot.
2. While adding and subtracting, arrange the amounts in such a way that all the dots fall in one line.

EXERCISE 6.2

1. **Solve the following.**
   a. ₹100 + ₹50 b. ₹500 + ₹100 + ₹30
   c. ₹700 + ₹100 d. ₹230 + ₹140 + ₹66
   e. ₹500 + ₹100 + ₹50 f. ₹100 + ₹50 + ₹20
2. **Solve the following.**
   a. ₹100 – ₹25 b. ₹500 – ₹432 c. ₹298 – ₹137 d. ₹960 – ₹923
3. **Solve the following.**

a.
```
    ₹   p
   12  45
+  19  20
---------

---------
```

b.
```
    ₹   p
    9  36
+  42  55
---------

---------
```

c.
```
    ₹   p
  169  48
+  20  09
---------

---------
```

d.
```
    ₹   p
   27  15
+ 165  20
---------

---------
```

4. **Add the following.**

a. ₹49.25, ₹12.72 and ₹63.50

b. ₹450.50, ₹19.25 and ₹7.15

c. ₹259.65, 35 p and ₹500

5. **Solve the following.**

a.
$$\begin{array}{rrr} & ₹ & p \\ & 25 & 14 \\ - & 12 & 13 \\ \hline & & \\ \hline \end{array}$$

b.
$$\begin{array}{rrr} & ₹ & p \\ & 95 & 75 \\ - & 29 & 50 \\ \hline & & \\ \hline \end{array}$$

c.
$$\begin{array}{rrr} & ₹ & p \\ & 63 & 15 \\ - & 29 & 49 \\ \hline & & \\ \hline \end{array}$$

d.
$$\begin{array}{rrr} & ₹ & p \\ & 240 & 49 \\ - & 89 & 52 \\ \hline & & \\ \hline \end{array}$$

6. **Subtract the following.**

a. ₹12.39 from ₹49.50

b. ₹20.25 from ₹155.45

c. ₹12.50 from ₹179.75

d. ₹36.89 from ₹63.98

WORD PROBLEMS

When we are given the price of 1 item and we need to find the price of many, we multiply the price by the quantity.

When we buy something from a shop, the shopkeeper gives us a **bill**. That bill explains to us as to how much we are paying for each item. It also tells us the **total amount we have to pay** for all the items bought.

A **rate chart** helps us to make the bill.

If 1 pen costs ₹15, then 3 pens will cost ₹45. We multiply the cost of one item with the number of items bought. This is explained below in a rate chart.

Particulars	Quantity	Rate	Amount
Pens	3	₹12	₹36

Example 14: If 1 pen costs ₹65, then how much will 7 pens cost?

Solution:

$$\begin{array}{r} ₹ \\ {}^{3}65 \\ \times\ 7 \\ \hline 455 \\ \hline \end{array}$$

So, 7 pens will cost ₹455.

Example 15: If I need to pay Santosh ₹372 and I give him a 500-rupee note, how much money will he return to me?

Solution:

$$\begin{array}{rrrr} & & M & \\ & & 9 & \\ & {}^{4}\not{5} & {}^{10}\not{0} & {}^{10}\not{0} \\ - & 3 & 7 & 2 \\ \hline & 1 & 2 & 8 \\ \hline \end{array}$$

Santosh will return ₹128.

Example 16: Lekha bought the following items from a stationery shop.

a. 5 pens at ₹12 each
b. 6 pencils at ₹9 each
c. 4 erasers at ₹5 each

Prepare a bill to calculate the total amount that Lekha has to pay.

Solution:

Prakash Stationery Store				
S. No.	**Particulars**	**Quantity**	**Rate**	**Amount**
1.	Pens	5	₹12	₹12 × 5 = ₹60
2.	Pencils	6	₹9	₹9 × 6 = ₹54
3.	Erasers	4	₹5	₹5 × 4 = ₹20
			Total amount	₹134

Answer: Lekha has to pay **₹134** for the items she bought.

Example 17: Vivaan went to Jumbo Toy Shop and bought the following items.

a. 2 dolls at ₹50 each
b. 1 aeroplane at ₹150
c. 3 balls at ₹20 each
d. 5 marbles at ₹6 each

Prepare a bill to calculate the total amount that Vivaan has to pay.

Solution:

Jumbo Toy Shop				
S. No.	**Particulars**	**Quantity**	**Rate**	**Amount**
1.	Dolls	2	₹50	₹50 × 2 = ₹100
2.	Aeroplane	1	₹150	₹150 × 1 = ₹150
3.	Balls	3	₹20	₹20 × 3 = ₹60
4.	Marbles	5	₹6	₹6 × 5 = ₹30
			Total amount	₹340

Answer: Vivaan has to pay **₹340** for the items bought.

Exercise 6.3

Solve the following.

1. If 1 pencil costs ₹35, what will be the cost of 6 pencils?

2. If each person gives ₹51 for charity, how much money will be collected from 6 people?

3. Tenzin bought a globe for ₹280 and a pen for ₹49. How much did he spend in all?

4. Sufiya bought a toy for ₹179. She gave the shopkeeper a 500-rupee note. How much money would the shopkeeper return to her?

5. Ajay bought vegetables worth ₹395. But he has only ₹255 with him. How much more money does he need?

6. If one book costs ₹68, what will be the cost of 9 such books?

7. Rashi bought a dress for ₹780. She gave the shopkeeper one 500-rupee note and three 100-rupee notes. How much money will the shopkeeper return to Rashi?

8. To pay ₹100 to a shopkeeper, I can pay
   ______ 100-rupee note or ______ 50-rupee notes.

9. To pay ₹200 to a shopkeeper, I can pay
   ______ 100-rupee notes.

10. To pay ₹500 to a shopkeeper, I can pay
    ______ 500-rupee note or ______ 100-rupee notes.

11. To pay ₹60 to a shopkeeper, I can pay
    ______ 10-rupee notes or ______ 5-rupee coins.

12. **Jeniya went to an ice cream shop and bought the following ice creams.**
    a. 3 chocolate ice creams at ₹20 each
    b. 8 vanilla ice creams at ₹15 each
    c. 10 orange bars at ₹12 each

    Prepare a bill to calculate the total amount that Jeniya has to pay.

13. **Shahid went to Yummy Bakery and bought the following items.**
    a. 2 loaves of bread at ₹30 each
    b. 6 pastries at ₹25 each
    c. 4 patties at ₹20 each
    d. 1 cake at ₹200

    Prepare a bill to calculate the total amount that Shahid has to pay.

14. **Rachit went to Uncle's Gift Shop and bought the following gifts for his cousins.**
    a. 3 puzzle games for ₹62 each
    b. 4 crayon sets for ₹35 each
    c. 2 bracelets for ₹77 each
    d. 1 diary for ₹110

    Prepare a bill to calculate the total amount that Rachit has to pay.

Key Concepts

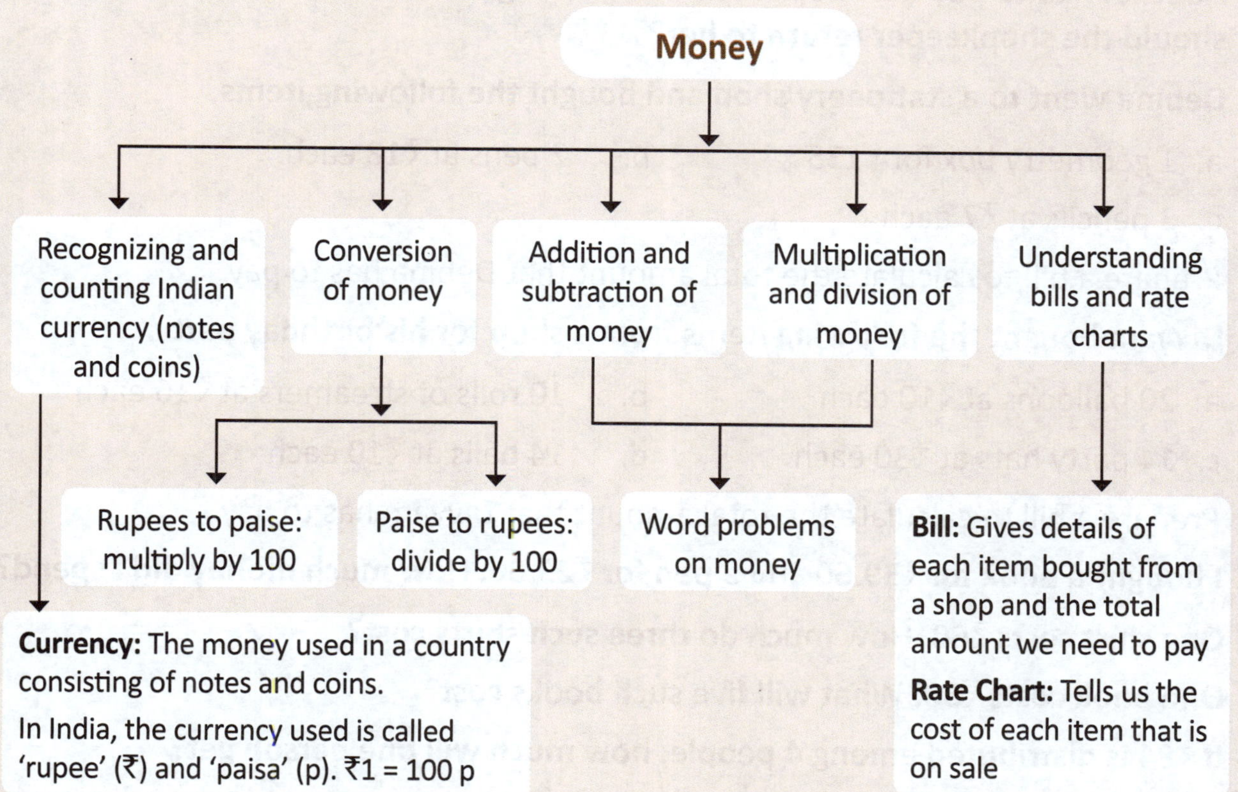

Revision Exercise

1. **Convert the following to paise.**

   a. ₹8 b. ₹19 c. ₹73 d. ₹4.80
   e. ₹27.35 f. ₹5 g. ₹20 h. ₹150
   i. ₹4.45 j. 7 rupees 12 paise k. ₹9 l. ₹24
   m. ₹1500 n. ₹5009 o. ₹9.40 p. ₹23.47

2. **Convert the following to rupees.**

   a. 300 paise b. 2700 paise
   c. 8 rupees 43 paise d. 15 rupees 29 paise
   e. 400 paise f. 3529 paise
   g. 7 rupees 42 paise h. 900 paise
   i. 1700 paise j. 125 paise
   k. 820 paise l. 3640 paise
   m. 7345 paise n. 2 rupees 35 paise

3. **Add ₹57.18, ₹13.69 and ₹42.56.**
4. **Subtract ₹34.50 from ₹73.25.**
5. **Sanjana wants to buy 5 hats. Each hat costs ₹94. How much money does she need?**
6. **Aanchal had to pay the shopkeeper ₹814. She gave him ₹900. How much money should the shopkeeper return to her?**
7. **Debina went to a stationery shop and bought the following items.**

   a. 1 geometry box for ₹135 b. 2 pens at ₹18 each
   c. 3 pencils at ₹7 each

   Prepare a bill to calculate the total amount that Debina has to pay.

8. **Divyam bought the following items from a shop for his birthday party.**

   a. 20 balloons at ₹10 each b. 10 rolls of streamers at ₹16 each
   c. 14 party hats at ₹30 each d. 14 balls at ₹10 each

   Prepare a bill to calculate the total amount that Divyam has to pay.

9. **I bought a book for ₹59.60 and a pen for ₹25.00. How much money did I spend?**
10. **One shirt costs ₹60. How much do three such shirts cost?**
11. **One book costs ₹50. What will five such books cost?**
12. **If ₹84 is distributed among 4 people, how much will one person get?**
13. **If I need to pay the shopkeeper ₹375 and I give him ₹500, how much money will he return to me?**

7 Geometry

Prior Knowledge

- Straight lines and curved lines
- Different types of straight lines
- Identifying attributes of flat and solid shapes
- Creating 2D shapes through paper folding and paper cutting
- Identifying rolling and sliding objects

Learning Objectives

- Dot grid and making different shapes on a dot grid
- Tangram shapes
- 2D and 3D shapes
- Tessellation
- Map reading

Let's Get Started

Many puzzles make use of geometry. Virat has created this figure using blocks of different sizes and colours. Observe the figure and answer the questions.

1. How many square blocks are there in all? ____________
2. How many rectangular blocks are there in all? ____________
3. How many yellow blocks has Virat used? ____________

STRAIGHT AND CURVED LINES

Straight Line

A straight line does not have any curve in it. It can be horizontal, slanted or vertical.

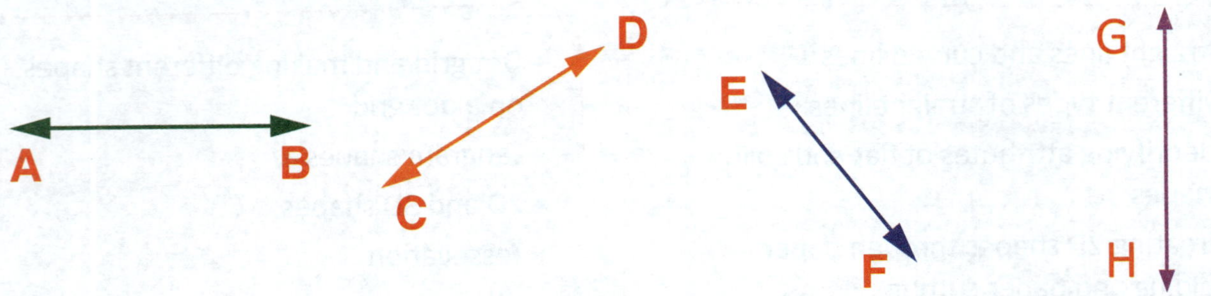

Horizontal line　　　Slanting lines　　　Vertical line

Curve

A curve is a collection of points that do not follow a straight path. AB is a curve.

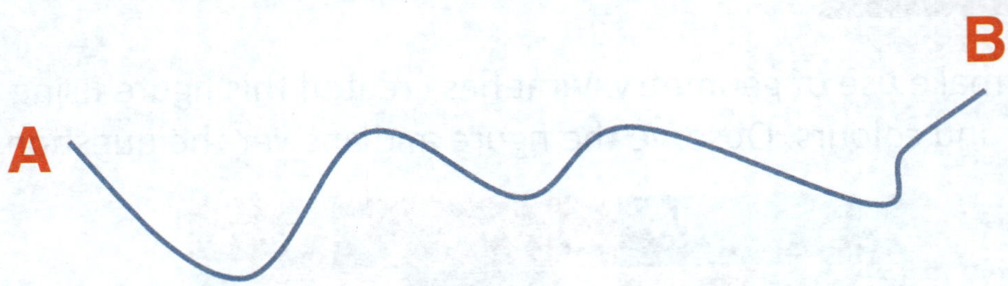

DOT GRID

A dot grid is a set of evenly spaced dots where we can create vertical, horizontal and diagonal lines as well as curves by joining the dots. A dot grid is shown below.

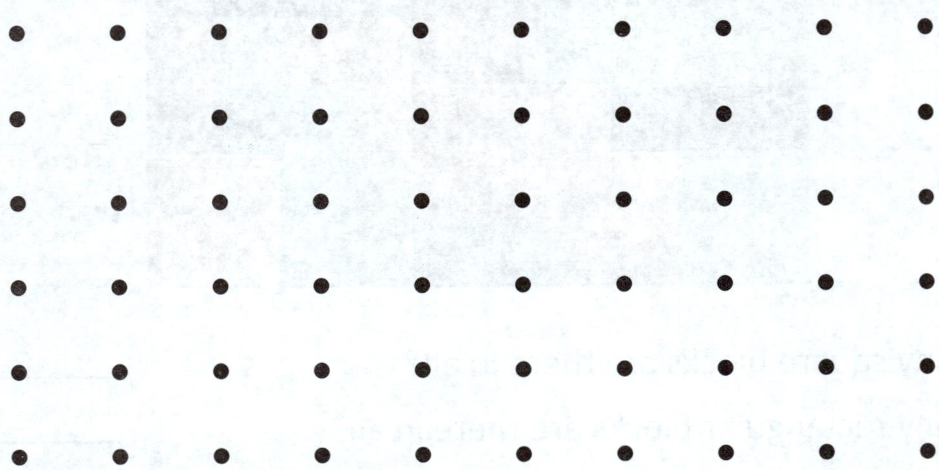

Making Vertical Line Segments

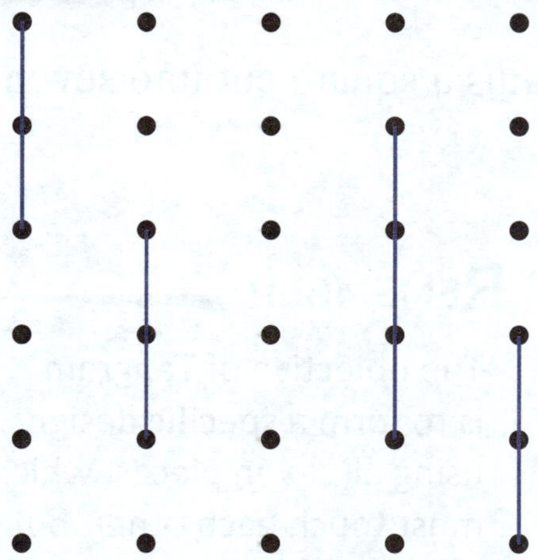

Making Horizontal Line Segments

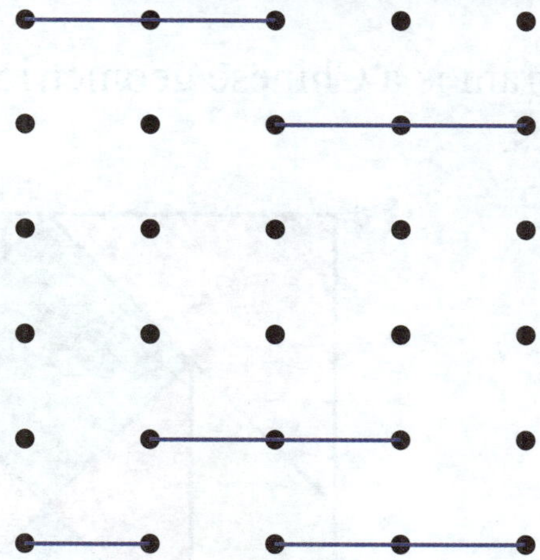

Making Curves

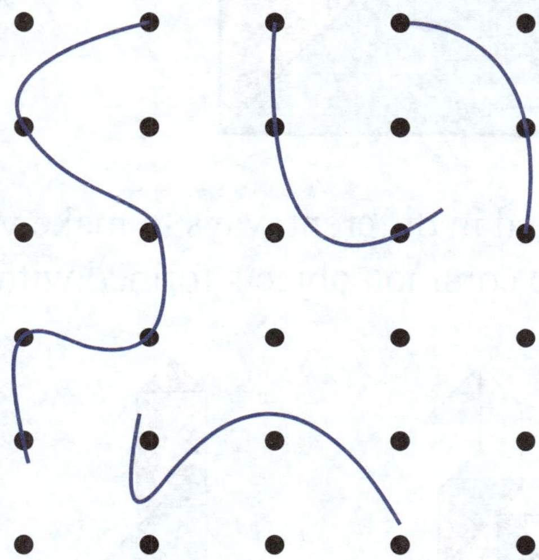

Making Different Shapes on a Dot Grid

Different shapes can be formed on a dot grid with the help of lines and curves.

 This is a straight line.  This is a curve.

Let us make some shapes and figures on a dot grid.

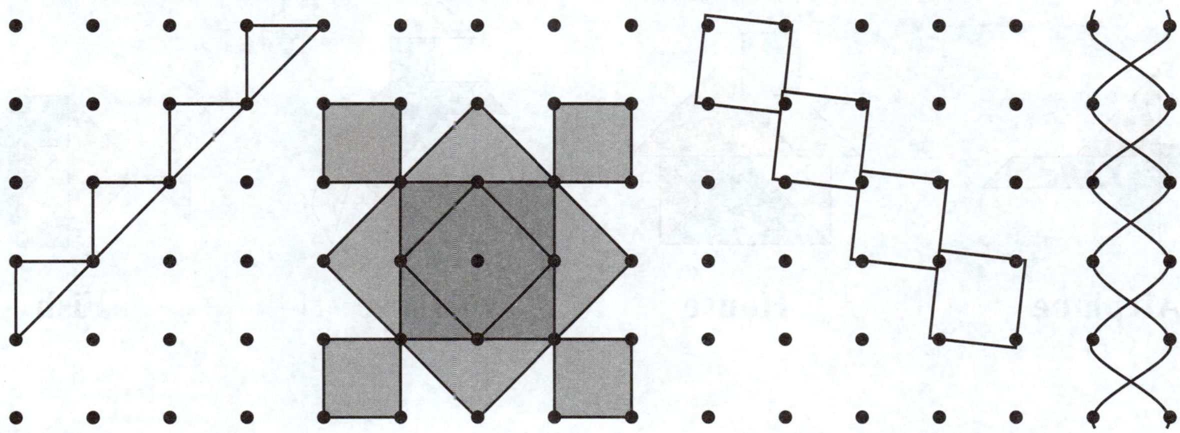

TANGRAM SHAPES

Tangram is a Chinese geometrical puzzle that contains a square cut into seven pieces.

REMEMBER

The objective of Tangram is to form a specific design using all seven pieces, which must touch each other, but not overlap.

These pieces can be arranged in different ways to make various shapes and figures. Look at the shapes of some common objects formed with Tangram pieces.

Candle

Swan

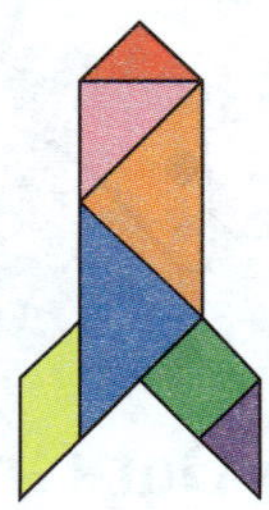

Rocket

Boat

Airplane

House

Horse

Fish

Exercise 7.1

1. **Draw the following in the dot grid.**

   a. Slanting line b. Square c. Triangle d. Rectangle

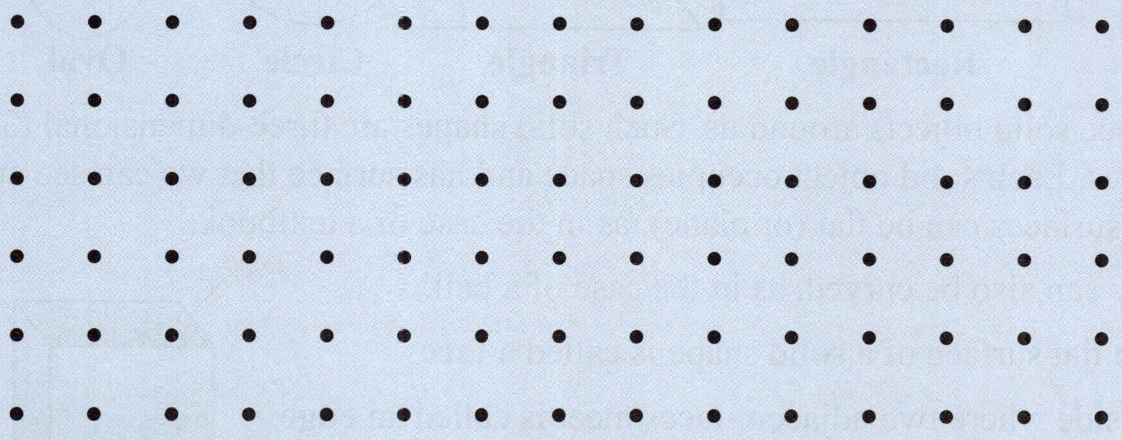

2. **Identify the following figures and make them using tangram puzzle.**

a.

b.

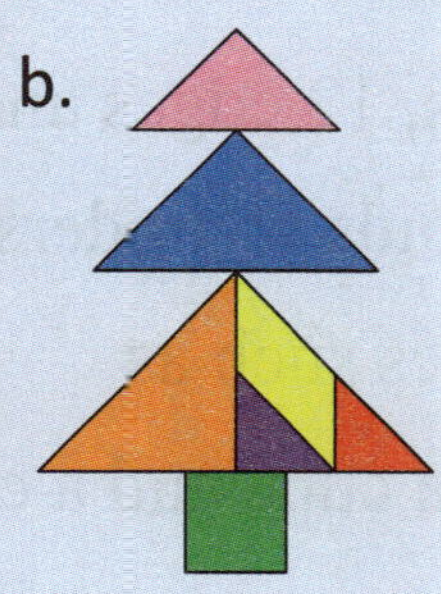

c.

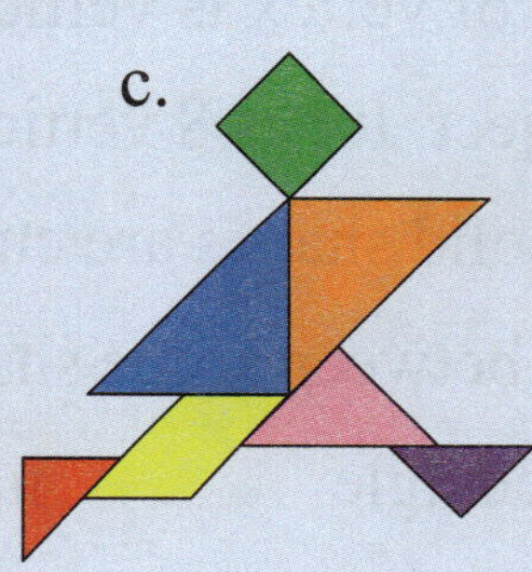

d.

_______________ _______________ _______________ _______________

2D AND 3D SHAPES

A two-dimensional (2D) shape can be drawn on any plane surface. 2D shapes have only length and width.

A square is an example of a 2D shape. It has 4 vertices and 4 sides as shown below.

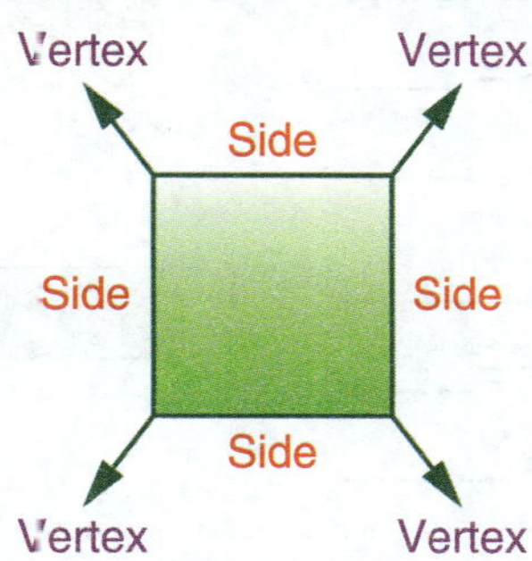

Other examples of 2D shapes are rectangles, circles, triangles and ovals.

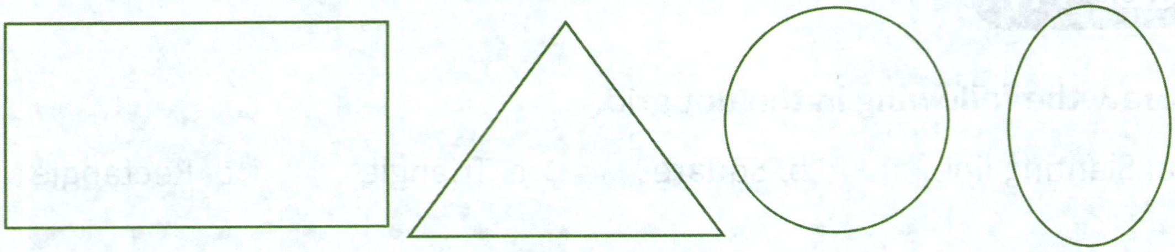

Rectangle **Triangle** **Circle** **Oval**

We see solid objects around us. Such solid shapes are three-dimensional (3D) shapes. Each solid object occupies space and has surface that we can see and feel. The surfaces can be flat (or plane), as in the case of a textbook.

They can also be curved, as in the case of a ball.

Each flat surface of a solid shape is called a **face**.

The side where two adjacent faces meet is called an **edge**.

The corner where two or more edges meet is called a **vertex**. The plural of vertex is vertices.

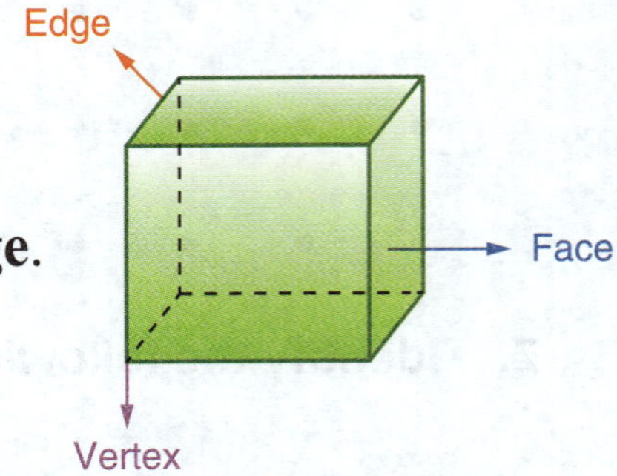

A cube is a solid object. It has 8 vertices, 12 edges and 6 faces, as shown.

Other examples of solid shapes are cuboids, cylinders, spheres and cones.

We find similarities between some shapes such as

i. a square and a rectangle ii. a cube and a cuboid

Exercise 7.2

1. Look at the figures and fill in the blanks.

a. 
Name: ____________
Number of vertices = ____
Number of sides = ______

b. 
Name: ____________
Number of vertices = ____
Number of sides = ______

c. 
Name: ____________
Number of vertices = ____
Number of sides = ______

d. 
Name: ____________
Number of vertices = ____
Number of sides = ______

e. 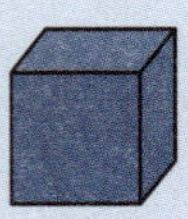
Name: ____________
Number of vertices = ____
Number of edges = ______
Number of faces = ______

f. 
Name: ____________
Number of vertices = ____
Number of edges = ______
Number of faces = ______

g. 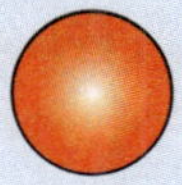

Name: ______________

Number of vertices = ____

Number of edges = ______

Curved face = __________

h. 

Name: ____________

Curved face = ______

Flat circles = _______

i. 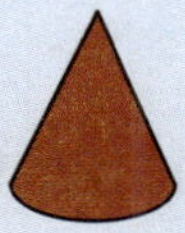

Name: ______________

Number of vertices = ____

Curved face = __________

Flat circle = ___________

REMEMBER

In the case of a cone, the corner where the curved surfaces meet is called the vertex or apex.

2. Compare the following shapes. Write the similarities between them.

a. Square and rectangle

Both have ______________.

Both have ______________.

b. Cuboid and cube

Both have ______________.

Both have ______________.

3. Match the shapes to their properties.

Column A	Column B
a. Triangle	i. 4 equal sides, 4 vertices
b. Circle	ii. 3 sides, 3 vertices
c. Square	iii. 4 sides, 4 vertices
d. Cone	iv. 1 curved face, 1 flat circle, 1 vertex
e. Rectangle	v. 1 curved face, 0 vertex

LINE DRAWINGS OF 3D OBJECTS ON PAPER OR ON FLAT SURFACE

2D figures are figures without any height. When we give height to a 2D figure, it becomes a 3D figure.

a. Square

When we give height to a square, it becomes a cube.

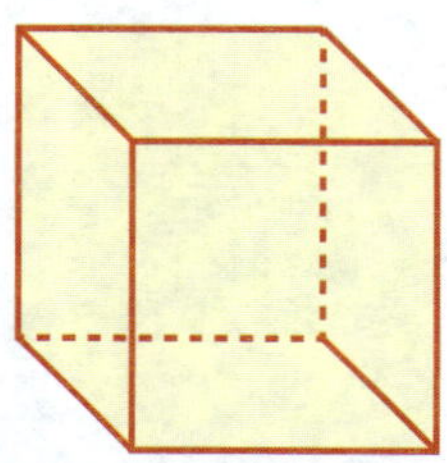

A cube has 6 square faces and 12 edges. If you look at a cube from any side, it will look like a square.

b. Rectangle

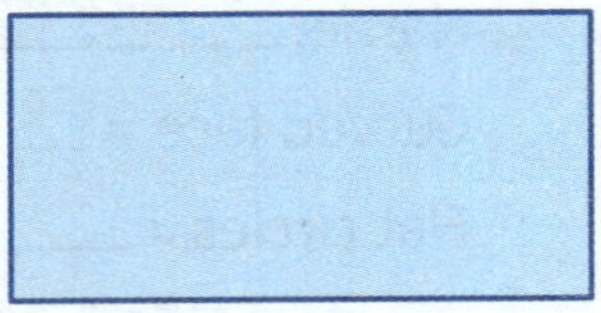

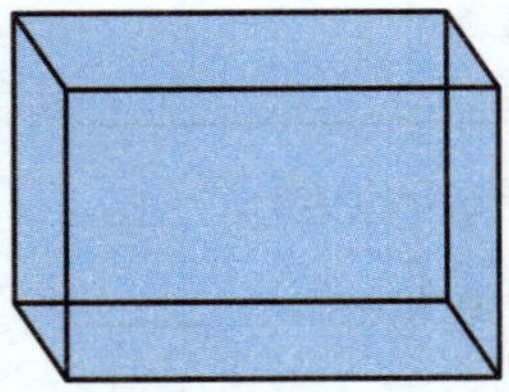

When we give height to a rectangle, it becomes a cuboid.

A cuboid has 6 rectangular faces and 12 edges.

If you look at a cuboid from the top, it will look like a rectangle.

c. Cylinder

If you give height to a circle, it becomes a cylinder.

If you look at a cylinder from the top, it will look like a circle.

d. Square Pyramid

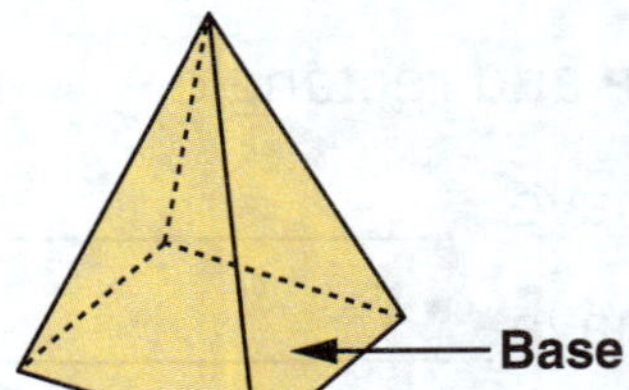

A square pyramid has five faces. One face (called the base) is a square, and the other four faces are triangular. If you look at the pyramid from one side, it looks like a triangle.

e. Sphere

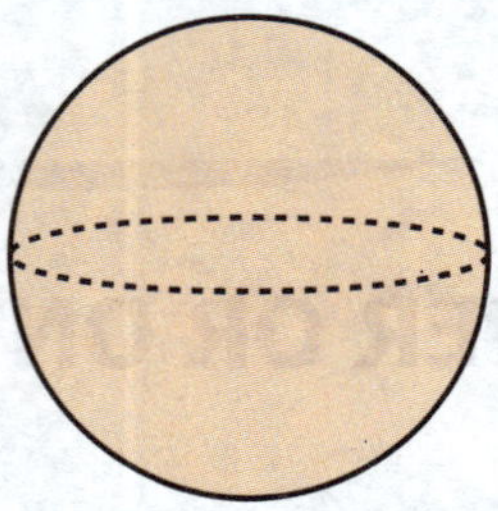

A sphere is a 3-dimensional version of a circle.

f. Cone

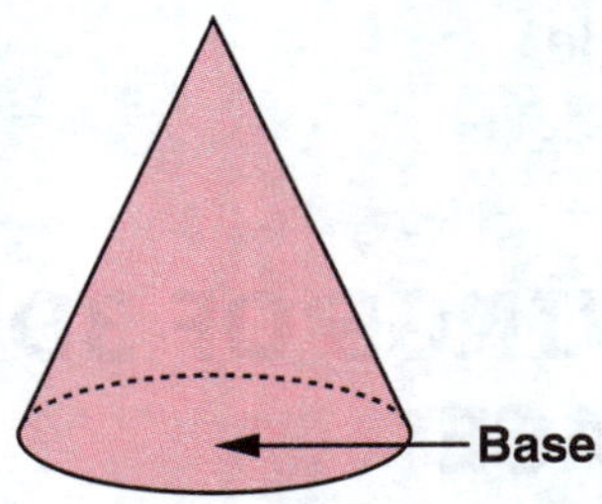

The base of a cone is a circle. It has a curved surface that is pointed at the top.

EXERCISE 7.3

Fill in the blanks.

1. When we view a cube from top, it will look like a ___________.
2. A cuboid has ___________ faces.

3. When we give height to a circle, it becomes a ____________.
4. Sphere is a _________-dimensional figure.
5. The base of a cone is ____________.
6. A square pyramid has ____________ faces.
7. A cube has ____________ edges.
8. The base of a square pyramid is _________ in shape.
9. A ____________ has six square faces.
10. A cuboid has ____________ vertices.

TESSELLATION

A **tessellation** is created when a shape is repeated over and over again covering a surface without any gaps or overlaps. Tessellation can also be called **tiling**.

Examples:

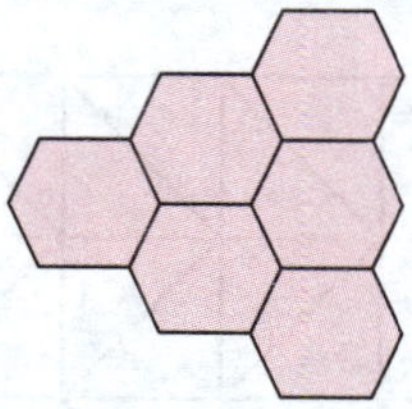

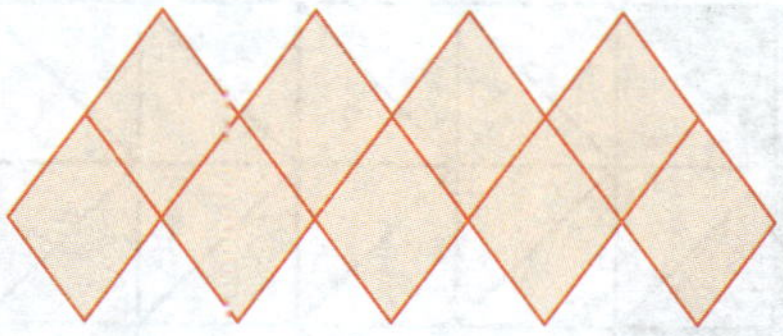

The shapes given above tessellate. These shapes can be used for tiling.

Shapes that leave a gap cannot be used for tiling. Shapes such as a circle do not tessellate.

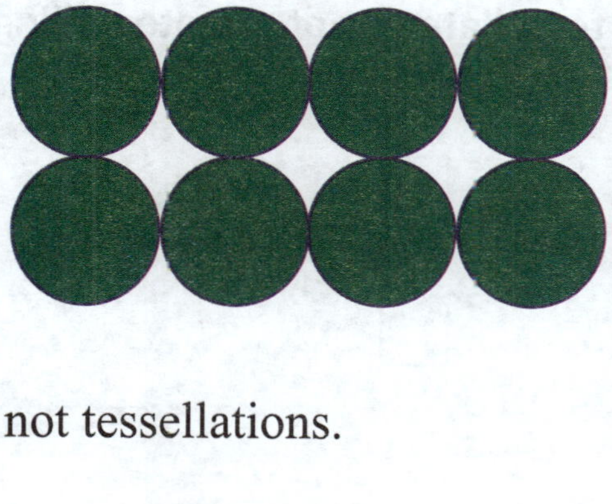

These are not tessellations.

Exercise 7.4

1. **Colour and complete the tiling pattern.**

a.

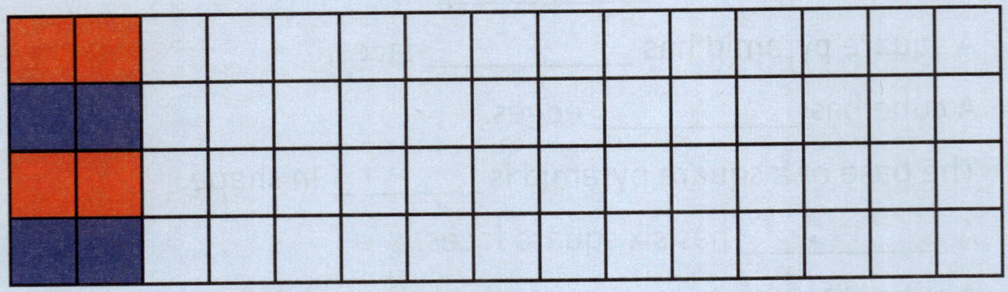

b.

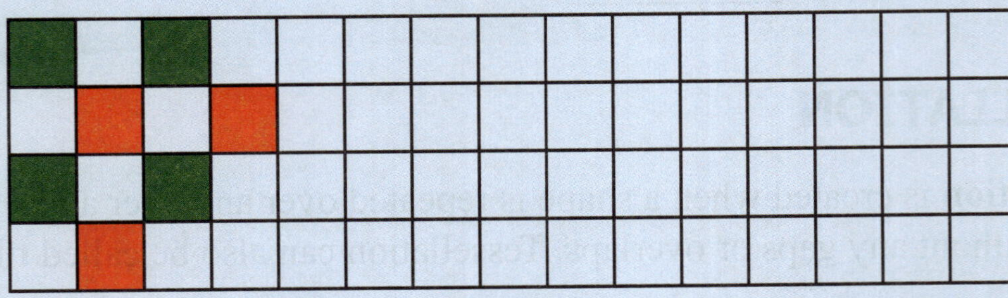

c.

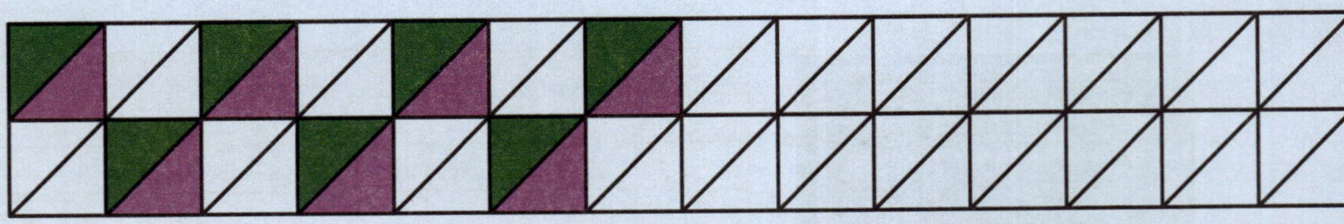

d.

2. **Identify whether the given shapes tessellate or not. Create a tiling pattern using the shapes in your notebook.**

a.

b.

c.

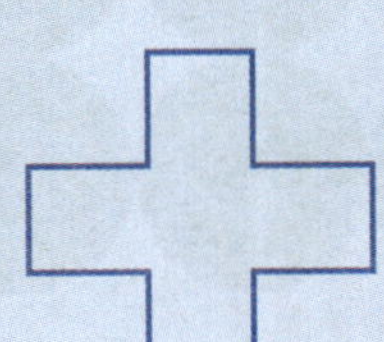

d.

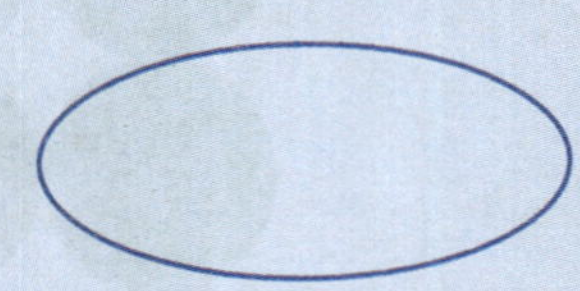

MAP READING

A **map** is a drawing of an area showing roads, buildings, parks, rail and bus stations and other important places. The first thing we need to know before we read maps are the four directions: North, South, East and West.

REMEMBER

Maps are very useful things. They help us to get the idea of direction and distance. The distances shown in maps are much lesser than the actual distances of real places.

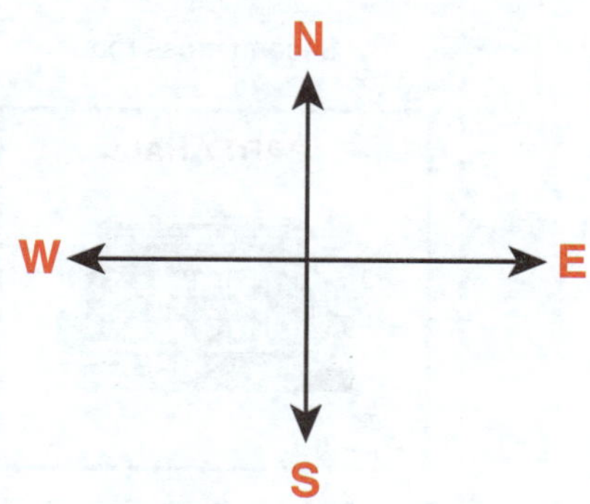

Every map must show the North direction and then we can figure out the other three directions.

EXERCISE 7.5

1. **Mark the South, East and West directions in the following.**

a. 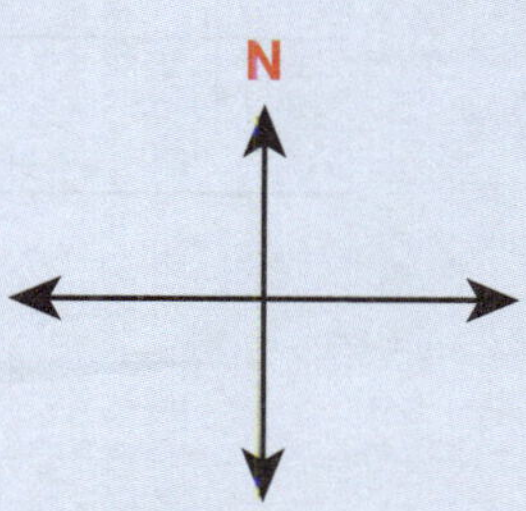

b. 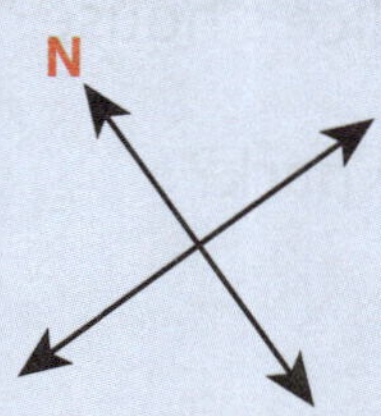

c. 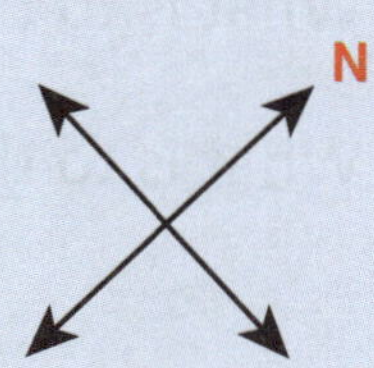

2. **Read the map and answer the following questions.**

a. What is to the north of the market? ________________

b. What is to the south of the market? ________________

c. What is to the east of the market? ________________

d. What is to the west of the market? ________________

e. What is to the south of Alice's house? ________________

f. What is to the east of the park? ________________

g. In which direction is the party hall located from the hospital? ______________

h. Rohan wants to go from his house to Diya's house.
In which direction should he walk? ______________

i. In which direction from the park is the hospital located? ______________

j. What is to the east of Romila's house? ______________

KEY CONCEPTS

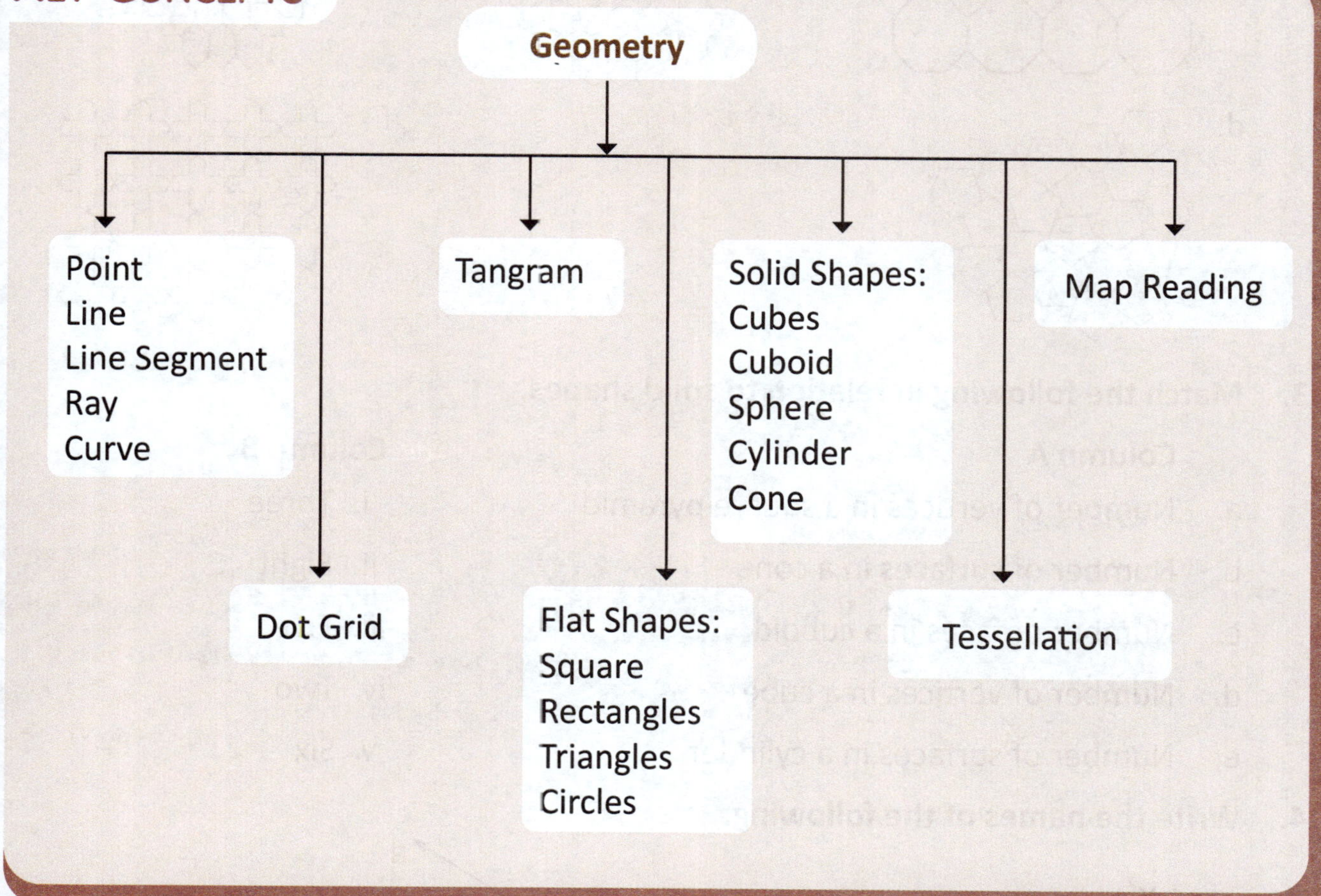

REVISION EXERCISE

1. Draw rectangles of four different sizes in the dot grid.

2. Tick the tessellations and cross out the non-tessellations.

a. 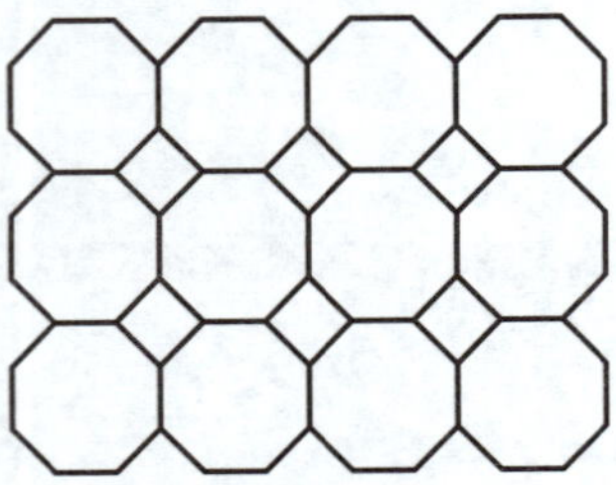

b. 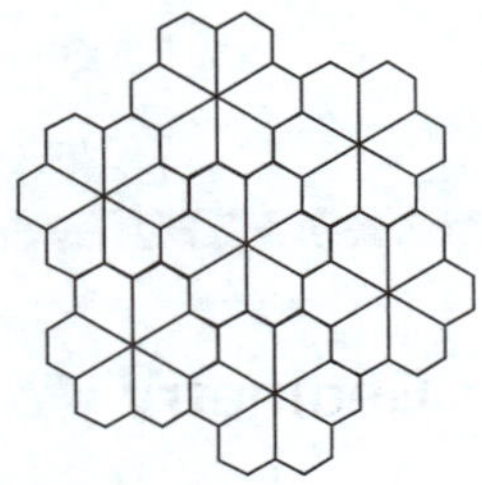

c. 

d. 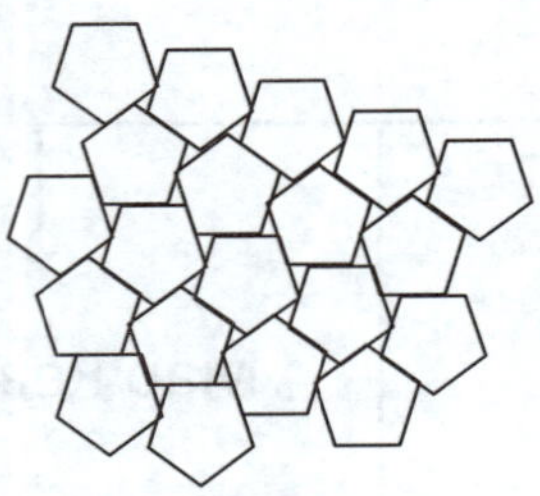

e. 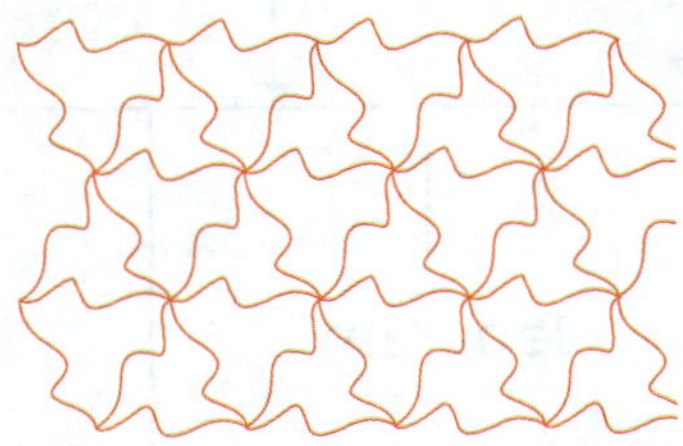

f. 

3. Match the following in relation to solid shapes.

Column A	Column B
a. Number of vertices in a square pyramid	i. Three
b. Number of surfaces in a cone	ii. Eight
c. Number of faces in a cuboid	iii. Five
d. Number of vertices in a cube	iv. Two
e. Number of surfaces in a cylinder	v. Six

4. Write the names of the following.

a. . X = __________

b. 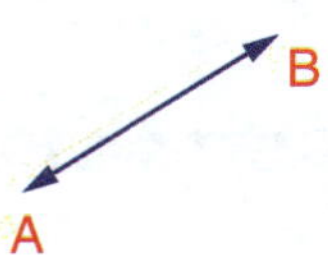

= __________

c. 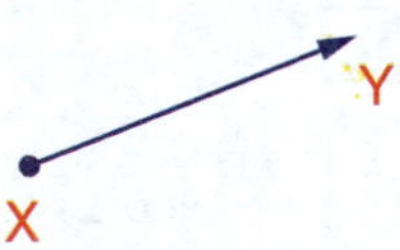

= __________

d. 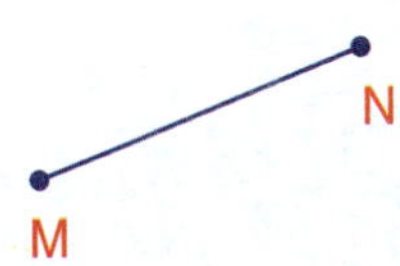

= __________

5. **Fill in the blanks based on the shape given here.**

Number of corners: ______________________________

Number of sides: ______________________________

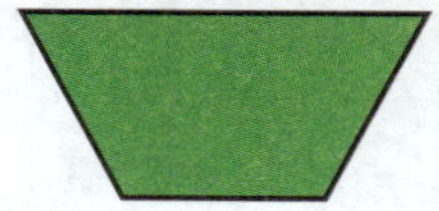

6. **Look at the figures and fill in the blanks.**

a. Name : ______________________________

Number of vertices = ______________________________

Number of sides = ______________________________

b. Name : ______________________________

Number of vertices = ______________________________

Number of edges = ______________________________

Number of faces = ______________________________

7. **How many edges and vertices are there in the given shapes?**

a. 

Number of edges = ________

Number of vertices = ________

b. 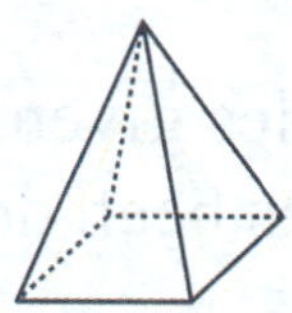

Number of edges = ________

Number of vertices = ________

8. **Read the map and answer the questions.**

a. On which side of the lake lies the mountain? ________

b. On which side of the river is the farm located? ________

c. What is to the south of the lake? ________

d. In which direction from the city is the farm located? ________

8 Length, Mass and Capacity

Prior Knowledge

- Measuring lengths using non-standard units
- Comparing two or more objects as heavier than/lighter than
- Using simple balance to compare mass
- Measuring the capacity of a container with non-standard units

Learning Objectives

- Standard units of measurement
- Measuring length using a scale or a ruler
- Drawing and measuring line segments
- Measurement of mass
- Measurement of capacity or volume
- Conservation of volume

Let's Get Started

Look at the weighing scales given below. Rank the scales from 1 to 6 in order of increasing values. One has been done for you.

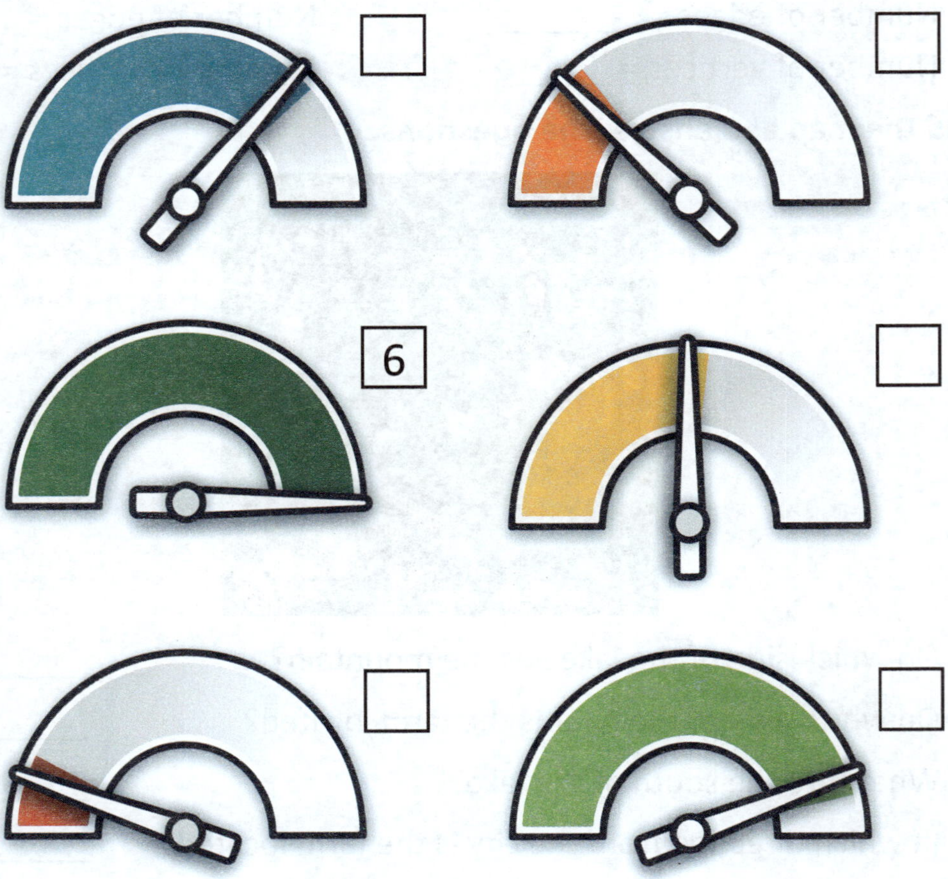

MEASUREMENT

Measurement is vital to our daily life. To **measure** something means to **find out the exact size or amount** of something. Commonly, we measure length, mass and capacity of objects.

MEASUREMENT OF LENGTH

Length of an object is the distance between the two ends of the object.

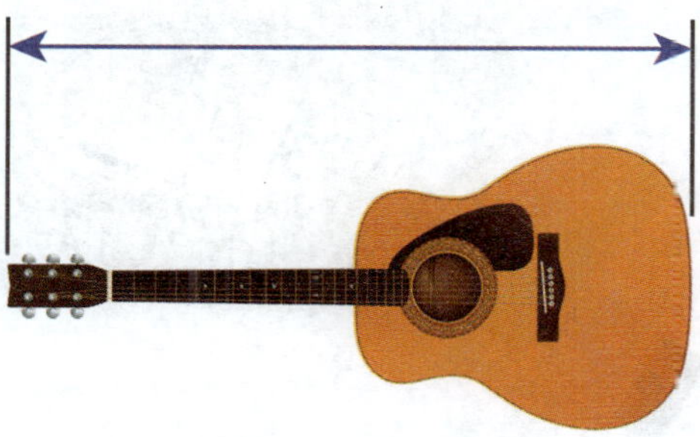

Length of a guitar

Length of a pencil

In earlier times, people used handspan, cubit and footspan to measure lengths of various items. These are non-standard units for measuring length.

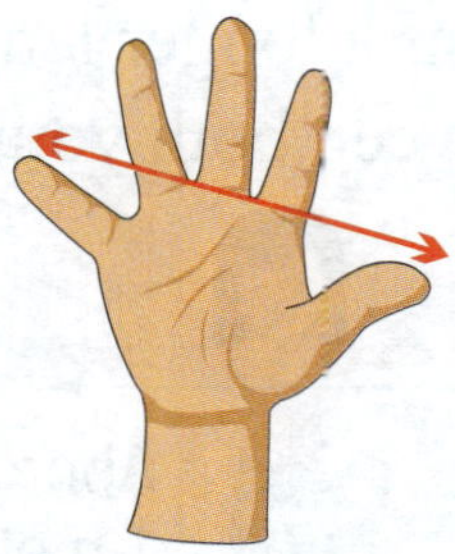

Handspan

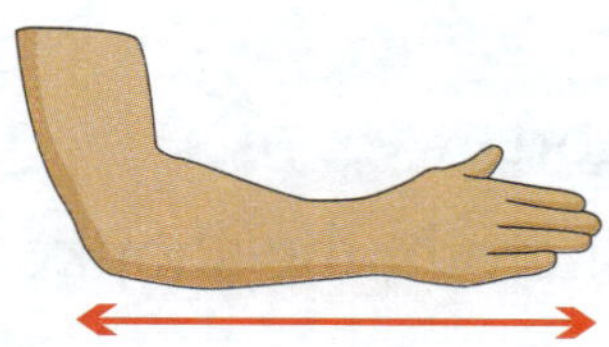

Cubit

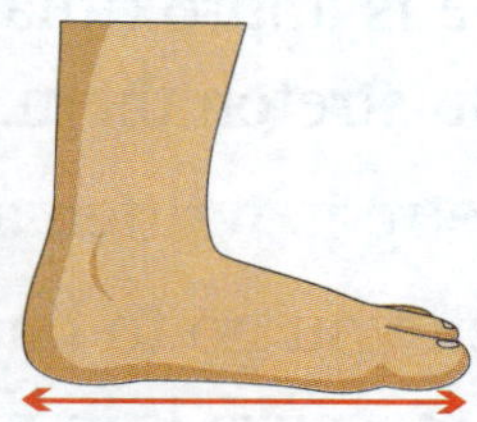

Footspan

Sonam and her father measured the length of a blackboard using cubits.

Sonam found that it was 6 cubits.

Sonam's father found that it was 4 cubits.

The measurements came out to be different because Sonam has a shorter cubit than her father.

Since the lengths of hands, arms and feet of different people are different, the need for a standard measurement system arose and we adopted the metric system. In the metric system, to measure length, we use centimetre (cm), metre (m) and kilometre (km).

STANDARD UNITS FOR MEASURING LENGTH

To make sure that everyone gets the same measurement, we use standard units of measurements. To measure length, we use fixed measurements called **metre** and **centimetre**.

We generally use tools such as ruler (scale) and measuring tape for measuring length.

Ruler or scale

Measuring tape

Metre

Metre is the standard unit of length. A metre is used to measure longer lengths. A metre is approximately equal to the distance, as shown, between both your hands if you stretch them.

A metre is written as '**m**' in short.

When you go to buy a piece of cloth, the shopkeeper will measure it in metres.

Remember, **1 metre = 100 centimetres.**

Approximately 1 metre

Metres are used to measure the length of a cloth, the height of a door or a wall, the length of a house or a swimming pool and so on.

Centimetre

A centimetre is used to measure short lengths. A centimetre is written as '**cm**'. The length of a centimetre is approximately the width of one's forefinger.

Look at a ruler to see the length of a centimetre.

This length is equal to 1 cm.

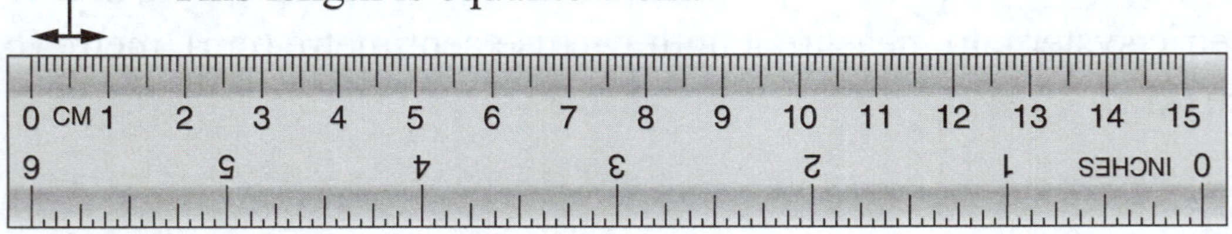

Kilometre

Kilometres are used to measure very long distances, such as the distance between two towns.

1 kilometre = 1000 metres

A kilometre stone on a highway tells the distance from that point to the place mentioned on the stone.

EXERCISE 8.1

1. **Circle the longest measurement and tick the shortest measurement.**

   centimetre   metre   kilometre

2. **Tick the pictures you think are longer than 1 metre.**

Height of a house

Length of an eraser

Height of a tea cup

Length of a cell phone

Height of a door

Length of a rolling pin

3. **Choose the correct measurement unit (m, cm or km) that is used to measure the following.**

   a. Length of a pencil ______ 

   b. Distance from one town to an another ______

   c. Length of a field ______

   d. Length of a worm ______

   e. Height of a tree ______

   f. Length of a hall ______

   g. Thickness of a book ______

   h. Length of a road ______

MEASURING LENGTH USING A SCALE OR A RULER

Let us measure the length of a pencil using a centimetre ruler.

1. Place the pencil against the ruler in such a way that one end of the pencil is at the 0 cm mark of the ruler.

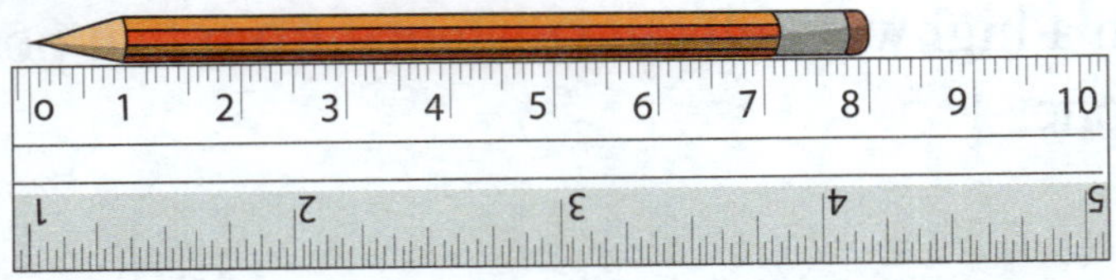

Measuring the length of a pencil with a scale

2. Check the mark where the other end of the pencil touches the ruler.
3. The reading at the other end of the pencil gives the measurement of its length. Here, the other end of the pencil is at 8 cm mark.

So, length of the pencil = 8 cm.

DRAWING AND MEASURING LINE SEGMENTS

To Draw a Line Segment With a Ruler

Let us draw a line segment 8 cm long with a ruler.

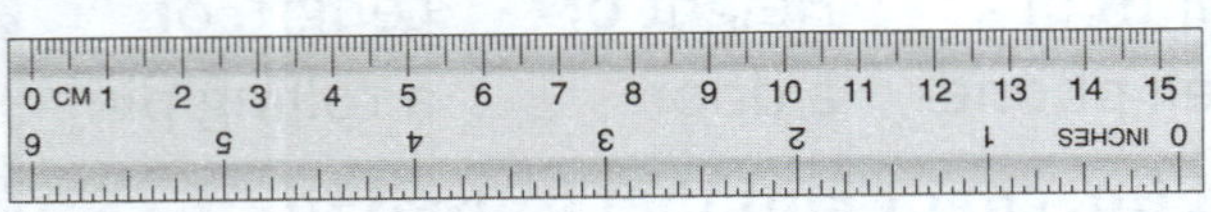

Place the ruler where the line segment is to be drawn.

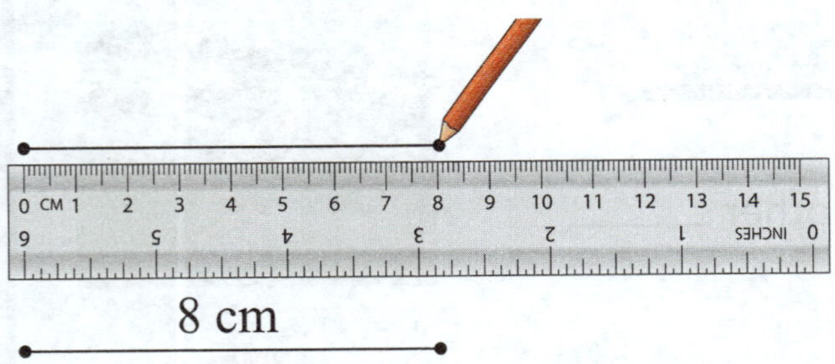

Start drawing a line segment from mark 0 to the mark 8 along the ruler.

Remove the ruler and the pencil, and you will get a line segment 8 cm long.

To Measure the Segment

When a line segment is given and we have to measure its length, place the ruler against the line segment with one end of the line segment at mark 0.

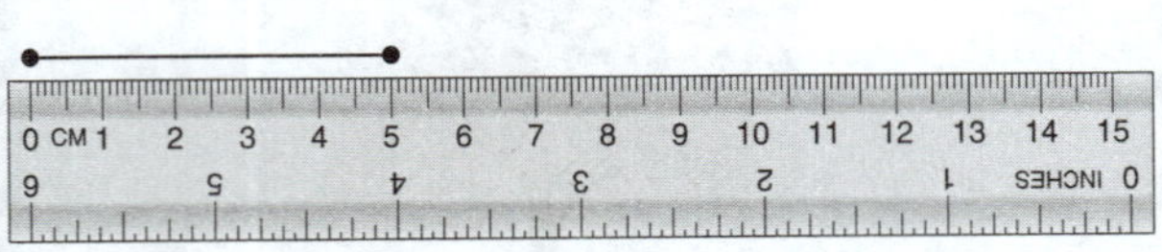

Note the point at which the other end of the line segment ends. The number on the scale in front of the other end of the line segment gives the length of the given line segment.

Here, the line segment ends at 5 cm mark. So, the length of the line segment is 5 cm.

Exercise 8.2

1. Write the lengths of the following objects by looking at the rulers.

a.

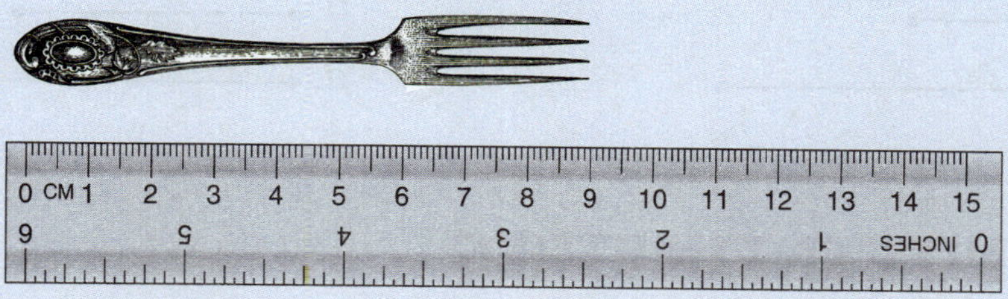

Length of the spoon = __________ cm.

b.

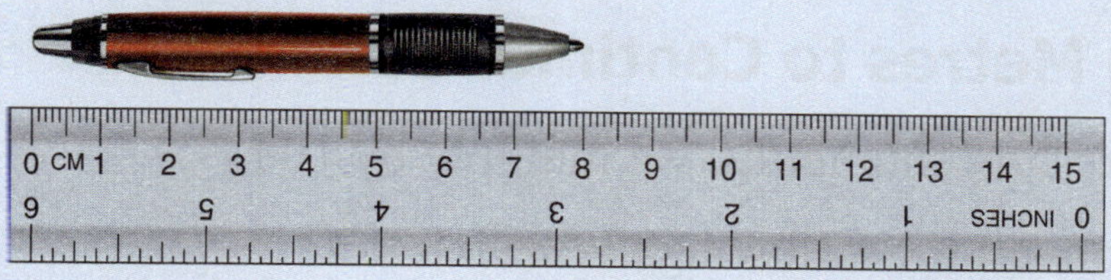

Length of the pen = __________ cm.

c.

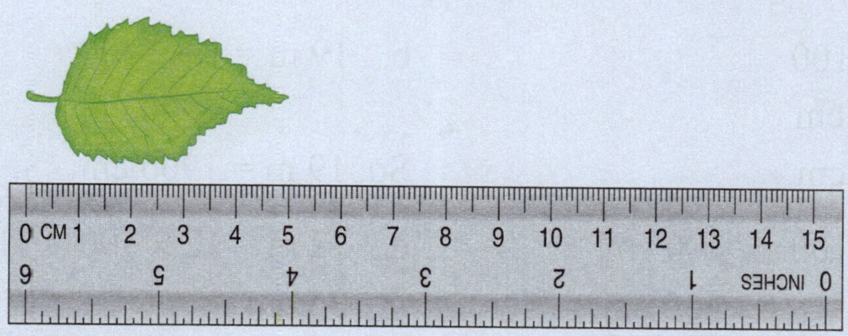

Length of the leaf = __________ cm.

d.

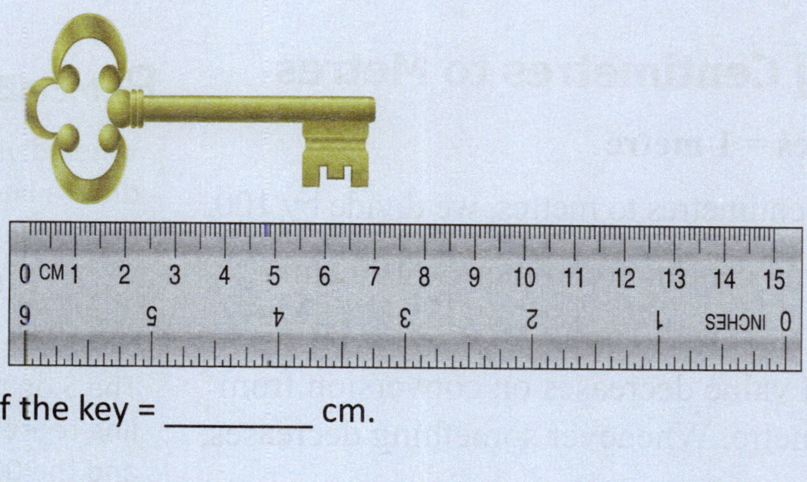

Length of the key = __________ cm.

2. Draw a line segment for each of the lengths given below.

a. 2 cm b. 3 cm c. 5 cm d. 6 cm e. 7 cm f. 9 cm

3. Measure the lengths of the following line segments with the help of a ruler.

a. •————• b. •————————•

c. •——————————• d. •————————————————•

METRES AND CENTIMETRES

1 metre = 100 centimetres

Converting Metres to Centimetres

To convert metres to centimetres, we multiply by 100.

Example 1: Convert the following.

a. 3 m to cm b. 19 m to cm c. 2 m 50 cm to cm d. 12 m 35 cm to cm

Solution:

a. 3 m = 3 × 100
= 300 cm

So, 3 m = 300 cm.

b. 19 m = 19 × 100
= 1900 cm

So, 19 m = 1900 cm.

c. 2 m = 2 × 100 = 200 cm
50 cm = + 50 cm
250 cm

So, 2 m 50 cm = 250 cm.

d. 12 m = 12 × 100 = 1200 cm
35 cm = + 35 cm
1235 cm

So, 12 m 35 cm = 1235 cm.

Converting Centimetres to Metres

100 centimetres = 1 metre

So, to convert centimetres to metres, we divide by 100.

While converting centimetre to metre, '100 cm' becomes '1 m'.

The numerical value decreases on conversion from centimetre to metre. Whenever something decreases, we divide.

REMEMBER

When dividing by 100, draw a line after the hundreds place.

H T O
5|0 0

The 5 on the left of the line represents metres and the 00 on the right represents centimetres.

Example 2: Convert the following.

a. 500 cm to m   b. 349 cm to m and cm

Solution:

a. 500 cm = 5|00 ÷ 100

= 5 m

$$\begin{array}{r} 5 \\ 100\overline{)500} \\ -500 \\ \hline 000 \\ \hline \end{array}$$

So, 500 cm = 5 m

b. 349 cm = 3|49 ÷ 100

= 3 m 49 cm

$$\begin{array}{r} 3 \\ 100\overline{)349} \\ -300 \\ \hline 49 \\ \hline \end{array}$$

So, 349 cm = 3 m 49 cm

REMEMBER

When a number is divided by 100, the number formed by the ones and tens digits gives the remainder and the remaining digits give the quotient. The quotient represents metres, and the remainder represents centimetres.

EXERCISE 8.3

1. **Convert the following m to cm.**

   a. 2 m = ________ cm   b. 7 m = ________ cm

   c. 11 m = ________ cm   d. 13 m = ________ cm

2. **Convert the following m and cm to cm.**

   a. 1 m 30 cm = ________ cm   b. 5 m 45 cm = ________ cm

   c. 2 m 15 cm = ________ cm   d. 7 m 50 cm = ________ cm

3. **Convert the following cm to m.**

   a. 400 cm = ________ m   b. 900 cm = ________ m

   c. 700 cm = ________ m   d. 1300 cm = ________ m

4. **Convert the following cm to m and cm.**

   a. 315 cm = ________ m ________ cm   b. 542 cm = ________ m ________ cm

   c. 276 cm = ________ m ________ cm   d. 198 cm = ________ m ________ cm

5. **Match the values in column A to those in column B.**

Column A	Column B
a. 3 m	i. 412 cm
b. 15 m	ii. 9 m
c. 4 m 12 cm	iii. 300 cm
d. 900 cm	iv. 1500 cm
e. 234 cm	v. 2 m 34 cm

6. **Write >, < or =.**

   a. 5 m ________ 650 cm   b. 3 m 10 cm ________ 7 m

   c. 400 cm ________ 4 m   d. 729 cm ________ 143 cm

MEASUREMENT OF MASS

We have learnt the meaning of heavier and lighter objects. How do we find out how heavy an object is?

We use a **simple balance** or a **weighing scale** to determine the mass of an object.

If we put a book on one side of the scale and a pencil on the other side, then the scale will tilt towards the side with the book. This will happen because the book is heavier than the pencil or the pencil is lighter than the book.

We see fruit and vegetable vendors using a weighing scale to measure the mass of fruits and vegetables. The weighing scale has two sides or pans.

If we put three tomatoes on one side only and nothing on the other side, the weighing scale will tilt towards the side of the tomatoes as shown here.

Now, if we put 2 potatoes on the other side of the weighing scale, and if the weighing scale balances, then this means that the 3 tomatoes weigh the same as 2 potatoes.

Let us use stones to compare the weight of different objects.

This means that 6 tomatoes, 4 potatoes and 1 pineapple weigh the same as each of them is equal to 3 stones.

Here, we are using stones as the '**unit**' of measurement. Stones are **non-standard units**.

EXERCISE 8.4

1. **The mass of the objects is measured using balls as units. Study the picture and fill in the blanks.**

   a. Mass of book = __________ balls.
   b. Mass of book and cup together = __________ balls.
   c. Mass of cup = __________ balls.

2. **In each of the weighing scales, the mass of the items is being measured using stones. Look at the picture and fill in the blanks.**

   a. Mass of the orange = __________ stones.
   b. Mass of the carrot = __________ stones.
   c. Mass of the jam bottle = __________ stones.
   d. Mass of orange and carrot together = __________ stones.
   e. Difference in masses of jam bottle and orange = __________ stones.

STANDARD UNITS OF MEASURING MASS

We use standard measures of kilogram and gram of the metric system for weighing objects.

Kilogram is written as **kg**.

Gram is written as **g**.

Grams are used to measure lighter objects.

Kilograms are used to measure heavier objects.

A paper clip weighs about 1 gram.

A tablespoon of salt weighs about 15 grams.

REMEMBER

In everyday usage, we use the term 'weight' rather than the term 'mass'. In higher classes, you will learn the difference between mass and weight.

An apple weighs about 200 grams.

A newborn baby weights about 3 kilograms.

Given below are some standard weights that are used for weighing objects.

50 g　　100 g　　500 g　　1 kg　　2 kg　　5 kg

EXERCISE 8.5

1. Tick the approximate measurements of the objects shown.

a.  100 g ☐ or 100 kg ☐

b.  90 g ☐ or 9 kg ☐

2. Fill in the blanks with g or kg.

a.  It weighs about 9 ______.

b.  It weighs about 100 ______.

3. Tick the approximate measurements of the objects shown.

a.  20 g ☐ or 2 kg ☐

b.  10 g ☐ or 10 kg ☐

4. Fill in the blanks with g or kg.

a.  It weighs about 250 ______.

b.  It weighs about 200 ______.

c.  It weighs about 2 ______.

d. 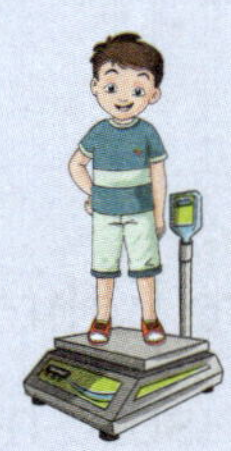 He weighs about 30 ______.

MEASUREMENT OF CAPACITY OR VOLUME

Capacity of a container is the measure of an object's ability to hold a substance such as a solid, a liquid or a gas. Volume is the amount of space taken up by an object. Only hollow objects have the capacity. However, both solid and hollow objects have volume.

Hazel is baking a cake. In a big bowl, she is mixing 2 cups of flour with 1 cup of milk. She is also adding an egg.

'**Cup**' is a non-standard unit for measuring volume. In the kitchen, we often measure water or milk using cups. Other everyday containers are also used as non-standard units.

For example:

- 1 **bowl** of soup
- 2 **spoonfuls** of medicine
- 2 **glasses** of water
- 5 **bottles** of water

The sizes of cups, spoons, bowls, glasses and bottles vary and are not fixed.

Let us compare the capacity of different containers.

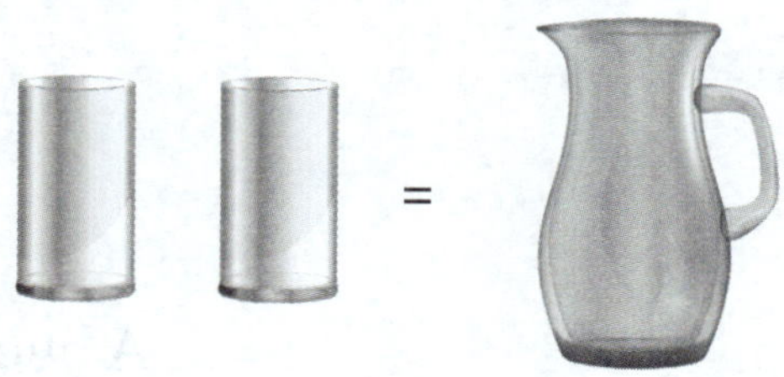

Two glasses of water fill up the given jug.

Also, 3 cups of water fill up the same jug.

So, the capacity of 2 glasses is equal to the capacity of 3 cups, which is equal to the capacity of the jug.

STANDARD UNITS FOR MEASURING CAPACITY

Capacity is measured in litres and millilitres in the metric system.

Litres measure larger quantities of liquid and millilitres measure smaller quantities of liquid.

Litre is written as **ℓ**. **Millilitre** is written as **mℓ**.

A drop of water is about 1 mℓ.

A tablespoon is about 15 mℓ.

A teaspoon is about 5 mℓ.

A glass of water is about 200 mℓ.

A bucket of water is about 15 ℓ.

EXERCISE 8.6

1. **Study the pictures and fill in the blanks.**

a. If  = , then 2 bowls = ________ cups.

b. If 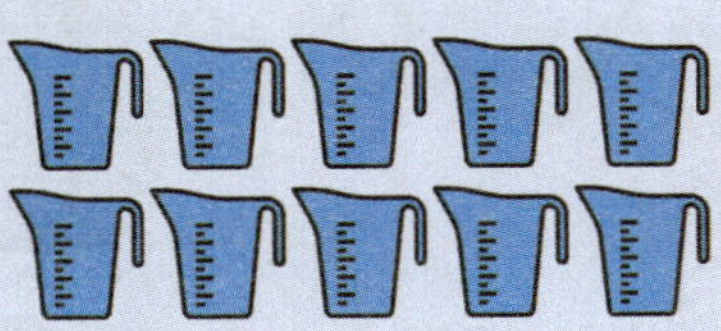 = , then half bucket = _______ mugs.

2. **Tick the measurement you think is correct.**

a. 

1 mℓ or 1 ℓ

b. 

5 mℓ or 5 ℓ

c. 

200 mℓ or 2 ℓ

d. 

250 mℓ or 250 ℓ

e. 

200 mℓ or 200 ℓ

CONSERVATION OF VOLUME

Suppose there are two identical containers A and B. A and B have the same volume of water.

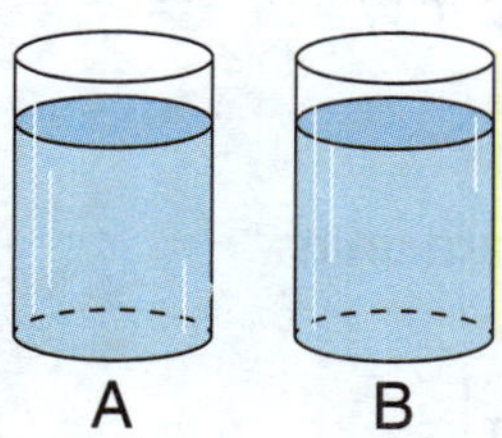

Now, all the water from container B is poured into another container C.

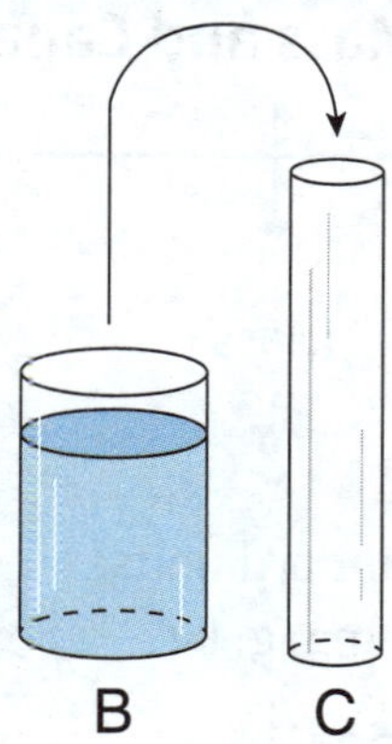

Take a look at containers A and C now. Which has more water?

Both containers A and C have the same volume of water. This is because volume of water in A and B was equal in the beginning, and the water of B was poured into C. So, the volume of water **is conserved (has remained the same)** after pouring from one container to another.

Exercise 8.7

1. **Look at the picture. Then, tick the correct option.**

- Jug A has more water.
- Jug B has more water.
- Jug A and Jug B have the same amount of water.

2. **If we pour a glass of water into container A and the same glass of water into container B, which container has more water: A or B?**

Key Concepts

Length, Mass and Capacity

Length

Standard units: m, cm, km

relation

1 m = 100 cm
1 km = 1000 m

Centimetre: A smaller unit of length, written as **cm**

Metre: A larger unit of length, written as **m**

Kilometre: A much larger unit of length, written as **km**

Mass

Standard units: mg, g, kg

relation

1 g = 1000 mg
1 kg = 1000 g

Milligram: A very small unit of mass, written as **mg**

Gram: A small unit of mass, written as **g**

Kilogram: A larger unit of mass, written as **kg**

Capacity

Standard units: mℓ, ℓ

relation

1ℓ = 1000 mℓ

Millilitre: A smaller unit of capacity, written as mℓ

Litre: A larger unit of capacity, written as ℓ

REVISION EXERCISE

1. **Use a pencil and a ruler to draw line segments of the following lengths in your notebook.**

   a. 3 cm

   b. 7 cm

2. **Circle the unit of measurement you would use to measure the following.**

   a. Length of a book

   cm m km

   b. Height of a wall

   cm m km

   c. Distance from Delhi to Jaipur

   cm m km

3. **Convert the following to cm.**

   a. 45 m = ______cm

   b. 3 m 75 cm = ______cm

4. **Convert the following to m and cm.**

   a. 300 cm = ______m ______cm

   b. 625 cm = ______m ______cm

5. **Put a tick against the lengths that you think are less than one metre.**

   a. Length of a paint brush ________

   b. Height of a flagpole ________

   c. Height of a giraffe ________

   d. Length of your shoe ________

   e. Thickness of a door ________

   f. Length of your cubit ________

6. **Fill in the blanks with 'grams' or 'kilograms'.**

   a. A coconut weighs about 900 __________.

   b. A cup of atta will weigh about 120 __________.

   c. The weight of one banana is about 100 __________.

   d. A dog will weigh about 30 __________.

   e. A bag full of books weighs about 5 __________.

7. **Number the containers in order of their increasing capacities.**

Bucket	Overhead tank	Syringe	Tea cup	Jug
________	________	________	________	________

8. **Read the sentence and circle the correct option.**

   a. 4 glasses of water will fill a **bucket/jug**.

   b. One bottle of medicine has about 20 **spoonfuls/bowls of medicine**.

   c. 5 cups of water will fill a **bottle/spoon**.

   d. To cook noodles, Reena boiled 5 **jugs/cups of water**.

9 Time

Prior Knowledge

- Reading the time at every hour
- Understanding the appropriate time of activities
- Days of the week
- Months of the year

Learning Objectives

- Calendar
- Reading time on a clock
- Concept of A.M. and P.M.
- Time duration
- 24-hour clock
- Conversion of days to hours and hours to minutes
- Timetable

Let's Get Started

Look at this clock and write the time shown.

______ or ______

When the hour hand is between 6 and 7, and the minute hand is at 6, the time is ______ or ______.

CALENDAR

Given below is the calendar of 2023. Look at it and answer the questions that follow.

a. When is your birthday? ____________

b. On which day does your birthday fall in the year 2023? ____________

c. When is the last Sunday of October? ____________

d. Dipti wants to organise a party on the first Saturday of April. Which date is that? ____________

e. How many full weeks are there in March 2023? ____________

f. How many full weeks are there in May 2023? ____________

g. On which day does 15 August fall? ____________

h. On which day does 29 September fall? ____________

READING TIME ON A CLOCK

A clock tells us the time. It has two hands. The long hand is called the **minute hand**, and the short hand is called the **hour hand**.

The minute hand moves faster than the hour hand. When the minute hand does one full round of the clock, the hour hand moves from one number to the next and the time taken is **one hour**.

In the clock given here, the time is 8 o'clock or 8:00.

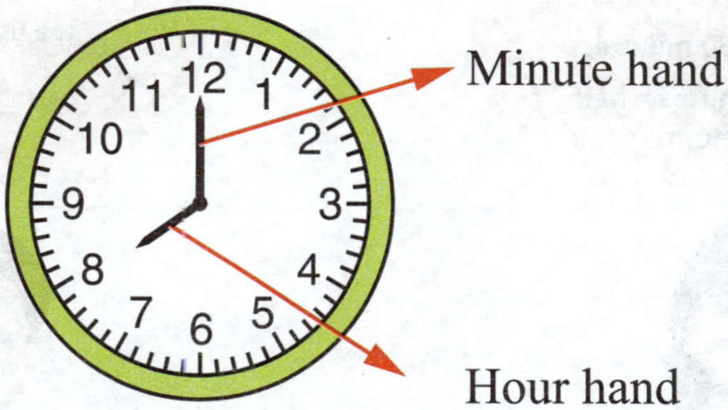

Reading Time to Half Past or 30 Minutes Past

In this clock, the hour hand is between 12 and 1, and the minute hand is at 6.

For the minute hand, the time between two numbers on a clock is equal to 5 minutes. So, when the minute hand is at 6, it has moved 30 minutes since it left 12.

Therefore, when the minute hand is at 6, the time is 30 minutes past or half past because **half an hour is equal to 30 minutes.**

12:30 or Half past 12

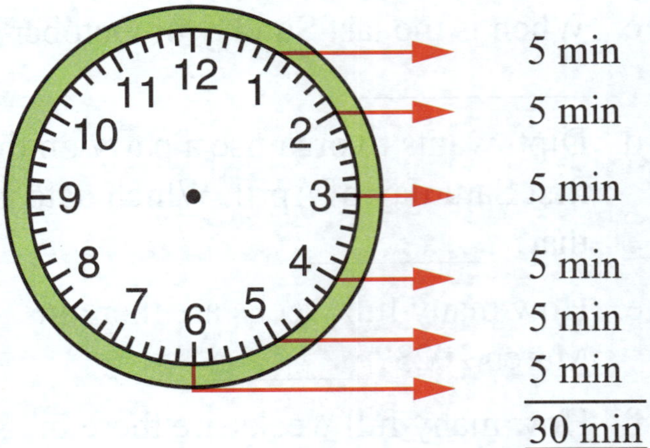

When the hour hand is between 4 and 5, and the minute hand is at 6, the time is 4:30 (four thirty) or half past 4.

When the hour hand is between 8 and 9, and the minute hand is at 6, the time is 8:30 (eight thirty) or half past 8.

Quarter Past or 15 Minutes Past

In this clock, the hour hand is between 12 and 1, and the minute hand is at 3.

So, when the minute hand is at 3, it has moved 15 minutes since it left 12.

Therefore, when the minute hand is at 3, the time is 15 minutes past or quarter past because a quarter is equal to 15 minutes.

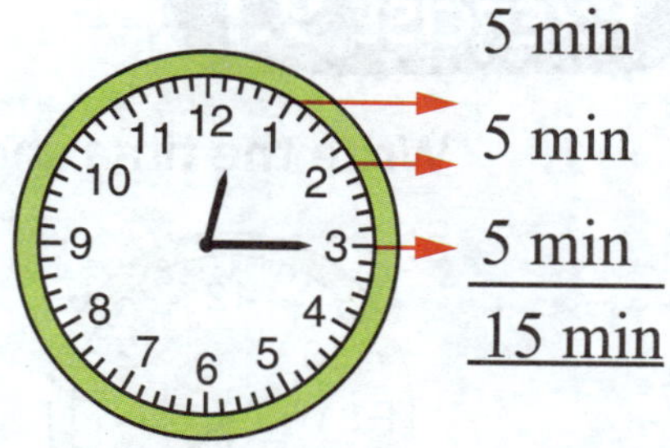

12:15 or quarter past 12

Quarter to or 15 Minutes to

In this clock, the hour hand is between 12 and 1, and the minute hand is at 9.

The time in the clock is 45 minutes past 12. It is written as 12:45.

The time is also expressed as 15 minutes to 1 or quarter to 1. Therefore, 12:45 is the same as quarter to 1.

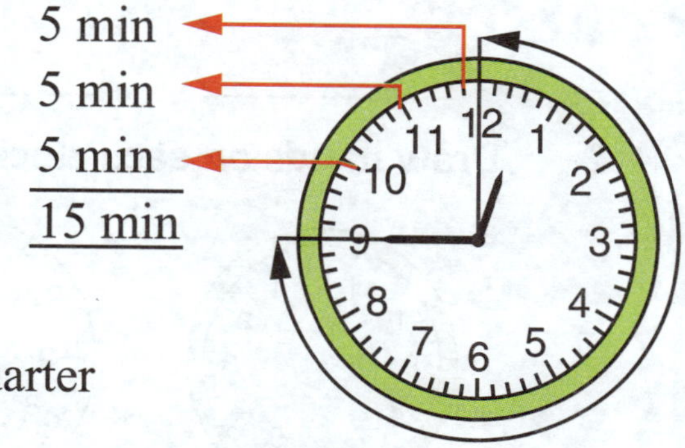

12:45 or quarter to 1

Example 1: Calculate the time taken by the minute hand to move from

a. 12 to 2

b. 4 to 8

Remember

1 hour = 60 minutes

Half an hour = 30 minutes

Quarter of an hour = 15 minutes

Solution:

a.

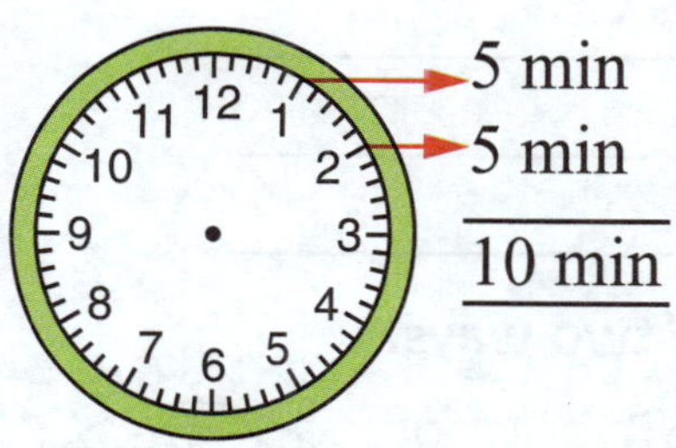

The minute hand takes 10 minutes to move from 12 to 2.

b.

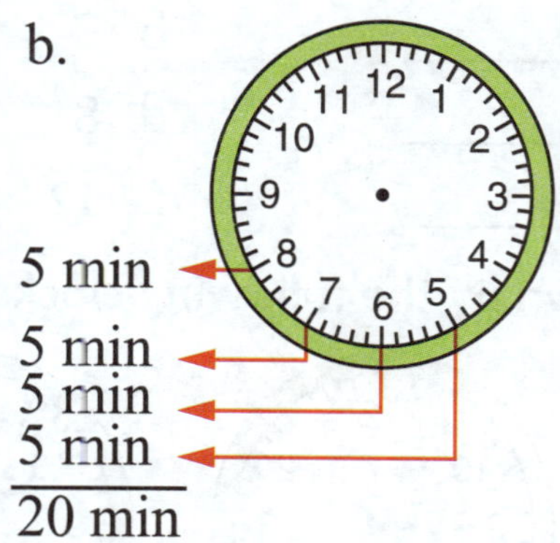

The minute hand takes 20 minutes to move from 4 to 8.

Exercise 9.1

1. Write the time shown by the following clocks in both the ways.

a. 

______ or ______

b. 

______ or ______

c. 

______ or ______

d. 

______ or ______

2. Draw hands on each clock according to the given time.

a. 

2:15

b. 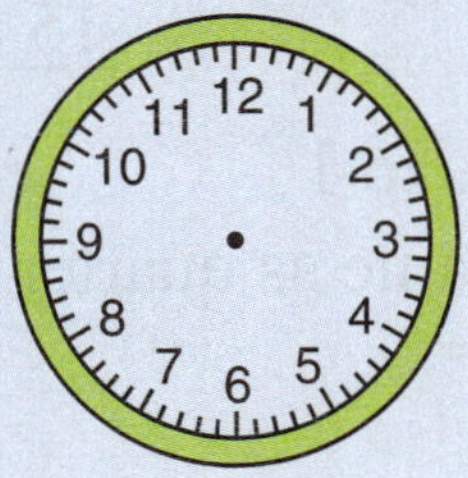

3:30

c. 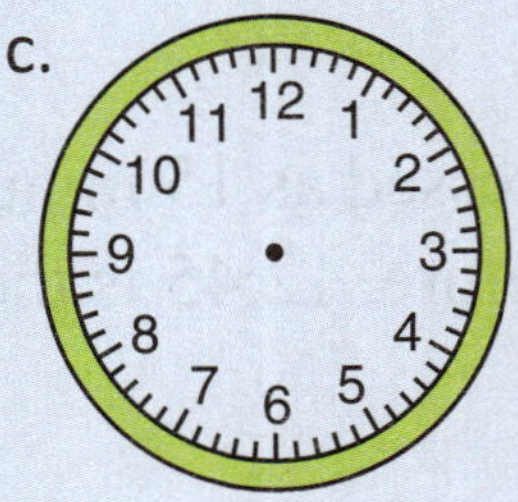

10:15

d. 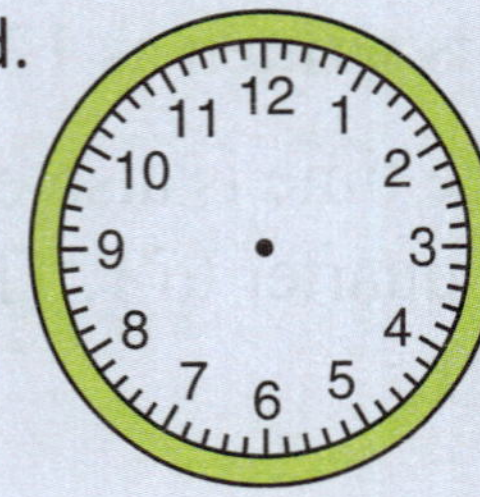

5:45

3. How many minutes does the minute hand take to move from 12 to each one of the following?

a. 2 ______ b. 3 ______

c. 5 ______ d. 8 ______

e. 11 ______ f. 12 ______

4. Write the time shown by the following clocks in two ways.

a. 

______ or ______

b. 

______ or ______

c. 

______ or ______

d. 

______ or ______

5. **Draw the hands on each clock according to the given time.**

a. 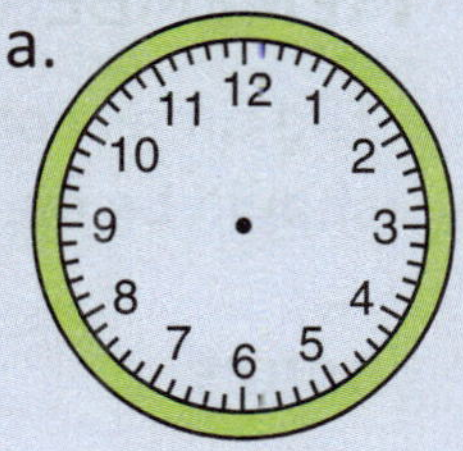
7:25

b. 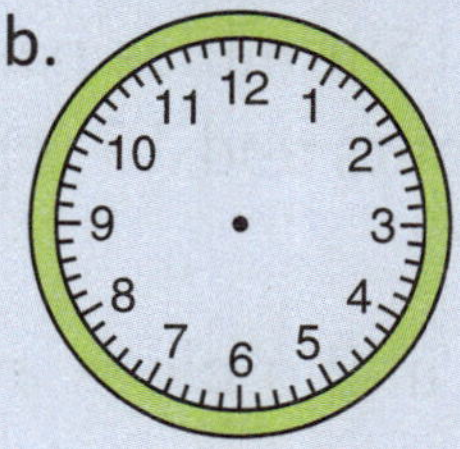
9:10

c. 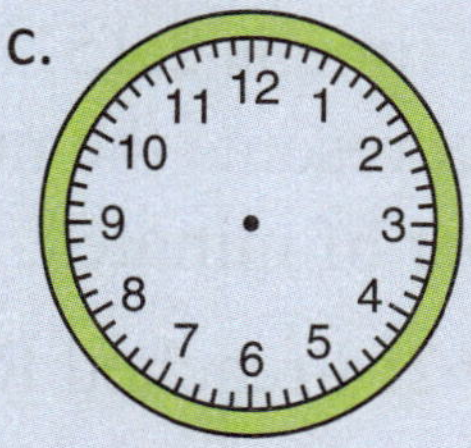
5:55

6. **Match the clocks in row A to the time in row B.**

A    

B 1:30 12:45 5:00 11:15

A.M. AND P.M.

We know that a day has 24 hours. The 12-hour system divides the 24 hours into two periods. Each period lasts 12 hours. The first 12-hour period starts from 12 o'clock at night and lasts till 12 o'clock during the day. The second period, marked **p.m.**, covers the 12 hours from noon to midnight. 12 o'clock during the day is called noon. After noon, we write **p.m.** with the time till 12 o'clock at night. 12 o'clock at night is called midnight. After midnight till noon, we use **a.m.** with the time. We do not use a.m. or p.m. with 12 o'clock. We say noon or midnight.

Midnight to 11:59 a.m.

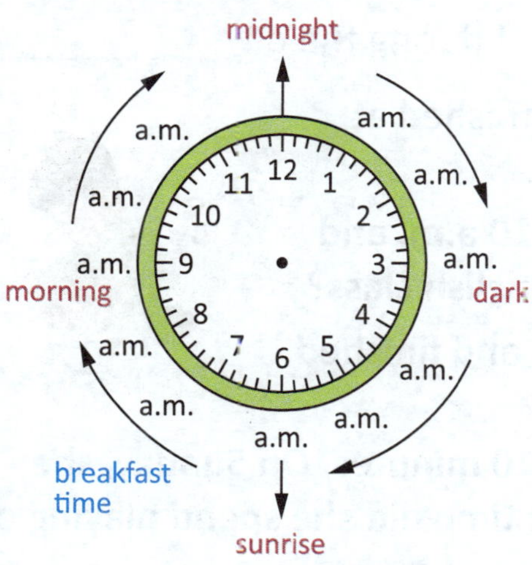

Noon to 11:59 p.m.

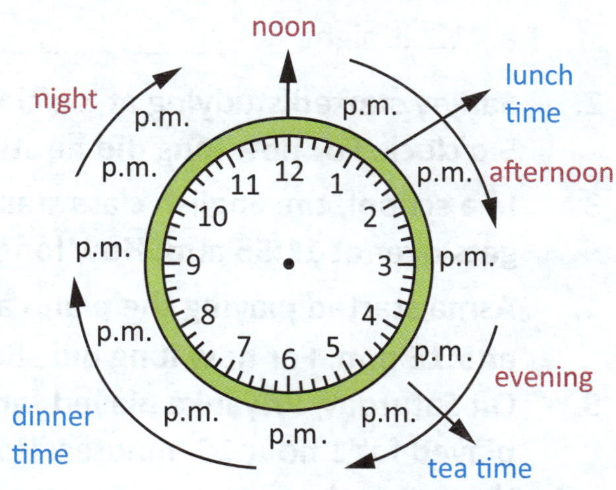

Timings for the day are shown above. After noon, we start with 1 o'clock again, but in this case, it is 1 p.m.

TIME DURATION

When the time is 2:15, it indicates 15 minutes past 2.
Here, 2 represents the number of hours and 15 represents the number of minutes.

REMEMBER

The time I come back should be on top.

Example 2: I reached Rita's house at 2 o'clock and left her house at 3 o'clock.
How much time did I spend at her house?

Solution: I spent 1 hour at Rita's house.

hours
3
− 2
1

Example 3: A movie began at 2:15 and finished at 4:55. How long was the movie?

Solution:

	Hours	minutes	
	4	55	Finishing time
−	2	15	Starting time
	2	40	

REMEMBER

We write the time of leaving on top while subtracting.

The movie was 2 hours 40 minutes long.

EXERCISE 9.2

1. **Write a.m., p.m., noon or midnight for the following.**
   a. 5 o'clock in the morning ________ b. 7 o'clock in the evening ________
   c. 2 o'clock in the afternoon ______ d. 11 o'clock during the day ________
   e. 12 at night ____________________ f. 12 during the day _______________
2. **Sanjay started studying at 2 o'clock and finished at 5 o'clock. For how long did he study?**

3. **In a school, the English class starts at 11:10 a.m. and gets over at 11:55 a.m. How long is the English class?**
4. **Asma started playing the piano at 4 p.m. and finished at 5:15 p.m. For how long did she play it?**
5. **On Saturday, Priyanka played for 1 hour 10 minutes. On Sunday, she played for 1 hour 15 minutes. How much time did she spend playing on these two days?**

6. **At Saloni's birthday party, the children played games for 2 hours 10 minutes and then ate for 1 hour 5 minutes. How much time did the children spend at the party?**

7. **Meera entered a grocery store at 6:10 p.m. and left the store at 6:35 p.m. For how long did she stay at the store?**

24-HOUR CLOCK

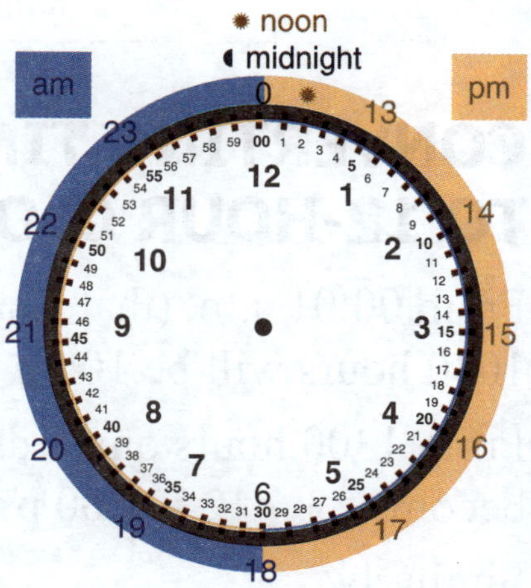

So far, we have read time according to the 12-hour clock.

In **12-hour clock**, we use a.m. and p.m. The 12-hour clock runs from 1 a.m. to noon and then from 1 p.m. to midnight.

In **24-hour clock**, we do not use a.m. or p.m. A complete day runs from 00:00 (midnight) to 23:59 (just before midnight). Time is written as hours.

The figure alongside shows the relationship between 12-hour clock and 24-hour clock.

The inner reading denotes the 12-hour clock. After noon, we write the time as p.m. After midnight, we read the time as a.m.

The outer reading denotes the time in 24-hour clock.

After noon, we write 1:00 p.m. as 1300 hours, 2:00 p.m. as 1400 hours, 3:00 p.m. as 1500 hours and so on.

From 12:01 a.m. (that is after midnight) to 12:59 p.m., numbers in the 24-hour clock remain the same as the 12-hour clock.

After 12:59 p.m. is 1:00 p.m. and from 1:00 p.m. onwards, we add 12 to the hours in the 24-hour clock.

So, **1:00 p.m.** will be **1 + 12 = 1300 hours** in the 24-hour clock.

And, **4:00 p.m.** will be **4 + 12 = 1600 hours** in the 24-hour clock.

Also, **7:00 p.m.** will be **7 + 12 = 1900 hours** in the 24-hour clock.

Example 4: Convert the given time in 12-hour clock to 24-hour clock.

a. 2:00 a.m. b. 11:50 a.m. c. Noon d. 12:59 p.m.

e. 1:00 p.m. f. 9:15 p.m. g. Midnight

Solution:

12-hour clock	24-hour clock
2:00 a.m.	0200 hours
11:50 a.m.	1150 hours
Noon	1200 hours
12:59 p.m.	1259 hours
1:00 p.m.	1300 hours
9:15 p.m.	2115 hours
Midnight	0000 hours

CONVERTING TIME FROM 24-HOUR CLOCK TO 12-HOUR CLOCK

From 00:01 a.m. (that is after midnight) to 12:59 p.m., the numbers are the same. 1030 hours will be 10:30 a.m. and 1240 hours will be 12:40 p.m.

From 1300 hours onwards, we subtract 12 from the hour, that is 1300 hours will become 13 – 12 = 1:00 p.m.

Similarly,

1600 hours will be **16 – 12 = 4:00 p.m.**

1700 hours will be **17 – 12 = 5:00 p.m.**

2015 hours will be **20 – 12 = 8:15 p.m.**

Example 5: Convert the given time in 24-hour clock to 12-hour clock.

a. 0100 hours b. 1200 hours c. 1259 hours d. 1300 hours

e. 1530 hours f. 2320 hours g. 0000 hours

Solution:

24-hour clock	12-hour clock
0100 hours	1:00 a.m.
1200 hours	Noon
1259 hours	12:59 p.m.
1300 hours	1:00 p.m.
1530 hours	3:30 p.m.
2320 hours	11:20 p.m.
0000 hours	Midnight

REMEMBER

- Till 1159 hours (that is before noon), we write a.m. with time in the 12-hour clock.
- After 1200 hours (that is from 1201 hours), we use p.m. in the 12-hour clock.

Exercise 9.3

1. **Write a.m., p.m., noon or midnight for the following.**

a. 1 at night ________ b. 6 in the morning ________
c. 10 in the morning ________ d. 10:45 in the morning ________
e. 12 during the day ________ f. 12:30 during the day ________
g. 1:15 during the day ________ h. 3:20 in the afternoon ________

2. **Write the time in the 24-hour clock for the given timings.**

12-hour clock	24-hour clock	12-hour clock	24-hour clock
a. 2:45 a.m.		b. Noon	
c. 6:30 a.m.		d. 12:20 p.m.	
e. 7:55 p.m.		f. 10:45 p.m.	

3. **Write the time in the 12-hour clock for the given timings.**

24-hour clock	12-hour clock	24-hour clock	12-hour clock
a. 0150 hours		b. 1040 hours	
c. 1430 hours		d. 1210 hours	
e. 2225 hours		f. 0059 hours	
g. 1630 hours		h. 1300 hours	

CONVERSION OF DAYS TO HOURS

We know that **1 day = 24 hours.**

When we have to convert days to hours, 1 day becomes 24 hours. The value increases numerically. So, we multiply with 24.

So, 1 day = 24 hours, 2 days = 2 × 24 hours = 48 hours

Example 6: Convert 6 days into hours.

Solution: 6 days = 6 × 24 hours
= 144 hours

		[2]2	4
×			6
	1	4	4

Example 7: Convert 9 days into hours.

Solution: 9 days = 9 × 24 hours
= 216 hours

		[3]2	4
×			9
	2	1	6

Example 8: 3 days 5 hours = ________ hours

Solution: 3 days = 3 × 24 = 72 hours

5 hours = + 5 hours

77 hours

Thus, 3 days 5 hours = 77 hours.

CONVERSION OF HOURS TO MINUTES

We know that **1 hour = 60 minutes**.

When we have to convert hours to minutes, 1 hour becomes 60 minutes. The value increases numerically. So, we multiply with 60.

So, 1 hour = 60 minutes.

2 hours = 2 × 60 = 120 minutes.

7 hours = 7 × 60 = 420 minutes.

Example 9: Convert 18 hours into minutes.

Solution: 18 hours = 18 × 60 = 1080 minutes.

$$\begin{array}{rrrr} & & {}^{3}1 & 8 \\ \times & & & 6 \\ \hline & 1 & 0 & 8 \end{array}$$

Example 10: Convert 2 hours 13 minutes into minutes.

Solution: 2 hours 13 minutes = ____________ minutes.

2 hours = 2 × 60 = 120 minutes.

13 minutes = +13 minutes

133 minutes

Thus, 2 hours 13 minutes = 133 minutes.

EXERCISE 9.4

1. **Convert the following.**
   a. 3 days = __________ hours b. 5 days = __________ hours
   c. 7 days = __________ hours d. 10 days = __________ hours
   e. 1 day 3 hours = __________ hours f. 2 days 5 hours = __________ hours
   g. 3 days 2 hours = __________ hours h. 6 days 4 hours = __________ hours
2. **Convert the following.**
   a. 3 hours = __________ minutes b. 5 hours = __________ minutes
   c. 6 hours = __________ minutes d. 8 hours = __________ minutes
   e. 1 hour 5 minutes = __________ minutes
   f. 2 hours 7 minutes = __________ minutes
   g. 5 hours 3 minutes = __________ minutes
   h. 8 hours 15 minutes = __________ minutes

TIMETABLE

A timetable is a chart that shows the departure and arrival times of trains, buses or aircrafts.

Departures

TIME	DESTINATION	FLIGHT	GATE	REMARK
09:45	BARCELONA	A4405	D17	ON TIME
09:57	NEW YORK	A1873	D08	ON TIME
10:03	DUBAI	A2960	C05	BOARDING
10:09	SHANGHAI	B0334	D14	DELAYED
10:14	DHAKA	B9700	F20	ON TIME
10:25	LONDON	C1503	F04	BOARDING
10:44	TOKYO	C5702	G11	ON TIME
10:59	SAO PAULO	D2013	G02	DELAYED
11:08	PARIS	D0869	E10	ON TIME
11:16	ISTANBUL	D7310	E06	ON TIME

Example 11: A railway schedule for trains from Mumbai to Kolkata is given below. Study it carefully and answer the following questions.

Train No./Name	Departure Station	Departure Time	Arrival Station	Arrival Time	Journey Duration
12261 - Howrah Duronto	CSMT Mumbai	17:15	HWH Howrah	20:15	1 Day 3 Hours
12859 - Gitanjali Exp	DR Mumbai	06:15	HWH Howrah	12:30	1 Day 6 Hours
12809 - Howrah Mail	DR Mumbai	21:25	HWH Howrah	06:00	1 Day 8 Hours
12101 - Jnaneshwari Exp	LTT Mumbai	20:35	SHM Kolkata	03:20	1 Day 6 Hours

a. Which is the slowest train from Mumbai to Kolkata?

Solution: Train No. 12809, Howrah Mail

b. Which train reaches Kolkata in the morning?

Solution: Train No.12859, Gitanjali Exp.

c. At what time will Jnaneshwari Exp depart from Mumbai?

Solution: 20:35 that is 8:35 p.m.

d. Which train will reach Howrah at 8:15 p.m.?

Solution: Train No. 12261, Howrah Duronto

Exercise 9.5

1. **A railway schedule for trains from Guwahati to Patna is given below. Study it carefully and answer the following questions.**

Train No./Name	Departure Station	Departure Time	Arrival Station	Arrival Time	Journey Duration
13247 - Capital Express	KYQ Guwahati	05:00	RJPB Patna	04:55	23 Hours 55 Mins
12423 - Rajdhani Exp	GHY Guwahati	07:00	PPTA Patna	21:40	14 Hours 40 Mins
15651 - Lohit Express	GHY Guwahati	13:10	SEE Sonpur	07:25	18 Hours 15 Mins
12505 - Northeast Exp	KYQ Guwahati	12:40	PPTA Patna	05:35	16 Hours 55 Mins

a. Which is the fastest train from Guwahati to Patna?

b. Which train reaches Patna during the night?

c. How long does Northeast Exp take to reach Patna from Guwahati?

d. Which train leaves Guwahati at 1:10 p.m.?

2. Study the timetable of a chef and answer the following questions.

Items to be baked	Time
Cheesecake	9:00 a.m. to 9:45 a.m.
Baked potatoes	9:50 a.m. to 10: 35 a.m.
Roasted vegetables	10:45 a.m. to 11:40 a.m.
Apple Pie	11:50 a.m. to noon
Potato chips	12:05 p.m. to 12:20 p.m.
Plum cake	12:30 p.m. to 1:40 p.m.
Puff pastries	1:50 p.m. to 2:35 p.m.

a. Which items will take less than 30 minutes to bake?

b. Which items will take more than 1 hour to bake?

c. How long does it take to bake a plum cake?

d. Which item needs the longest time to bake?

e. How long does it take to bake a cheesecake?

KEY CONCEPTS

Time

- Reading time
  - Half past or 30 minutes past the hour
  - Quarter past or 15 minutes past the hour
  - 45 minutes past or quarter to or 15 minutes to the hour
  - To 5-minute intervals
  - To the nearest hour
- Telling the time before and after
- Estimating time
- Calendar
  - A page or series of pages showing the days, weeks and months of a particular year

REVISION EXERCISE

1. **State True or False.**

   a. 1 week has 7 days. ____________

   b. One hour has 30 minutes. ____________

   c. There are 7 months that have 31 days. ____________

   d. Quarter of an hour has 30 minutes. ____________

   e. There are 5 months that have 30 days. ____________

   f. July and August have 31 days each. ____________

   g. February has 29 days in a leap year. ____________

   h. September and March have 30 days each. ____________

2. **Write the time for each of the following clocks.**

a.

____________ or ____________

b.

____________ or ____________

c.

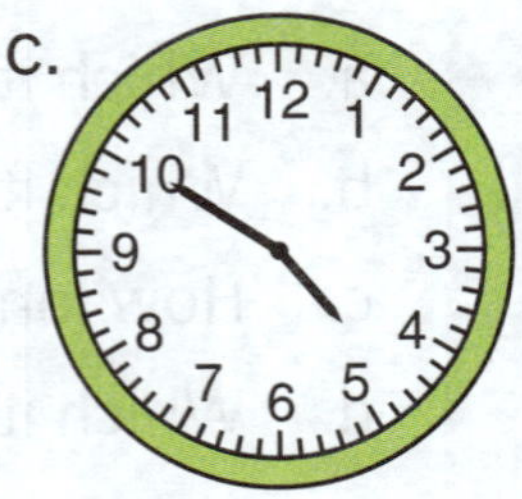

____________ or ____________

3. **How many minutes does the minute hand take to move from 12 to 5?** ____________

4. **Draw the hands of each clock for the given time.**

a.

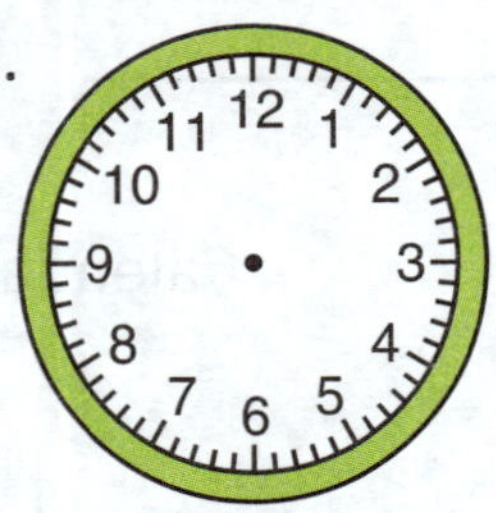

11:30 or Half past 11

b.

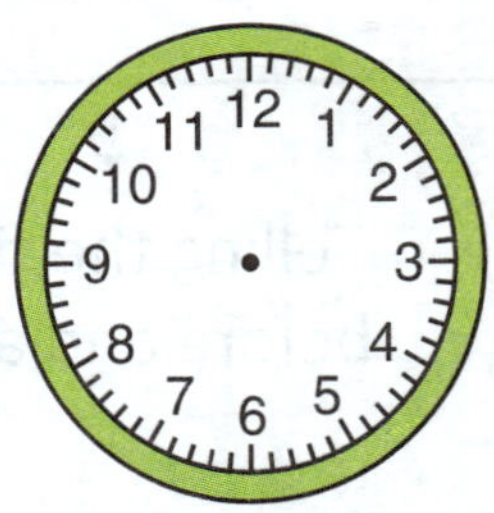

6:40 or 40 minutes past 6

5. **I went out to play in the park at 4:30 p.m. and came back at 5:45 p.m. For how long did I play in the park?**

	Hours	minutes
	5	4 5
–	4	3 0

I played in the park for ____________ hours ____________ minutes.

6. **Rajesh took 1 hour 15 minutes to reach his school and 1 hour 25 minutes to come back. How much time did he take to go to and come back from his school?**

	Hours	minutes
	1	15
+	1	25

Rajesh took __________ hours __________ minutes to go to and come back from his school.

7. **Write a.m., p.m., noon or midnight for the following.**

   a. 6 o'clock in the morning ____________________

   b. 10 o'clock during the day ____________________

   c. 9 o'clock in the evening ____________________

   d. 12 during the day ____________________

   e. 3 o'clock in the afternoon ____________________

   f. 12 at night ____________________

8. **Write the time in the 24-hour clock.**

   a. 6:15 p.m. = ______________ b. 7:05 a.m. = ______________

   c. 12:30 a.m. = ______________ d. 11:45 p.m. = ______________

9. **Write the time in the 12-hour clock.**

   a. 1515 hours = ____________ b. 1210 hours = ____________

   c. 2325 hours = ____________ d. 0820 hours = ____________

10. **Convert the following into hours.**

   a. 9 days = _______ hours b. 12 days = _______ hours

   c. 5 days 15 hours = _______ hours d. 10 days 12 hours = _______ hours

11. **Convert the following into minutes.**

   a. 9 hours = ________ minutes

   b. 11 hours = ________ minutes

   c. 3 hours 6 minutes = ________ minutes

   d. 6 hours 35 minutes = ________ minutes

10 Data Handling

Prior Knowledge

- Organizing and interpreting data
- Understanding data in the form of charts
- Interpreting and drawing pictographs

Learning Objectives

- Pictographs
- Tally marks
- Recording data using tally marks

Let's Get Started

Piyush loves to play with block toys. He has made this figure using all his blocks. In his block set, there were 5 green blocks, 2 yellow blocks, 7 blue blocks and 6 red blocks.

Count the blocks in the figure.

a. How many green blocks are there?

____

b. How many blue blocks are there?

____

c. How many red blocks are there?

____

d. How many yellow blocks are there?

____

e. Has Piyush lost any blocks? If yes, write the numbers.

____

PICTOGRAPHS

A pictograph uses pictures or symbols to give information. It has a title. The title says what the pictograph represents. Using pictorial representations, a pictograph helps in comparing information to arrive at a conclusion.

Example 1: Ramu sells fruits at the market. The following pictograph shows his sales for Sunday. Look at the pictograph and answer the questions given below.

a. How many apples did he sell in total?

b. Which fruit was sold the most?

c. Which fruit was sold the least?

d. How many kinds of fruits did Ramu sell on Sunday?

e. How many fruits were sold in all?

Solution:

a. Ramu sold 8 apples in total.

b. Orange was sold the most.

c. Watermelon was sold the least.

d. Ramu sold 5 kinds of fruits.

e. Total number of fruits sold = 8 + 13 + 10 + 5 + 3 = 39

Now, look at the following examples.

If  = 1 apple, then  = 2 apples

 = 3 apples  = $\frac{1}{2}$ apple

Sometimes, a symbol represents more than one item. Look at the following example.

If  = 2 apples, then  = 4 apples

 = 6 apples  = 1 apple

Example 2: The following pictograph shows the number of apples Vinny and Romila ate during the week.

Look at the pictograph and answer the given questions.

Number of apples eaten during a week	
Days	**Number of apples eaten**
Monday	
Tuesday	
Wednesday	
Thursday	
Friday	
Saturday	

Each  = 2 apples

a. How many apples is  equal to?

b. Find the number of apples they ate on the following days.

   i. Tuesday

   ii. Wednesday

   iii. Saturday

c. What is the total number of apples Vinny and Romila ate on Monday, Tuesday and Saturday?

d. What is the title of the pictograph?

Solution: a. 2 apples

b. i. 4 apples (2 × 2 = 4)

   ii. 7 apples (3 × 2 + 1 = 6 + 1 = 7)

   iii. 6 apples (3 × 2 = 6)

c. The total number of apples they ate on Monday, Tuesday and Saturday
= (2 + 1) + 4 + 6 = 3 + 4 + 6 = 13 apples

d. The title of the pictograph is **Number of apples eaten during a week**.

EXERCISE 10.1

1. **The following pictograph shows how much pocket money Shubham earned every day from Monday to Friday. Answer the following questions.**

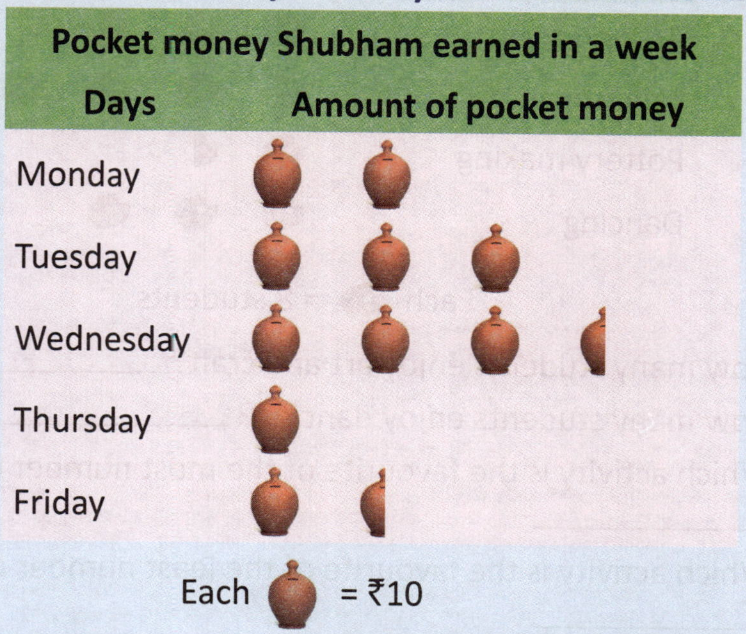

a. How much money did Shubham earn on the following days?

i. Monday ______ ii. Tuesday ______

iii. Wednesday ______ iv. Thursday ______

v. Friday ______

b. On which day did he earn the maximum money? ____________

c. On which day did he earn the least money? ____________

d. On which day did he earn ₹30? ____________

2. **The following pictograph shows how many students of Class 3 like different flavours of pastry.**

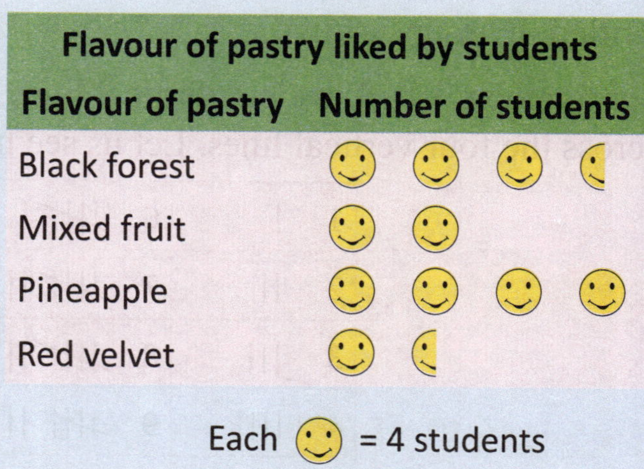

a. How many students like black forest flavour?

____

b. How many students like mixed fruit flavour?

____

c. Which flavour is liked the most by students?

____

d. Which flavour is liked the least by students? ____________

3. **The pictograph shows the favourite summer activity of students of Class 3.**

Favourite summer activity	
Favourite activity	**Number of students**
Art and craft	
Swimming	
Pottery making	
Dancing	

Each  = 8 students

a. How many students enjoy art and craft? ______________

b. How many students enjoy dancing? ______________

c. Which activity is the favourite of the most number of students?

____

d. Which activity is the favourite of the least number of students?

____

e. How many more students enjoy swimming than dancing? ______________

RECORDING DATA USING TALLY MARKS

We will now learn how to record data using tally marks, represent it pictorially and draw conclusions.

Tally Marks

Tally marks are a way of recording the number of observations. Tally marks are written in groups of five.

For numbers 1 to 4, we put vertical lines. For the number 5, we put a slanting line across the four vertical lines. Let us see how we write them.

1 |	6 𝍸 |	11 𝍸 𝍸 |
2 ||	7 𝍸 ||	12 𝍸 𝍸 ||
3 |||	8 𝍸 |||	13 𝍸 𝍸 |||
4 ||||	9 𝍸 ||||	14 𝍸 𝍸 ||||
5 𝍸	10 𝍸 𝍸	15 𝍸 𝍸 𝍸

Example 3: Given below is the tally chart showing the number of books Sushmita read in January, February, March and April.

Month	Tally marks	Number of books
January	𝍸	5
February	𝍷𝍷𝍷	3
March	𝍸 𝍷𝍷	7
April	𝍷𝍷𝍷𝍷	4

This tally chart is shown in the pictograph below.

Study the given pictograph and answer the questions.

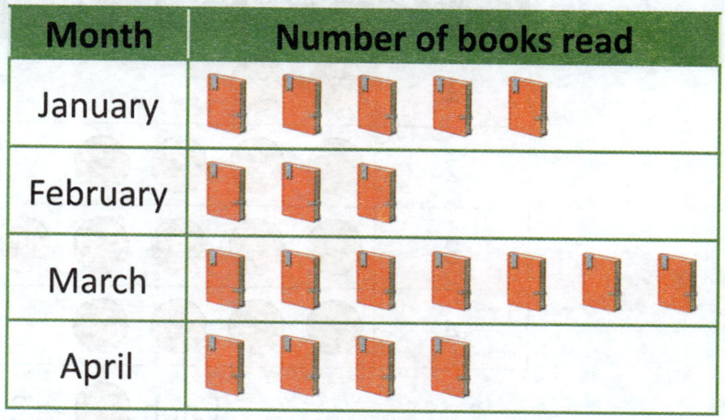

Each [book] = 1 book

a. How many books did Sushmita read in the following months?
   i. January
   ii. February
   iii. March
   iv. April

b. In which month did she read the maximum number of books?

c. How many books did she read in January and February?

d. How many more books did she read in March than April?

Solution: a. i. In January, Sushmita reads 5 books.

ii. In February, Sushmita reads 3 books.

iii. In March, Sushmita read 7 books.

iv. In April, Sushmita read 4 books.

b. In March, she reads the maximum number of books.

c. Total number of books read in January and February = 5 + 3 = 8 books

d. Number of books read in March = 7

Number of books read in April = 3

7 – 4 = 3

Thus, Sushmita read 3 more books in March than April.

Example 4: Given below is the tally chart showing the number of students in Classes 1, 2, 3 and 4 who like to play football.

Class	Tally marks	Number of students who like to play football
1	𝍷𝍷𝍷𝍷	4
2	𝍸 𝍷𝍷𝍷	8
3	𝍸 𝍸 𝍷𝍷	12
4	𝍸 𝍷𝍷𝍷	8

This tally chart is shown in the pictograph below.

Class	Number of students who like to play football
1	● ●
2	● ● ● ●
3	● ● ● ● ● ●
4	● ● ● ●

Each ● = 2 students

Study the above pictograph and answer the following questions.

a. How many students like football in the following classes?

i. Class 1 ii. Class 2

iii. Class 3 iv. Class 4

b. What is the total number of students from Class 1 to Class 4 who like football?

c. From which class do 4 students like football?

d. How many more students from Class 3 like football than from Class 4?

Solution: a. i. 4 ii. 8 iii. 12 iv. 8

b. The total number of students from Class 1 to Class 4 who like football = 4 + 8 + 12 + 8 = 32.

c. Class 1

d. The number of students from class 3 who like more football than from Class 4 = 12 – 8 = 4.

Example 5: A shopkeeper keeps the record of sales of grocery items by writing the name of the item each time it is sold.

rice   soap   sugar   oil   soap

oil   rice   rice   sugar   oil

sugar   rice   sugar   rice   sugar

oil   oil   soap   oil   soap

oil   sugar   soap   soap   soap

rice   soap   oil   sugar   rice

oil   sugar

The above data in the tabular form is given below.

Grocery items	Tally marks	Number of times
Rice	𝍸 II	7
Oil	𝍸 IIII	9
Sugar	𝍸 III	8
Soap	𝍸 III	8

Now, answer the following questions.

a. Which item is sold the least?

b. How many items are sold altogether?

c. How many times rice is sold?

d. Which item is sold the most?

e. Which two items are sold equal number of times?

Solution:

a. Rice

b. $7 + 9 + 8 + 8 = 32$

c. 7

d. Oil

e. Sugar and soap

Exercise 10.2

1. **Given below is the tally chart showing the number of cakes a baker baked on Monday, Tuesday, Wednesday and Thursday.**

Days	Number of cakes
Monday	||
Tuesday	卌
Wednesday	卌 ||
Thursday	|

Complete the pictograph given below and then answer the questions.

Days	Number of cakes
Monday	
Tuesday	
Wednesday	
Thursday	

Each ◈ = 1 cake

a. How many cakes did the baker bake on the following days?

i. Monday ________________ ii. Tuesday ______________

iii. Wednesday ______________ iv. Thursday ______________

b. On which day did the baker bake 7 cakes? ______________

c. How many total cakes did the baker bake on Monday and Tuesday?

____

d. How many more cakes did the baker bake on Wednesday than on Thursday? ________________

2. **Given below is the tally chart showing the number of seashells collected by four friends from a beach.**

Name	Number of seashells collected
Rashmi	卌 卌 ||
Preeti	卌 卌 ||||
Jayshree	卌 卌
Monika	卌 卌 卌 |

Complete the pictograph given below and then answer the questions.

Name	Number of seashells collected
Rashmi	
Preeti	
Jayshree	
Monika	

Each ▲ = 2 shells

a. How many shells were collected by each of the following friends?

i. Rashmi ____________ ii. Preeti ____________

iii. Jayshree ____________ iv. Monika ____________

b. Which friend collected 14 shells? ____________

c. How many shells were collected by Monika and Rashmi together?

____

d. How many more shells were collected by Preeti than Jayshree?

____

KEY CONCEPTS

Data handling

↓

To collect and organize data

↓

To record data using tally marks

↓

Tally Marks: A way of counting and recording the number of observations

↓

To represent data → Data

Pictograph → To interpret data and draw a conclusion

Pictograph → Pictures or symbols used to represent data

Revision Exercise

1. **The pictograph below shows the pocket money saved by four friends in their piggy banks.**

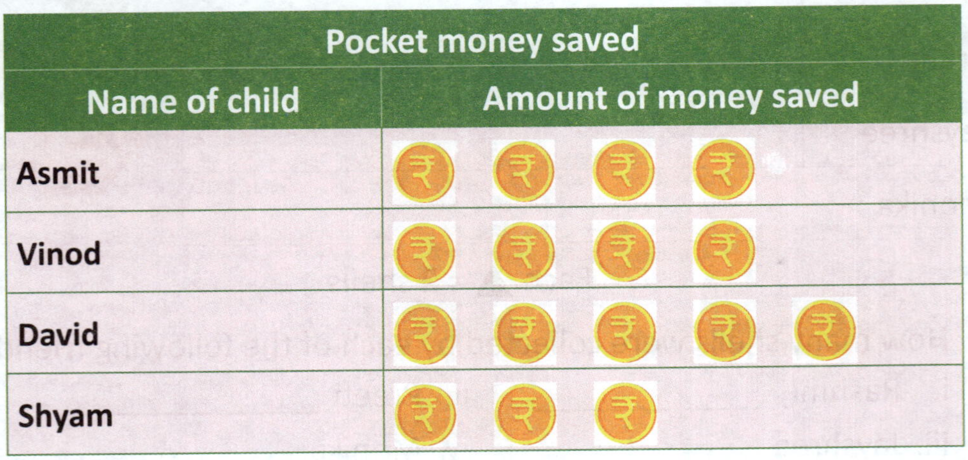

Each ₹ = ₹30

a. Who has saved the maximum money? ____________

b. Who has saved the least amount of money? ____________

c. How much money has Vinod saved? ____________

d. How much more money has David saved than Asmit? ____________

2. **The following pictograph shows the transport used by the teachers and students of a particular school.**

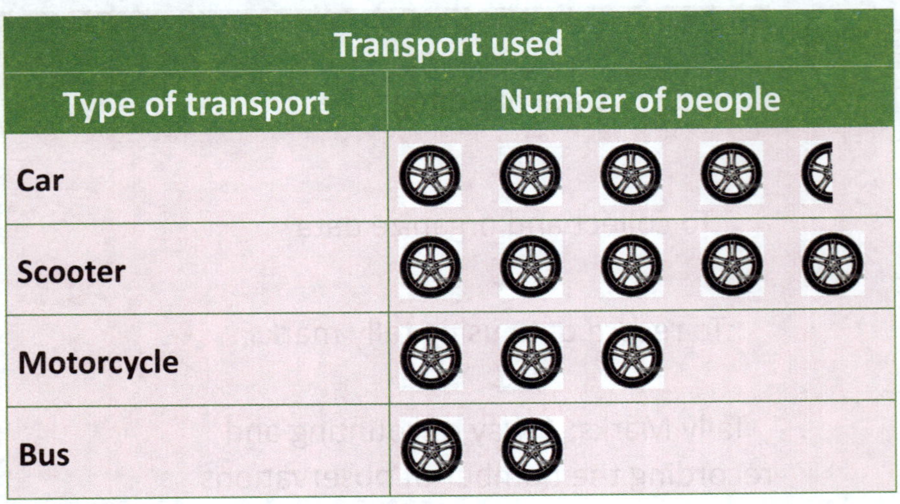

Each  = 20 people

a. How many people come by car? ____________

b. How many people come by motorcycle? ____________

c. Which transport is used by more people: scooter or motorcycle ____________

d. Which transport is used by the least number of people? ____________

3. **Rahul conducted a survey of the most sold vegetables of 20 vegetable sellers of the local market and tabulated the responses in the following manner.**

Onion	Pumpkin	Potato	Tomato	Capsicum	Potato
Carrot	Capsicum	Tomato	Tomato	Potato	Onion
Pumpkin	Tomato	Tomato	Potato	Onion	Pumpkin
Potato	Tomato	Onion	Capsicum	Pumpkin	Capsicum

Represent the above data in a tabular form using tally marks and answer the following questions.

a. Which vegetable is purchased the most?

b. Which vegetable is purchased the least?

c. How many pumpkins were sold?

d. How many vegetables were taken for the data?

4. **Udita is very fond of ornaments. She has the following ornaments in her jewellery box.**

Ornaments in Udita's jewellery box	
Ornament type	Number
Necklaces	12
Earring pairs	23
Bracelets	7
Finger rings	4

Represent the given data in the form of tally marks.

Draw a pictograph for the given data. Use the symbol ◯ to show 2 items.

Now, answer the following questions.

a. How many more bracelets does Udita have than finger rings? ____________

b. What is the total number of ornaments that she has? ____________

c. How many more earring pairs does she have than necklaces? ____________

d. How many more bracelets should she buy so that the number equals that of necklaces? ____________

e. If she buys 5 more necklaces, how many total necklaces will she have? ____________

11 Patterns

Prior Knowledge

- Observing and identifying unit of repeat
- Extending patterns based on identified unit of repeat
- Creating patterns from daily-life experiences

Learning Objectives

- Patterns around us
- Patterns with shapes
- Unit of repeat
- Patterns with numbers and letters
- Patterns with objects

Let's Get Started

Draw and colour to complete the picture.

What does the picture look like?

Can you see any pattern in the picture?

PATTERNS AROUND US

A **pattern** is formed when a design is repeated to form a structure or an object. We see many patterns around us.

In this cloth, designs are repeated over and over again to fill the entire object.

A design is repeated several times around the edge of a dinner plate to form a pattern.

A beautiful pattern is formed on a peacock's feathers.

Patterns are carved out in a building.

Patterns can be found in animals.

PATTERNS WITH SHAPES

Patterns can be formed with shapes, numbers, letters, objects and various other things.

Example 1: What will be the next two shapes in the pattern?

, ________, ________

Solution: Since  and  are being repeated every time, the answer will be

.

Example 2: Draw the next three shapes in the given pattern.

, ________, ________, ________

Solution: Since  are being repeated every time, the answer will be

.

UNIT OF REPEAT

To understand a pattern, we need to identify the 'unit of repeat'. Unit of repeat means **what is being repeated** in a given pattern.

Some patterns and the unit of repeat are given below.

Pattern	Unit of repeat

A B C D A B C D A B C D	A B C D
2 4 2 2 2 4 2 2 2 4 2 2	2 4 2 2

PATTERNS WITH NUMBERS AND LETTERS

Let us observe the following patterns.

Example 3: Find the next two terms in the given pattern.

A A A B B B ___ ___

Solution: Each letter is written three times. So, after B, there comes C.

Therefore, **A A A B B B** __C__ __C__

Example 4: Find the next three terms in the given pattern.

S U N S U N S U N ___ ___ ___

Solution: In this pattern, the unit of repeat is **S U N**.

Therefore, **S U N S U N S U N** __S__ __U__ __N__

Example 5: Find the rule and extend the given letter pattern.

AbB, CdD, EfF, GhH, _____, _____, _____

Solution: Here the rule is, starting with capital A, write the next letter of the alphabet first in small and then in capital. Then, start with the next letter and so on.

So, the next 3 terms will be **IjJ, KlL, MnN**.

Example 6: Identify the rule and extend the given pattern.

10, 11, 12, 13, _____, _____

Solution: Since 1 is being added every time to the given number, the rule will be

10, 11 (or 10 + 1), 12 (or 11 + 1), 13 (or 12 + 1), …

So, the next two terms will be 14 (or 13 + 1) and 15 (or 14 + 1).

Therefore, the pattern is extended as **10, 11, 12, 13,** __**14**__, __**15**__.

Example 7: Identify the rule and extend the given pattern.

21, 19, 17, 15, _____, _____, _____

Solution: Since 2 is being subtracted every time from the given number, the rule will be

21, 19 (or 21 – 2), 17 (or 19 – 2), 15 (or 17 – 2), …

So, the next three terms will be 13 (or 15 – 2), 11 (or 13 – 2) and 9 (or 11 – 2).

Therefore, the pattern is extended as **21, 19, 17, 15,** __**13**__, __**11**__, __**9**__.

Patterns With Objects

Let us extend some patterns based on objects.

Example 8: Identify the rule and find out which object will come next.

 ________

Solution: Here, the unit of repeat is . So, after pineapple, the next object will be a strawberry .

Example 9: Find out the next three objects in the pattern.

________ ________ ________

Solution: Here, the number of balls is decreasing by one on each repeat. So, the next three objects in the pattern will be

EXERCISE 11.1

1. Colour the shapes according to the pattern.

a. 

b. 

2. Circle the shape that will come next in the pattern.

a. 

b. 

c. 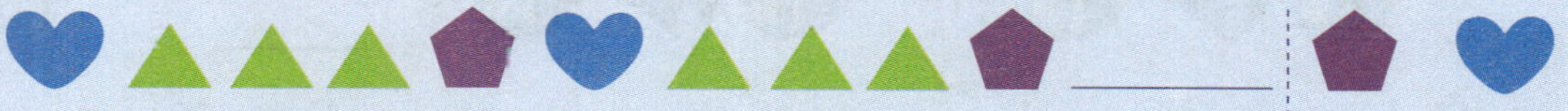

d. 

3. Find the rule and extend the number patterns.

a. 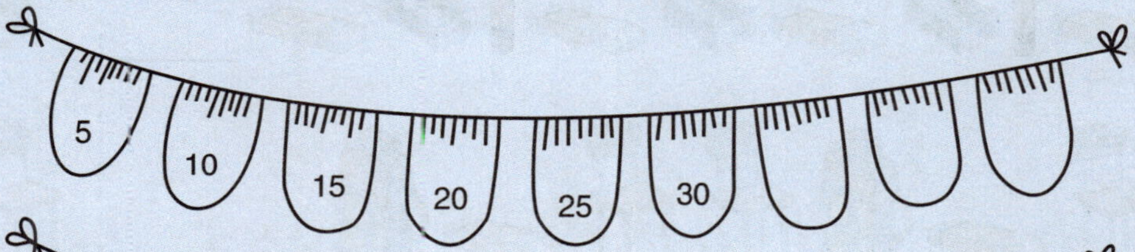

b. 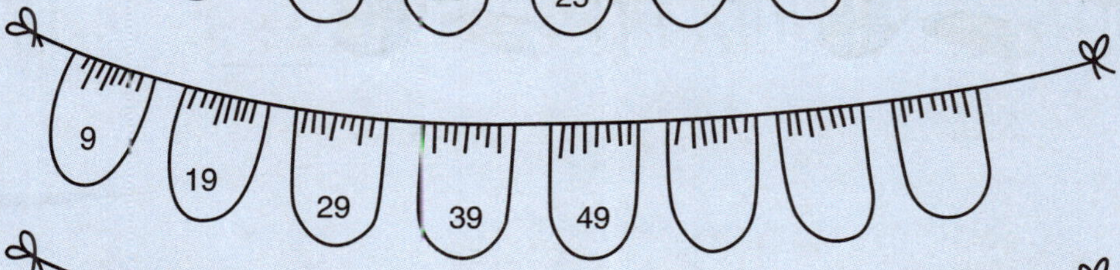

c. 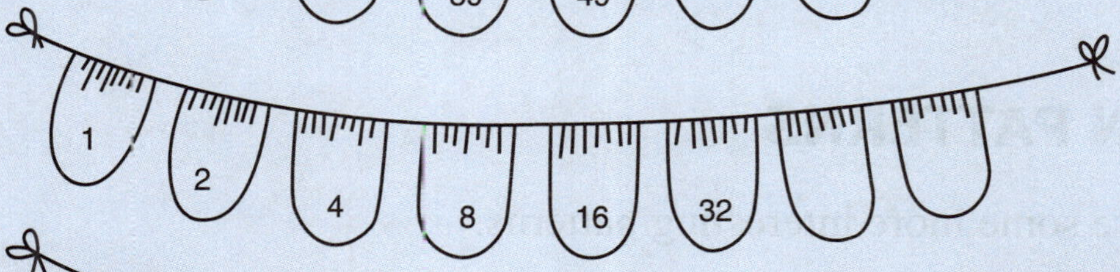

d. 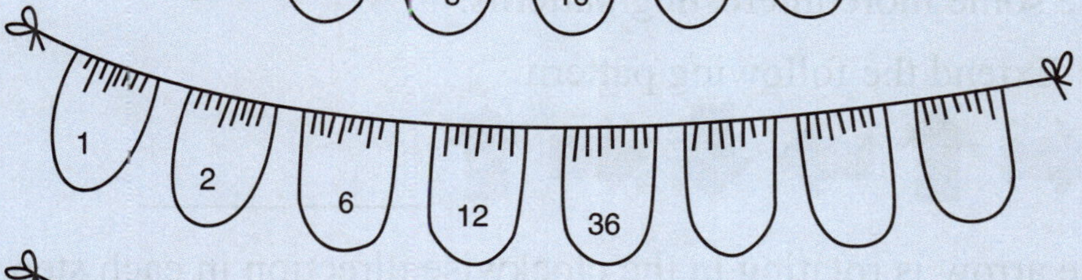

e. 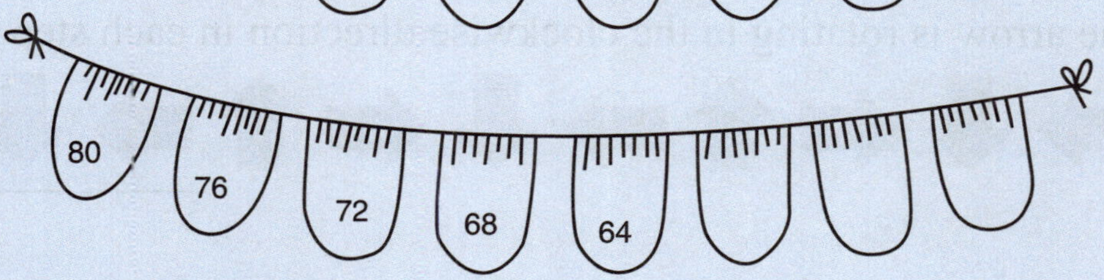

4. **Circle the object that will come next in the pattern.**

a.  ______ 

b. 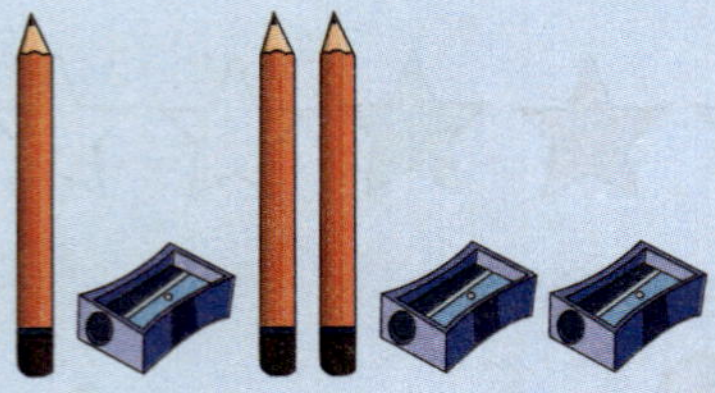 ______ 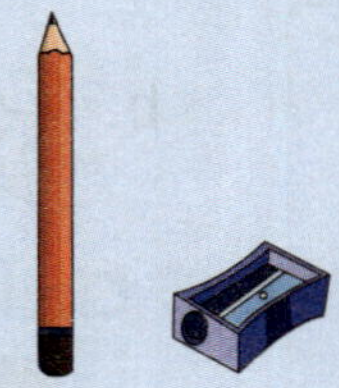

c.  ______ 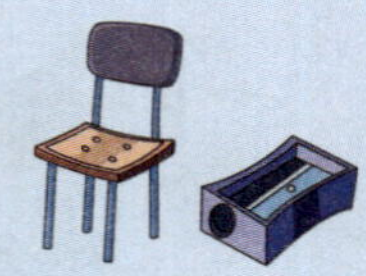

d. 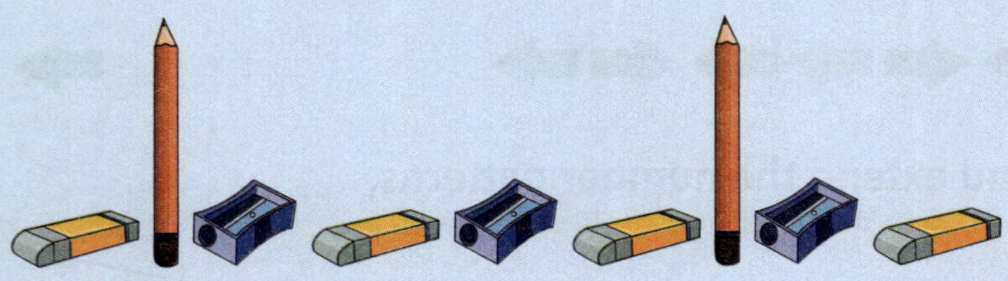 ______ 

e.  ______ 

MORE ON PATTERNS

Let us explore some more interesting patterns.

Example 10: Extend the following pattern.

 ______ ______

Solution: The arrow is rotating in the clockwise direction in each step.

Therefore, 

Example 11: Extend the given pattern.

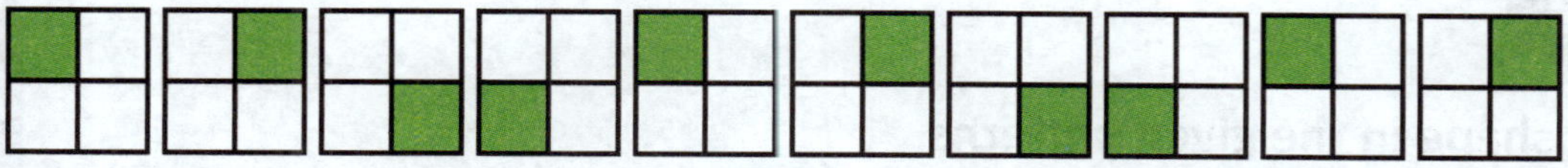 ______ ______

Solution:

Since the shaded square is moving in rotation, the answer will be 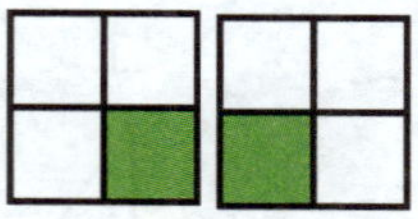

Example 12: What will be the next figure in the given pattern?

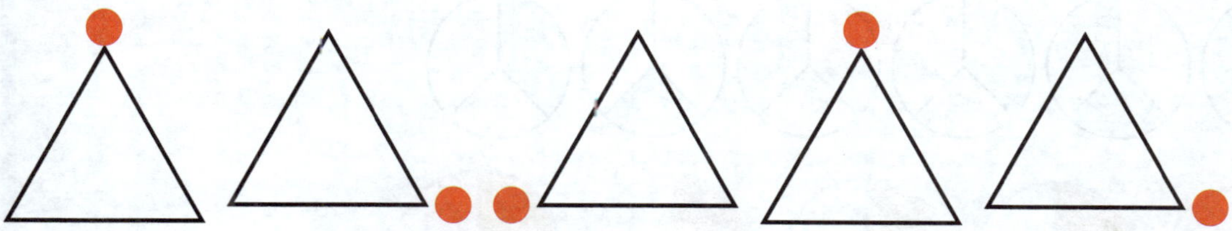 ______

Solution: In this pattern, the red dot is moving from one corner to the next in clockwise manner.

So, the next figure in the given pattern will be 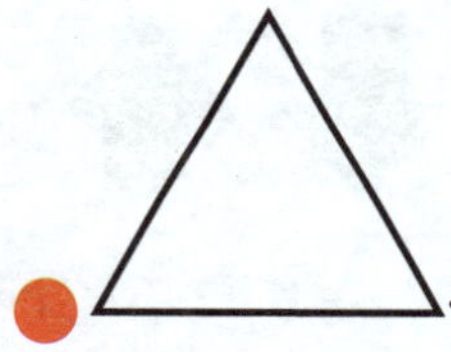.

Example 13: What will come next in the pattern?

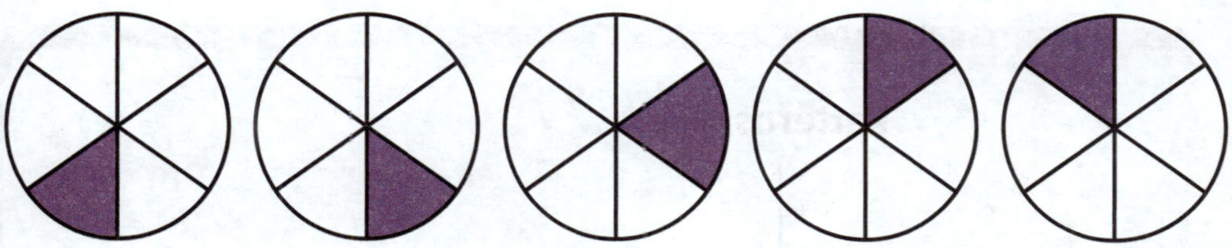 ______

Solution: Here, the shading is moving to the next part in anti-clockwise manner.

So, the next term in the pattern will be 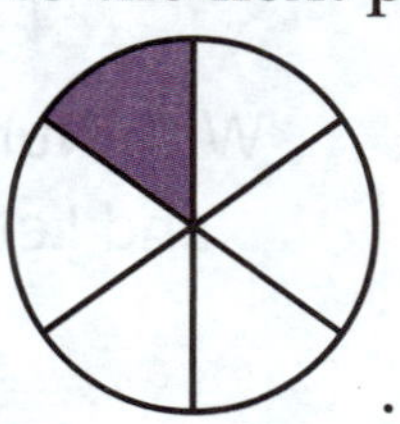.

Exercise 11.2

Draw the next shape in the given patterns.

1. 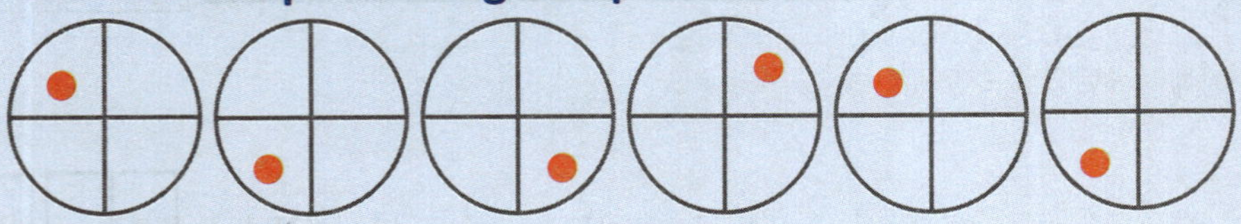

2. 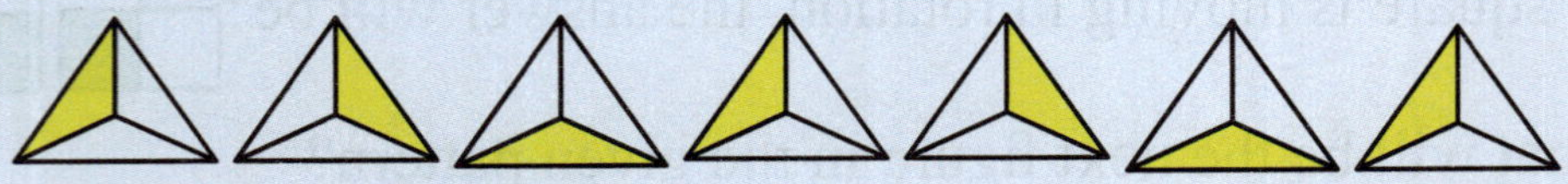

3. 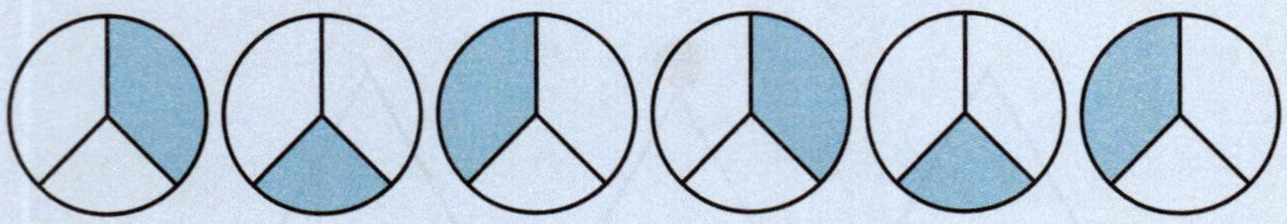

4. 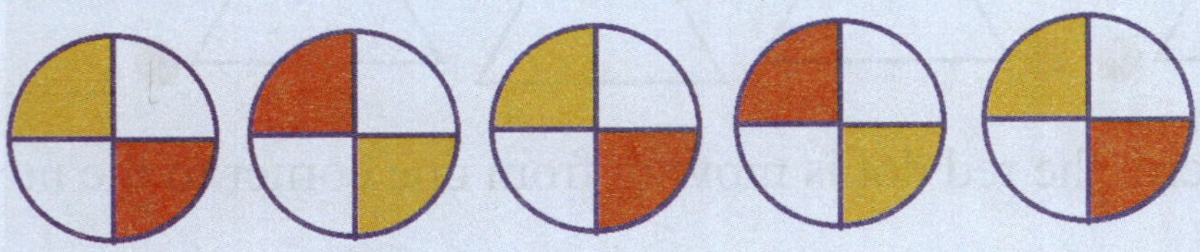

5. 

Key Concepts

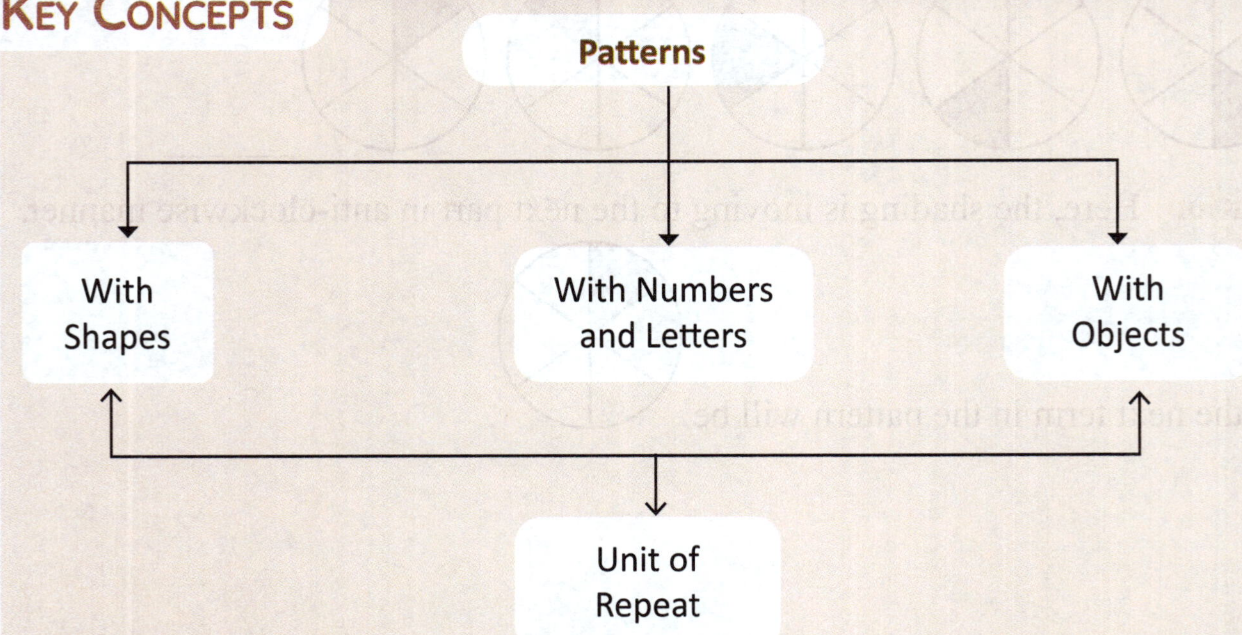

REVISION EXERCISE

1. Extend the following patterns.

a.  ____________

b. 11, 21, 31, 41, 51, ____________, ____________

c. 1, 3, 9, 27, ____________, ____________

d. Z, Z, Y, Y, X, X, ____________, ____________

e. N, E, X, T, N, E, X, T, N, E, X, ____________, ____________

f. A, AB, ABC, ABCD, ____________, ____________

2. Draw the next figure in each of the given patterns.

a. 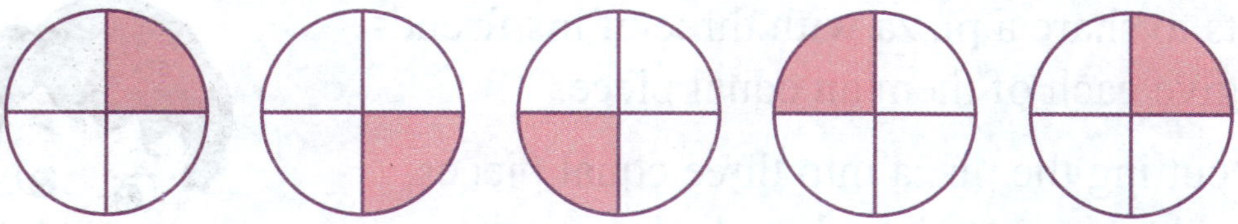 ____________

b. 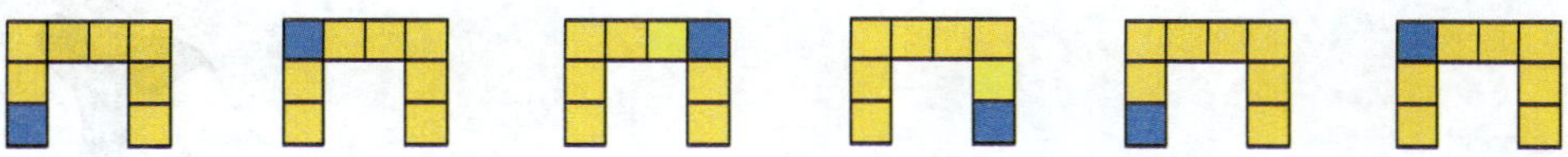 ____________

c. 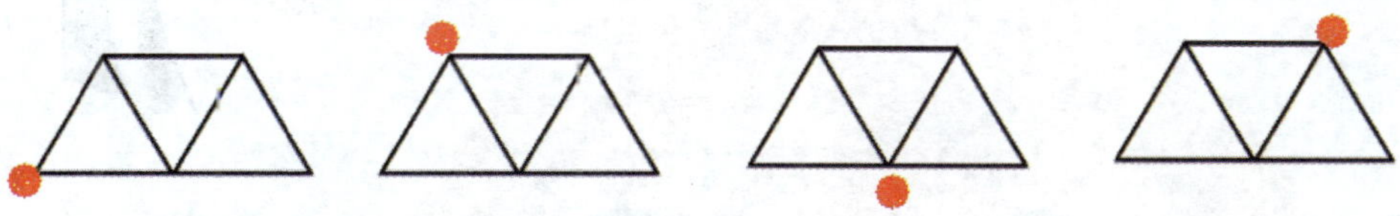 ____________

d. 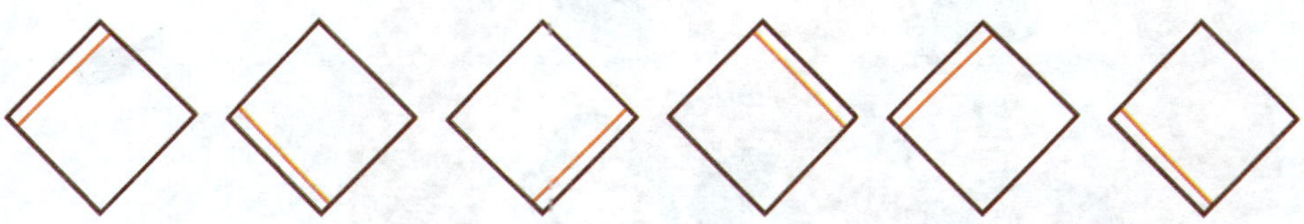 ____________

3. Follow the given rule and create patterns with the first 4 terms.

a. Start with capital B, write the next letter of the alphabet, first in small and then in capital. Then, start with the next letter and so on.

b. Start at 30, add 4 each time

c. Start at 50, add 10 each time

d. Start at 60, add 100 each time

e. Start at 90, subtract 2 each time

f. Start at 150, subtract 5 each time

12 Introduction to Fractions

Prior Knowledge

- Equal sharing
- Equal grouping
- Dividing a number by another number

Learning Objectives

- Fraction as a part of a whole
- One-half, one-third and one-fourth
- Fraction as a part of a collection

Let's Get Started

Subroto wants to share a pizza with three of his friends. He wants to give each of them an equal piece.

Help him by cutting the pizza into three equal pieces. Draw lines on the pizza to show how he can cut it.

You have just helped Subroto make fractions of the pizza. Let us learn about fractions.

FRACTION AS A PART OF A WHOLE

There are two chocolates. Each of them is cut into two pieces.

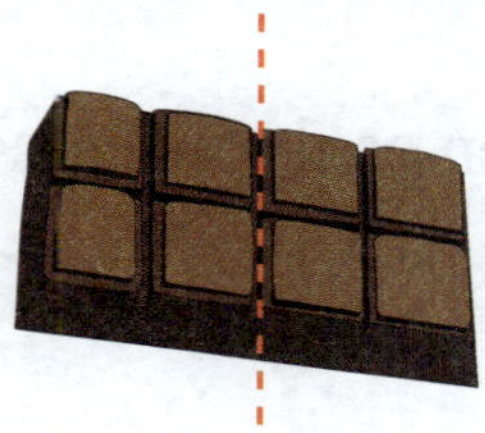

Here, both the parts are of the same size.

Here, the parts are not of the same size.

If we cut the chocolate through the middle into two equal parts, then each equal part is called a **half**.

Half is a fraction. Mathematically, it is written as $\frac{1}{2}$.

A fraction is a part of a whole object or a collection of objects.

REMEMBER

Plural of the word 'half' is 'halves'.

ONE-HALF

Any object cut into two equal parts is said to be cut into two equal halves. So, one-half is one of the two equal parts.

= half of the cake

$= \frac{1}{2}$ cake

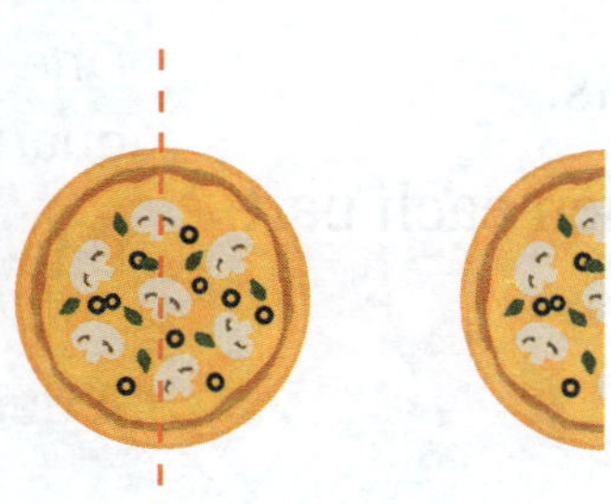

= half of the pizza

$= \frac{1}{2}$ pizza

More examples of one-half

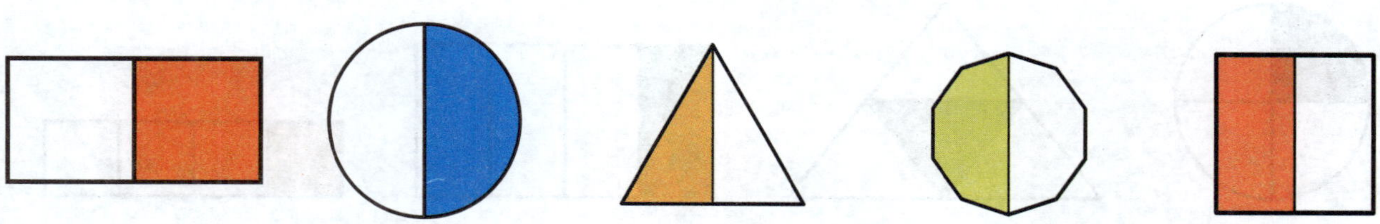

ONE-THIRD

Just like one-half is one part of two equal parts, one-third is one part of three equal parts.

If we cut a chocolate bar into three equal pieces, then each piece is called **one-third**.

One-third is a fraction. It is written as $\frac{1}{3}$.

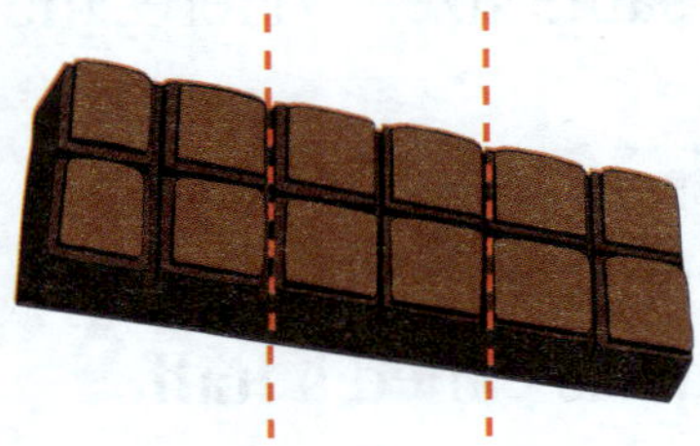

More examples of one-third

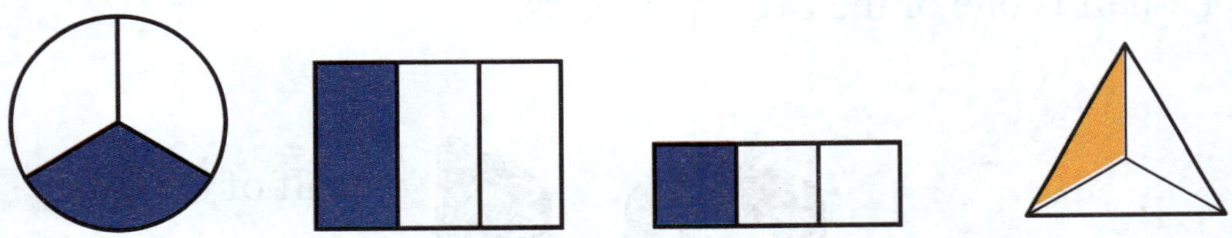

ONE-FOURTH

One-fourth is one part of four equal parts.

If we cut a cake into four equal parts, then each part is called **one-fourth**.

One-fourth is written as $\frac{1}{4}$.

> **REMEMBER**
>
> One-fourth is also called a quarter.
>
> One-fourth = $\frac{1}{4}$
>
> A quarter = $\frac{1}{4}$

More examples of one-fourth

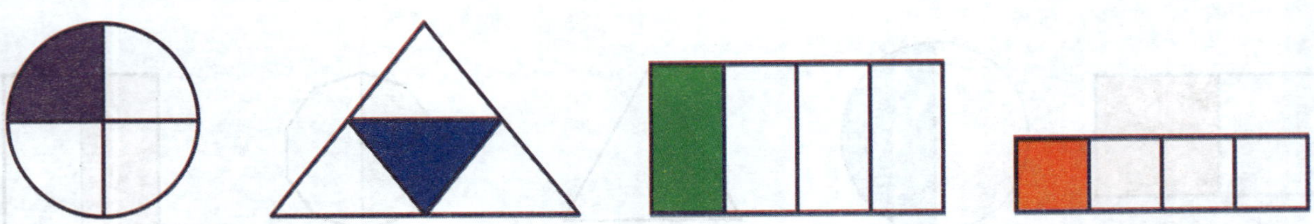

EXERCISE 12.1

1. **Write the fraction for the shaded portion in each figure.**

a. 

______

b. 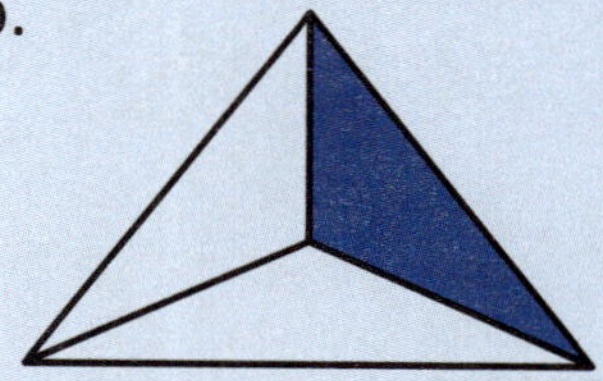

______

c. 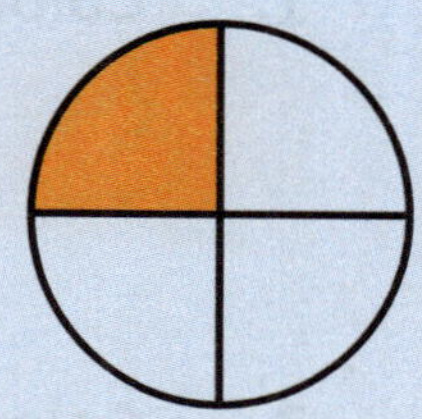

______

2. **Write the fraction for the unshaded portion in each figure.**

a. 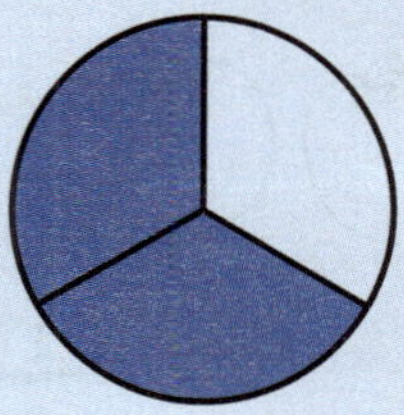

______

b. 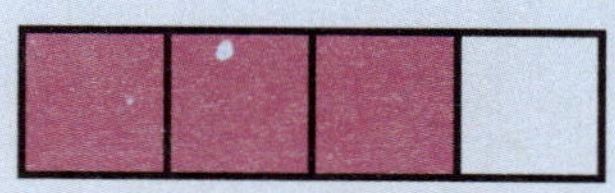

______

FRACTION AS A PART OF A COLLECTION

Example 1: There are two balloons. One balloon is blue.

Thus, $\frac{1}{2}$ of the balloons are blue.

Example 2: There are three apples.

One apple is red.

Thus, $\frac{1}{3}$ of the apples are red.

Example 3:

This is a group of four pencils.

One pencil is green.

Thus, $\frac{1}{4}$ of the pencils are green.

Exercise 12.2

1. Colour $\frac{1}{2}$ of the butterflies.

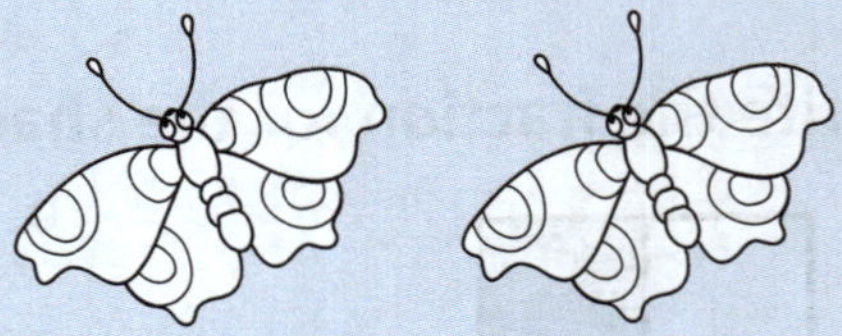

2. Colour $\frac{1}{3}$ of the carrots.

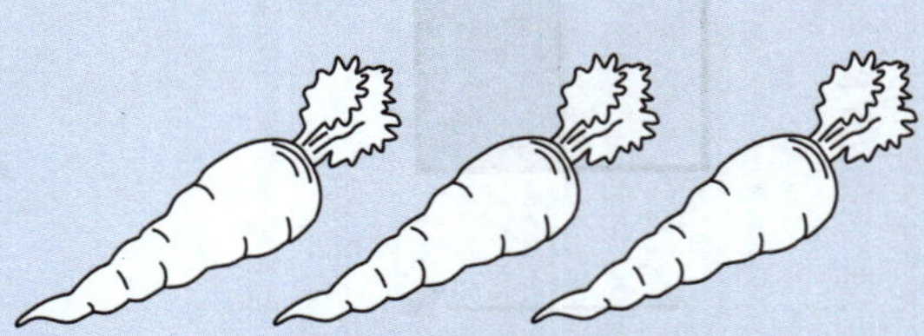

3. Colour $\frac{1}{4}$ of the tomatoes.

Key Concepts

Introduction to Fractions

Fractions as a part of a whole

Fractions as a part of a collection

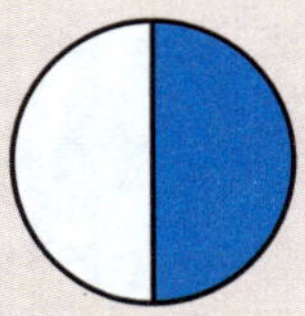 ← $\frac{1}{2}$ → 

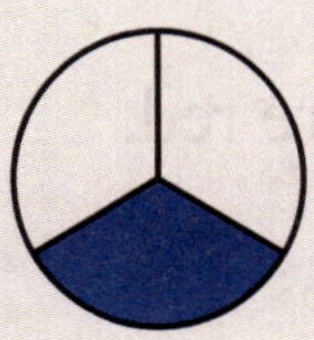 ← $\frac{1}{3}$ → 

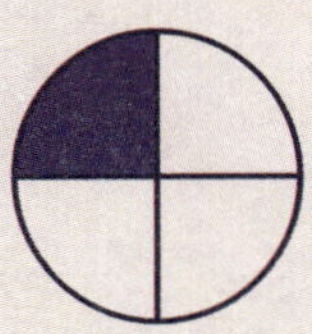 ← $\frac{1}{4}$ → 

Revision Exercise

1. Match the figures in column A to how much they represent in column B. The fractions represent the shaded portion in each figure.

	A		B
a.	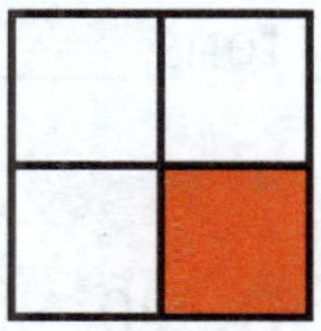	i.	$\frac{1}{2}$
b.	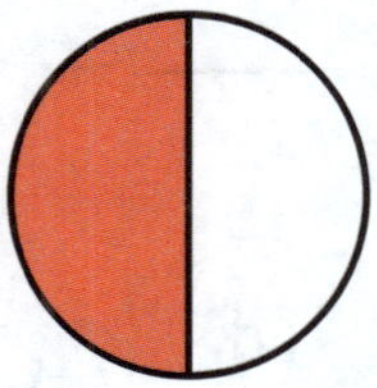	ii.	$\frac{1}{3}$
c.	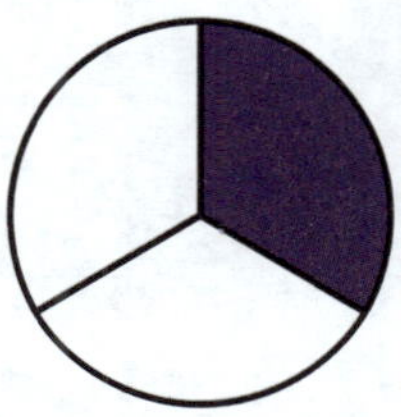	iii.	$\frac{1}{4}$

2. a. Colour $\frac{1}{4}$ of each picture.

i. 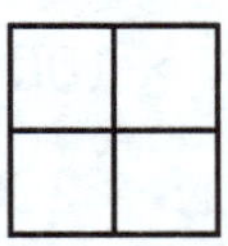 ii. 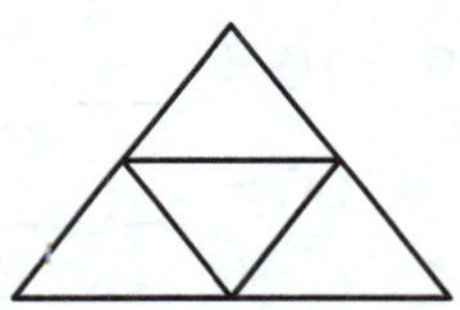 iii. 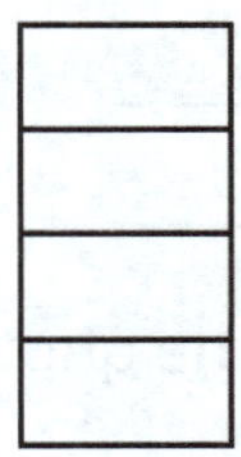 iv. 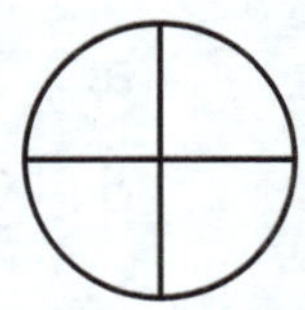

b. Colour $\frac{1}{3}$ of each picture.

i.  ii. 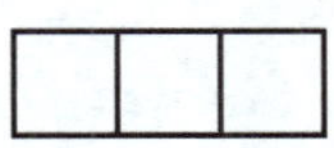 iii. 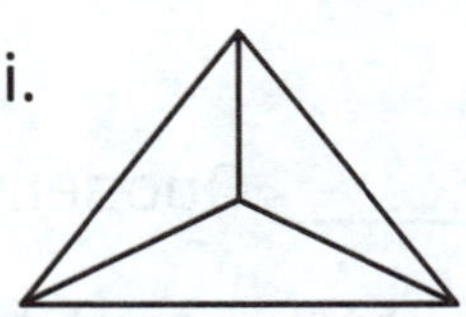 iv. 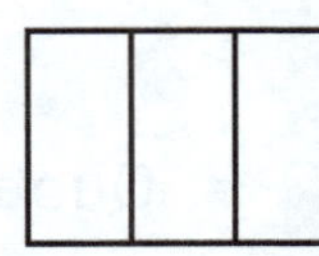

c. Colour $\frac{1}{2}$ of each picture.

i. 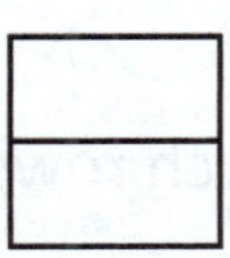 ii. 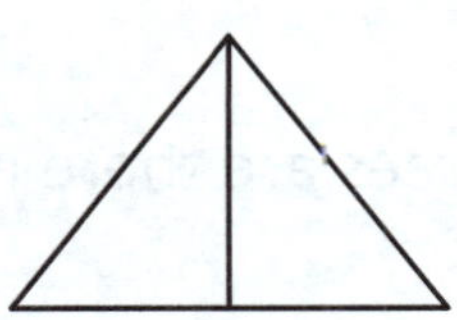 iii. 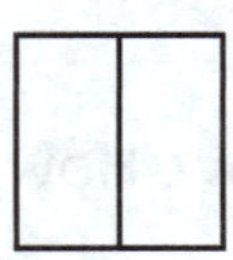 iv. 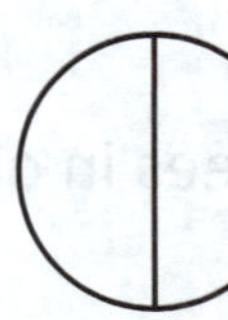 v. 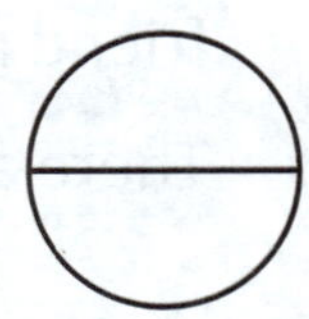

Test Paper 1

1. Fill in the blanks.

a. The number name of 70,070 is ____

____

b. 7923 = ________ thousands ________ hundreds ________ tens ________ ones

2. Write the place value of the underlined digits.

a. 56,0$\underline{9}$8 ______ b. $\underline{7}$194 ______ c. 3$\underline{8}$,923 ______ d. 50$\underline{1}$8 ______ e. 61,3$\underline{2}$0 ______ f. $\underline{2}$0,408 ______

3. Solve the following.

a.

	H	T	O
	7	8	5
+	1	6	3

b.

	H	T	O
	1	3	5
+	4	9	3

c.

	H	T	O
	8	0	0
+	4	6	5

d.

	H	T	O
		3	8
+			5

4. Use the short method to multiply the following.

a. 53 × 10 = ________ b. 79 × 10 = ________ c. 4 × 1000 = ________

d. 2 × 30 = ________ e. 5 × 200 = ________ f. 13 × 200 = ________

5. Divide and find the quotient.

a. $6\overline{)36}$ b. $5\overline{)45}$ c. $7\overline{)49}$ d. $8\overline{)56}$

Quotient: ________ Quotient: ________ Quotient: ________ Quotient: ________

6. Namita bought a T-shirt for ₹545 and a watch for ₹375. How much do the two items cost together?

7. Sameer distributed 54 crayons among his 6 friends. How many crayons did each friend get?

8. There are 36 trees in one row. How many trees are there in 7 such rows?

9. Vivaan read 148 pages of a book. The book had 208 pages. How many pages are left to read?

10. Write the fraction for the shaded and the non-shaded parts.

a.

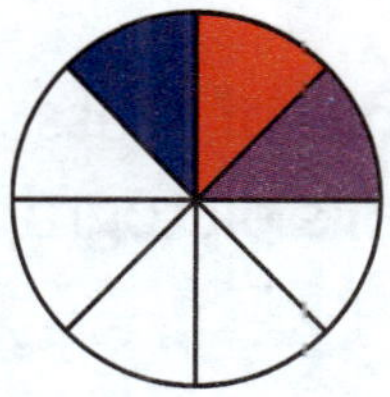

__________ is shaded.

__________ is not shaded.

b.

__________ is shaded.

__________ is not shaded.

11. Convert the following to cm.

a. 7 m = _____ cm   b. 12 m 35 cm = _____ cm

12. Convert 469 cm to m and cm.

13. Draw line segments with the following measurements

a. 6 cm   b. 1 cm

14. The children reached the playground at 4:15 and left at 5:30. How much time did they spend in the playground?

They spent _________ in the playground.

15. Radha spent her time shopping from 2:00 to 4:00 and then stopped for coffee from 4:00 to 5:00. How much time did she spend shopping and having coffee?

Radha spent _________ shopping and having coffee.

16. To pay a shopkeeper ₹460, I can pay

______ 100-rupee notes

\+

______ 50-rupee notes

\+

______ 10-rupee notes

or

I can pay the shopkeeper a 500-rupee note and he will return ₹______ to me.

$$\begin{array}{r} 5\ 0\ 0 \\ -\ 4\ 6\ 0 \\ \hline \\ \hline \end{array}$$

17. Tick the shapes that will tessellate.

a. b. c. b. e.

18. The following pictograph shows the channels that students of Class 3 like to watch. Answer the following questions and give a title to this pictograph.

TV Channels liked by Class 3 students	
Channel	**Number of students**
Channel A	
Channel B	
Channel C	

Each  = 4 children

a. How many students like to watch the following TV channels?

i. Channel A ____ ii. Channel B ____ iii. Channel C ____

b. How many more students watch Channel A than Channel B? ________

c. Which channel is enjoyed by the maximum number of students? ________

d. Which channel is liked by 22 students? ________

19. Draw the next term in each of these patterns.

a.  ____________

b.  ____________

20. Write the following time as per the 24-hour clock.

a. 5:40 p.m. ________ b. 12:20 a.m. ________

c. 7:12 a.m. ________ d. 11:56 p.m. ________

e. 2:43 p.m. ________ f. 3:00 a.m. ________

g. 10:05 p.m. ________ h. 9:24 a.m. ________

i. 6:39 a.m. ________ j. 1:24 p.m. ________

k. 8:46 a.m. ________ l. 12:25 p.m. ________

Test Paper 2

1. Write < or >.

a. 4049 ☐ 40,049 b. 10,090 ☐ 10,900

c. 8991 ☐ 8919 d. 60,143 ☐ 60,142

2. Fill in the blanks.

a. The smallest 4-digit number formed using the digits 2, 1, 9 and 7 is ______.

b. The largest 4-digit number using the digits 5, 1, 8 and 6 is ______.

c. The smallest 4-digit number formed using the digits 2, 8, 0 and 1 is ______.

d. The largest 4-digit number using the digits 7, 9, 3 and 0 is ______.

3. Solve the following.

a.

	H	T	O
	1	3	9
+	7	8	4

b.

	H	T	O
	9	8	8
−	4	9	0

c.

	H	T	O
		5	2
+			3

d.

	H	T	O
		8	9
+			2

4. Divide and find the quotient.

a. $4\overline{)28}$ b. $5\overline{)40}$ c. $3\overline{)27}$ d. $9\overline{)63}$

Quotient: ______ Quotient: ______ Quotient: ______ Quotient: ______

5.

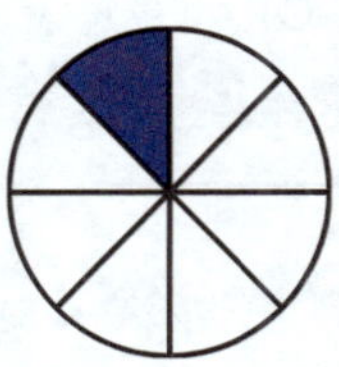

________ of the figure is shaded.

________ of the figure is not shaded.

6. Prerna has 42 buttons. She wants to use these buttons equally for stitching 6 shirts. How many buttons should she put on one shirt?

7. Hemant had ₹780 in his wallet. He used ₹265 to buy a game and ₹144 to buy a book. How much money is left with him now?

8. Neha packs 24 candles in one box. How many candles will she need to pack 9 such boxes?

9. A necklace costs ₹670. Mitali has ₹487 in her purse. How much more money does she need to buy the necklace?

10. Convert the following.

a. 564 cm to m and cm   b. 13 m to cm   c. 320 cm to m and cm

11. To pay ₹378 to a shopkeeper, I can pay

________ 100-rupee notes   ________ 50-rupees notes

________ 10-rupee notes   ________ 1-rupee notes

12. How many minutes does the minute hand take to move from

a. 3 to 6?   b. 2 to 7?   c. 10 to 12?

13. Fill in the blanks.

a. 

Name: ________________

Number of vertices = _____

Number of sides = _____

b. 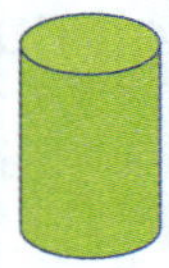

Name: __________

Curved face = _____

Flat circles = _____

14. Write the appropriate unit for each (g/kg/ℓ/mℓ).

a. A bottle of water contains about 500 _______ of water.

b. A basket of mangoes would weigh about 5 _______.

c. The weight of a bead necklace is about 150 _______.

d. The doctor asked Anish to take 8 _______ of medicine twice in a day.

15. Write the time for the following clocks.

a. 

_________ or _________

b. 

_________ or _________

16. Fill in the blanks.

a. 1 week = days   b. 1 year = months

c. 1 hour = minutes d. 1   d. $\frac{1}{2}$ hour = minutes

e. 10 minutes = _______ seconds   f. 30 minutes = _______ seconds

g. 45 minutes = _______ seconds   h. 60 minutes = _______ seconds

i. 60 seconds = _______ minutes   j. 80 seconds = _______ minutes

k. 120 seconds = _______ minutes   l. 360 seconds = _______ minutes

17. The following pictograph shows the types of activities that children like to play in a park

Children playing different activities	
Types of activities	**Number of children**
Swing	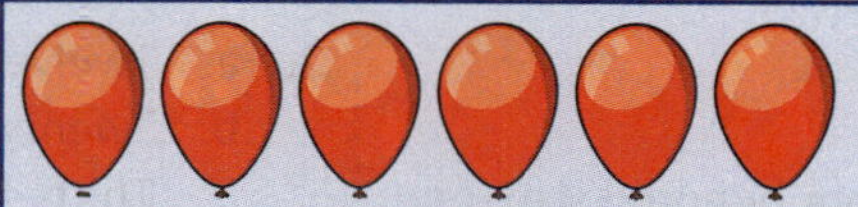
Seesaw	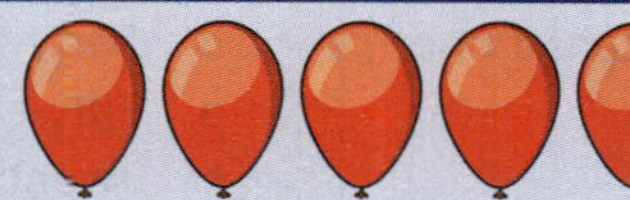
Slide	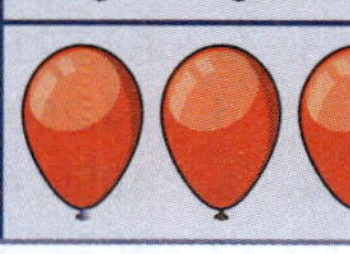

Each  = 10 children

a. How many children like the following?

i. Swing ________ ii. Seesaw ________ iii. Slide ________

b. Most children like the ________.

c. 35 children like the ________.

d. How many more children like the swing than the slide? ________.

18. Circle the figure/object that will appear next in the given patterns.

a.  _____ 

b.  _____ 

c.  _____ 

d.  _____ 

Answers

Chapter – 1

Exercise 1.1

1. a. 3 4 6 1

Number name: Three thousand four hundred sixty-one
Expanded form: 3 thousands 4 hundreds 6 tens 1 one
Or
3000 + 400 + 60 + 1

b. 6 5 2 8

Number name: Six thousand five hundred twenty-eight
Expanded form: 6 thousands 5 hundreds 2 tens 8 ones
Or
6000 + 500 + 20 + 8

2. a. Number: 8241
Number name: Eight thousand two hundred forty-one
Expanded form: 8 thousands 2 hundreds 4 tens 1 one
Or
8000 + 200 + 40 + 1

b. Number: 2175
Number name: Two thousand one hundred seventy-five
Expanded form: 2 thousands 1 hundred 7 tens 5 ones
Or 2000 + 100 + 70 + 5

3. a. 1 thousands 4 hundreds 6 tens 4 ones
b. 3 thousands 5 hundreds 4 tens 5 ones
c. 6 thousands 5 hundreds 8 tens 5 ones
d. 8 thousands 0 hundreds 1 ten 4 ones
e. 3 thousands 5 hundreds 5 tens 5 ones
f. 6 thousands 5 hundreds 9 tens 5 ones
g. 9 thousands 7 hundreds 6 tens 9 ones

4. b. 1154, 1155, 1156, 1157
c. 2451, 2452, 2453, 2454
d. 7870, 7871, 7872, 7873

5. b. 9620 c. 1507 d. 7028

6. a. 2509 b. 4186 c. 6380

7. a. 1844 b. 7388 c. 6119

Exercise 1.2

1. a.

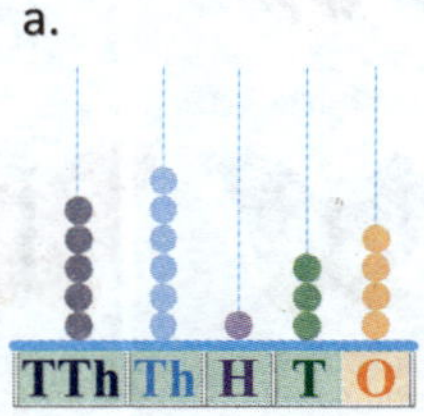

b.

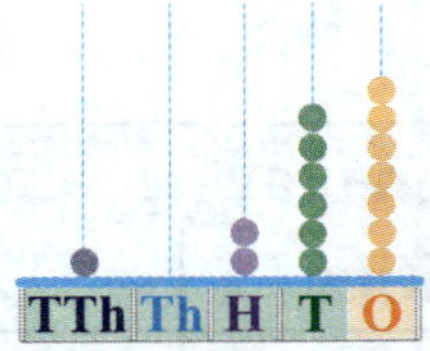

2. a. Twelve thousand eight hundred forty-seven
b. Twenty-nine thousand three hundred fifty-four
c. Thirty-five thousand four hundred sixty-one
d. Forty-six thousand seven
e. Fifty-eight thousand two hundred nine
f. Twenty thousand two hundred three

3. a. 63,571 b. 34,029 c. 87,000
d. 94,260 e. 70,004 f. 44,444

4. a. 4950, 4951, 4952, 4953
b. 3021, 3022, 3023, 3024
c. 7698, 7699, 7700, 7701
d. 20,001, 20,002, 20,003, 20,004
e. 32,492, 32,493, 32,494, 32,495
f. 53,043, 53,044, 53,045, 53,046

5. a. 32,565 b. 60,249 c. 51,004

6. a. 43,714 b. 72,627 c. 51,008

7. a. Place value = 80
Face value = 8
b. Place value = 6000
Face value = 6
c. Place value = 20
Face value = 2
d. Place value = 8
Face value = 8
e. Place value = 7000
Face value = 7
f. Place value = 8
Face value = 8
g. Place value = 300
Face value = 3
h. Place value = 7000
Face value = 7

8. a. 6330, 6340, 6350, 6360
b. 17,460, 17,470, 17,480, 17,490
c. 45,667, 45,677, 45,687, 45,697

9. a. 3344, 3444, 3544, 3644
b. 48,630, 48,730, 48,830, 48,930
c. 33,433, 33,533, 33,633, 33,733

10. a. 4003, 5003, 6003, 7003
b. 5522, 6522, 7522, 8522
c. 76,099, 77,099, 78,099

Exercise 1.3

1. a. < b. < c. <
d. < e. > f. <

2. a. < b. < c. <
d. < e. < f. =

Exercise 1.4

1. a. 8489 b. 9073
c. 39,879 d. 21,738

2. a. 4351 b. 6732
c. 48,058 d. 65,394

3. a. 1890 < 1987 < 2407 <6138
b. 3462 < 4989 < 8273 < 10,729
c. 2304 < 9001 < 61,812 < 71,103
d. 4279 < 5038 < 11,832 < 16,294

4. a. 7801 > 7008 > 6298 > 4612
   b. 18,824 > 8451 > 7963 > 5293
   c. 99,621 > 61,723 > 59,819 > 22,793
   d. 98,461 > 98,173 > 98,035 > 4920
5. a. 2891 b. 4020 c. 45,092
   d. 10,000 e. 99,992
6. a. 3999 b. 7998 c. 10,089
   d. 89,000 e. 9999

Exercise 1.5

1. a. Greatest: 8421 Smallest: 1248 b. Greatest: 6521 Smallest: 1256
   c. Greatest: 84321 Smallest: 12348 d. Greatest: 97532 Smallest: 23579
   e. Greatest: 86210 Smallest: 10268 f. Greatest: 8520 Smallest: 2058
   g. Greatest: 9730 Smallest: 3079 h. Greatest: 65410 Smallest: 10456
   i. Greatest: 98732 Smallest: 23789 j. Greatest: 96510 Smallest: 10569
2. a. 2237 b. 9552 c. 7322
   d. 2559 e. 1668 f. 2577
   g. 8850
3. (4) ✓ 5, (8) ✓ 9, (10) ✓ 27, (12) ✓ 51, (40) ✓ 593, (236) ✓ 7389, (1278)
4. a. True b. True c. False
   d. False e. True f. False
   g. True
5. a. Greatest: 9985 Smallest: 5589 b. Greatest: 7732 Smallest: 2237
   c. Greatest: 8810 Smallest: 1008 d. Greatest: 9964 Smallest: 4469
   e. Greatest: 5532 Smallest: 2235 f. Greatest: 8871 Smallest: 1178
   g. Greatest: 9960 Smallest: 6009 h. Greatest: 5510 Smallest: 1005
   i. Greatest: 4432 Smallest: 2234 j. Greatest: 8870 Smallest: 7008

Revision Exercise

1. 7 5 2 9

Number name: Seven thousand five hundred twenty-nine

Expanded form: 7 thousands 5 hundreds 2 tens 9 ones

Or

7000 + 500 + 20 + 9

2.

3. a. 7235, 7236, 7237, 7238
   b. 2310, 2311, 2312, 2313
   c. 8799, 8800, 8801, 8802
   d. 45,676, 45,677, 45,678, 45,679
4. a. Six thousand three hundred twenty-four
   b. Eighteen thousand one hundred nine
5. a. 8012 b. 50,003
6. a. (13,219) b. (4109)
7. a. > b. < c. <
8. a. 2435, 8400, 16,943, 65,791
   b. 11,269, 11,059, 9213, 8340
9. a. 5000 b. 9
10. a. 2359 b. 15,966 c. 998
11. 5450, 5460, 5470, 5480
12. 2694, 2794, 2894, 2994
13. 3242, 4242, 5242, 6242
14. (2) ✓ 39, (14) ✓ 875, (22) ✓ 1093, (340) ✓ 2049, (516) ✓ 9387, (1078) ✓ 9999, (5522) ✓ 12,489, (9370)

Chapter – 2

Exercise 2.1

1. 997 2. 887 3. 577 4. 699
5. 999 6. 959 7. 578 8. 987
9. 678 10. 868 11. 799 12. 669
13. 648 14. 926 15. 999 16. 978
17. 896 18. 865

Exercise 2.2

1. 370 2. 654 3. 651 4. 762
5. 852 6. 345 7. 795 8. 893
9. 688 10. 594 11. 586 12. 894

Exercise 2.3

1. 621 2. 772 3. 434 4. 542
5. 813 6. 620 7. 963 8. 823
9. 817 10. 853 11. 797 12. 953
13. 856 14. 749 15. 757

Exercise 2.4

1. 5675 2. 7868 3. 4999 4. 6689
5. 3799 6. 4998 7. 8598 8. 6054
9. 5430 10. 7718

Exercise 2.5

1. 83305 2. 77699 3. 75846 4. 68458
5. 65,375 6. 92,867 7. 152,405

Exercise 2.6

1. 588 2. 730 3. 390 4. 835
5. 887 6. 568 7. 990 8. 976
9. 359 10. 5377

Exercise 2.7

1. a. 40 b. 230 c. 460
d. 5260
2. a. 400 b. 900 c. 3300
d. 7800
3. a. 3000 b. 3000
c. 9000 d. 6000
4. a. Estimated sum = 400, Actual sum = 399
b. Estimated sum = 400, Actual sum = 381
c. Estimated sum = 700, Actual sum = 647
d. Estimated sum = 1000, Actual sum = 1022
e. Estimated sum = 1000, Actual sum = 972
f. Estimated sum = 400, Actual sum = 412
5. a. 5520 b. 11,400 c. 10,210
6. a. 8000 b. 12,600 c. 12,600
7. a. 18,000 b. 21,000 c. 13,000

Revision Exercise

1. a. 758 b. 477 c. 731 d. 878
e. 898 f. 595 g. 871 h. 923
i. 854 j. 8979 k. 8913 l. 10,142
m. 9178 n. 40,189 o. 80,383
2. 480 3. 920 4. 610
5. a. 810 b. 931 c. 879
d. 600 e. 7861 f. 6404
g. 8975 h. 9748 i. 64,588
j. 91,779
6. a. Estimated sum = 600, Actual sum = 588
b. Estimated sum = 700, Actual sum = 727

Chapter – 3

Exercise 3.1

1. a. 331 b. 471 c. 772 d. 100
e. 541 f. 163 g. 321 h. 200
i. 131 j. 143 k. 321 l. 400
m. 251 n. 322 o. 241 p. 222

Exercise 3.2

1. a. 107 b. 404 c. 319 d. 88
e. 342 f. 219 g. 416 h. 528
i. 158 j. 428 k. 578 l. 169
2. a. 46 b. 224 c. 218 d. 407
e. 132 f. 326 g. 543 h. 78
i. 109 j. 168 k. 153 l. 171
3. a. 115 b. 359 c. 459 d. 179
e. 477 f. 738 g. 468 h. 257
i. 514 j. 466 k. 308 l. 65

Exercise 3.3

1. a. 8731 b. 4657
c. 5187 d. 6623
2. a. 2412 b. 3811 c. 5531
d. 3512 e. 5543 f. 6031

Exercise 3.4

1. a. 2131 b. 4592 c. 2488
d. 1888 e. 1769 f. 5238
2. a. 4409 b. 6545 c. 8709
d. 1870 e. 5739 f. 4492

Exercise 3.5

1. 137 2. 21 3. 121 4. 26 5. 175
6. 730 7. 298 8. 69 9. 6541 10. 3230

Exercise 3.6

1. 429 2. 164 3. 590 4. 2 5. 140

Exercise 3.7

1. a. Estimated difference = 200
Actual subtraction = 260
b. Estimated difference = 300
Actual subtraction = 310
c. Estimated difference = 500
Actual subtraction = 551
d. Estimated difference = 300
Actual subtraction = 264
e. Estimated difference = 100
Actual subtraction = 126
f. Estimated difference = 100
Actual subtraction = 131
2. a. 1000 b. 3000 c. 1000
d. 2000 e. 1000 f. 1000

Exercise 3.8

1. a. 15890 b. 28911 c. 28891
d. 18889 e. 38988 f. 14789
2. a. 7409 b. 13,545 c. 15,709
d. 22,969 e. 34,738 f. 51492

Revision Exercise

1. a. 681 b. 312 c. 451 d. 366
e. 427 f. 272 g. 276 h. 552
i. 286
2. a. 702 b. 699 c. 605 d. 390
e. 45 f. 665 g. 40 h. 225
i. 407 j. 1546 k. 1735 l. 2568
m. 5729 n. 24,493 o. 13,589 p. 18,487
3. 287 4. 604 5. 595 6. 820 7. ₹8690
8. 8552 9. ₹5250 10. 2920 litres
11. Estimated vacant seats = 7500, Actual vacant seats = 7539
12. Estimated men = 28,000, Actual men = 28,080

Chapter – 4

Exercise 4.1

1. a. 30 b. 780 c. 940 d. 500
e. 6300 f. 4800
2. a. 60 b. 860 c. 280 d. 630
e. 800 f. 600 g. 1500 h. 1000
i. 1800
3. a. 400 b. 1410 c. 1400 d. 3040
e. 1500 f. 1750 g. 1350 h. 2100
i. 1680

Exercise 4.2

1. a. 396 b. 516 c. 696 d. 820
2. a. 690 b. 698 c. 1521 d. 696
e. 670 f. 1692

Exercise 4.3

1. a. 325 b. 368 c. 5486 d. 2938
e. 15,720 f. 10,168 g. 9492 h. 12,355

2. a. 966 b. 945 c. 1134 d. 390
e. 8046 f. 6702 g. 11,190 h. 5710
i. 4542 j. 11,056 k. 6204 l. 11,691

Exercise 4.4

1. 84 chocolates 2. 20 pictures 3. 159 4. 180
5. 285 6. 360 7. 78 8. 255
9. 288 10. 325 11. 360 12. 595
13. 3750

Exercise 4.5

1. a. Estimated product = 100
Actual multiplication = 108
b. Estimated product = 400
Actual multiplication = 336
c. Estimated product = 900
Actual multiplication = 828
d. Estimated product = 800
Actual multiplication = 756
e. Estimated product = 200
Actual multiplication = 176
f. Estimated product = 300
Actual multiplication = 252

Exercise 4.6

1. a.

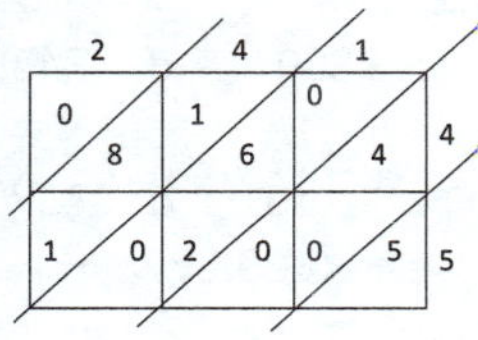

b.

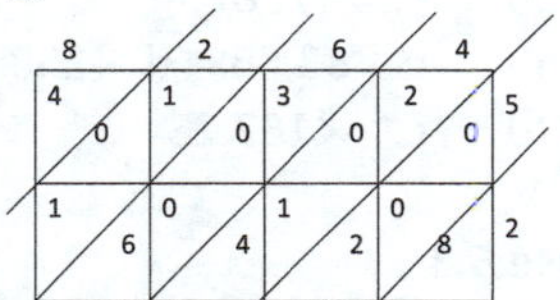

2. a.

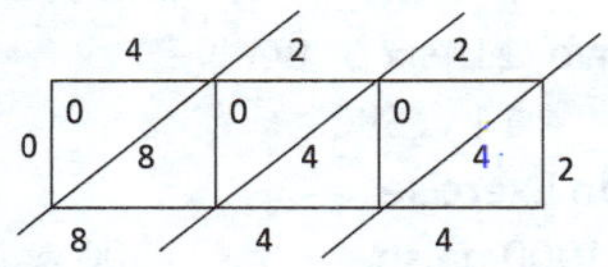

= 844

b.

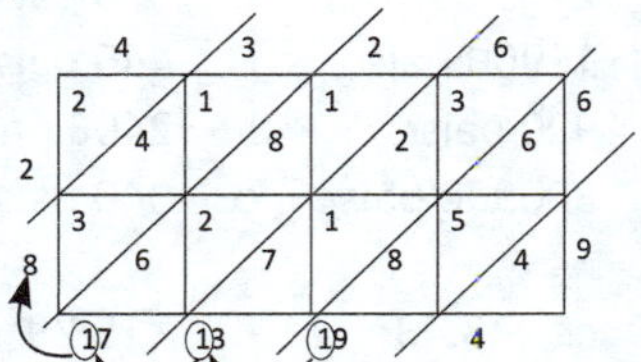

= 298494

c.

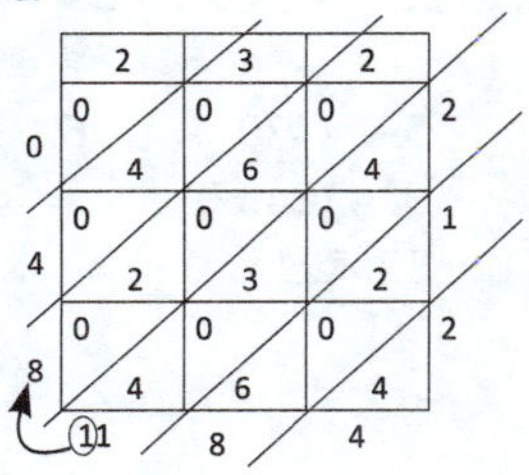

= 49184

d.

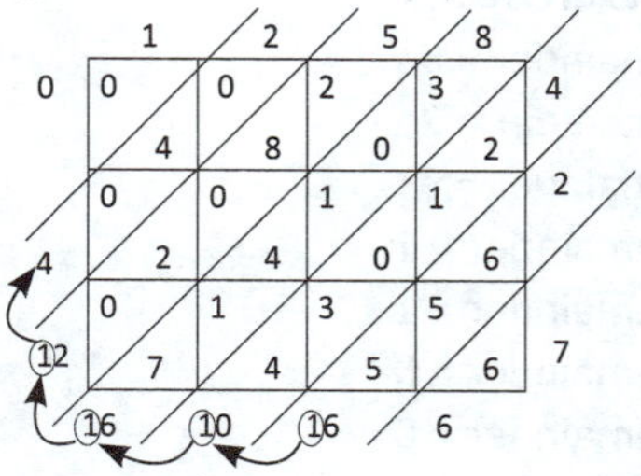

= 537166

e.

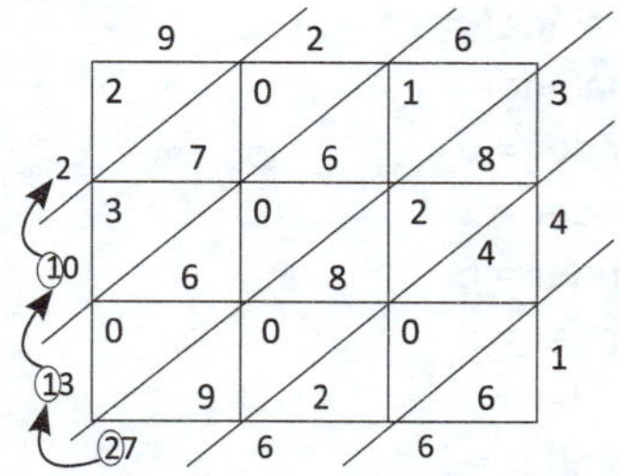

= 315766

Revision Exercise

1. a. 384 b. 1288 c 640 d. 552
e. 2646 f. 741 g. 396 h. 406
i. 860 j. 390 k. 804 l. 750
m. 8972 n. 9576 o. 69342 p. 10485
q. 600 r. 2400
2. a. 390 b. 720 c. 500 d. 2700
e. 9200 f. 2900
3. a. 70 b. 282 c. 376 d. 1132
e. 840 f. 17,361 g. 7981 h. 21,835
4. 288 5. 144 6. 325 7. 625
8. a. Estimated product = 600
Actual multiplication = 549
b. Estimated product = 500
Actual multiplication = 416
9. ₹795 10. 4015 days 11. 6000 children
12. ₹78,000 13. ₹9120 14. ₹4410
15. 10,108 pages

Chapter – 5

Exercise 5.1

1. Quotient = 12, Remainder = 0
2. Quotient = 13, Remainder = 0
3. Quotient = 11, Remainder = 2
4. Quotient = 36, Remainder = 0
5. Quotient = 18, Remainder = 1
6. Quotient = 12, Remainder = 0
7. Quotient = 21, Remainder = 1
8. Quotient = 10, Remainder = 0

Exercise 5.2

1. Quotient = 142, Remainder = 0
2. Quotient = 312, Remainder = 0
3. Quotient = 72, Remainder = 0
4. Quotient = 156, Remainder = 1
5. Quotient = 62, Remainder = 1
6. Quotient = 171, Remainder = 1
7. Quotient = 240, Remainder = 0
8. Quotient = 120, Remainder = 0

Exercise 5.3

1. Quotient = 642, Remainder = 0
2. Quotient = 978, Remainder = 2
3. Quotient = 405, Remainder = 3
4. Quotient = 1406, Remainder = 1
5. Quotient = 1062, Remainder = 1
6. Quotient = 2838, Remainder = 0
7. Quotient = 2490, Remainder = 0
8. Quotient = 1920, Remainder = 0
9. Quotient = 1113, Remainder = 1
10. Quotient = 1099, Remainder = 7
11. Quotient = 22, Remainder = 0
12. Quotient = 27, Remainder = 2
13. Quotient = 51, Remainder = 6
14. Quotient = 61, Remainder = 5
15. Quotient = 14, Remainder = 1
16. Quotient = 160, Remainder = 2
17. Quotient = 205, Remainder = 14
18. Quotient = 278, Remainder = 12
19. Quotient = 381, Remainder = 15
20. Quotient = 184, Remainder = 25

Exercise 5.4

1. 6 2. 106 rows 3. 25 cars
4. 21 toffees 5. 5 people 6. 12 books
7. ₹10 8. 6 packets and 5 biscuits left

Revision Exercise

1. a. $72 \div 9 = 8$, $72 \div 8 = 9$ b. $56 \div 7 = 8$, $56 \div 8 = 7$
2. a. 42 b. 36
3. a. 6 b. 5 c. 3 d. 4 e. 3 f. 7
4. a. Quotient = 52, Remainder = 4
   b. Quotient = 176, Remainder = 2
   c. Quotient = 137, Remainder = 1
   d. Quotient = 200, Remainder = 0
   e. Quotient = 131, Remainder = 1
   f. Quotient = 18, Remainder = 26
   g. Quotient = 16, Remainder = 20
   h. Quotient = 7, Remainder = 10
5. a. Quotient = 1075, Remainder = 1
   b. Quotient = 1350, Remainder = 0
   c. Quotient = 1038, Remainder = 0
   d. Quotient = 839, Remainder = 3
   e. Quotient = 701, Remainder = 4
   f. Quotient = 14, Remainder = 10
   g. Quotient = 39, Remainder = 8
   h. Quotient = 16, Remainder = 13
   i. Quotient = 38, Remainder = 8
   j. Quotient = 51, Remainder = 18
   k. Quotient = 119, Remainder = 11
   l. Quotient = 247, Remainder = 11
   m. Quotient = 218, Remainder = 1
   n. Quotient = 413, Remainder = 4
   o. Quotient = 151, Remainder = 20

6. 8 boats 7. 9 trays 8. 160 students
9. 40 cards 10. 12 crayons 11. 7 shirts
12. 20 baskets, 5 apples 13. 25 students
14. ₹700 15. ₹590 16. 446
17. 220 18. 282 packets and 16 biscuits will be left
19. 250 km 20. 165 trees
21. 349 oranges, yes, 16 oranges 22. 24 chocolates
23. 147 groups 24. 165 25. 374

Chapter – 6

Exercise 6.1

1. a. ₹7.78 b. ₹64.06 c. ₹409.08 d. ₹790.50
2. a. 7 rupees 25 paise b. 60 rupees 4 paise c. 63 rupees 8 paise d. 327 rupees 75 paise
3. a. 700 paise b. 1200 paise c. 900 paise d. 5600 paise e. 9000 paise f. 6200 paise g. 2200 paise h. 3800 paise
4. a. ₹8 b. ₹16 c. ₹7.25 d. ₹9.50 e. ₹5.50 f. ₹12.30 g. ₹15.05 h. ₹45.35
5. a. 530 paise b. 1545 paise c. 2309 paise d. 1250 paise e. 1512 paise f. 3809 paise
6. a. ₹3.12 b. ₹12.35 c. ₹17.03 d. ₹33.02

Exercise 6.2

1. a. ₹150 b. ₹630 c. ₹800 d. ₹436 e. ₹650 f. ₹170
2. a. ₹75 b. ₹68 c. ₹161 d. ₹37
3. a. ₹31.65 b. ₹51.91 c. ₹189.57 d. ₹192.35
4. a. ₹125.47 b. ₹476.90 c. ₹760
5. a. ₹13.01 b. ₹66.25 c. ₹33.66 d. ₹150.97
6. a. ₹37.11 b. ₹135.20 c. ₹167.25 d. ₹27.09

Exercise 6.3

1. ₹210 2. ₹306 3. ₹329 4. ₹321
5. ₹140 6. ₹612 7. ₹20 8. one or two
9. two 10. one or five 11. six or twelve
12. ₹300 13. ₹490 14. ₹590

Revision Exercise

1. a. 800 paise b. 1900 paise c. 7300 paise d. 480 paise e. 2735 paise f. 500 paise g. 2000 paise h. 15000 paise i. 445 paise j. 712 paise k. 900 paise l. 2400 paise m. 150000 paise n. 500900 paise o. 940 paise p. 2347 paise
2. a. ₹3 b. ₹27 c. ₹8.43 d. ₹15.29 e. ₹4 f. ₹35.29 g. ₹7.42 h. ₹9 i. ₹17 j. ₹1.25 k. ₹8.20 l. ₹36.40 m. ₹73.45 n. ₹2.35
3. ₹113.43 4. ₹38.75 5. ₹470 6. ₹86
7. ₹192 8. ₹920 9. ₹84.60
10. ₹180 11. ₹250 12. ₹21
13. ₹125

Chapter – 7

Exercise 7.1

1.
a. Slanting line b. Square c. Triangle d. Rectangle

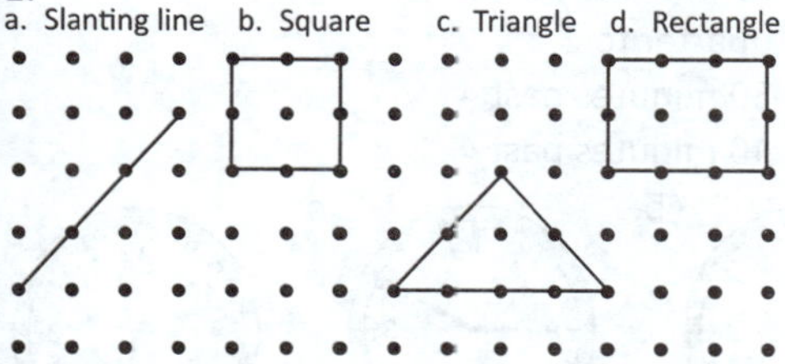

2. a. Helicopter b. Tree c. Running person
d. Rabbit

Exercise 7.2

1. a. Name : Square
Number of vertices = 4
Number of sides = 4

b. Name : Rectangle
Number of vertices = 4
Number of sides = 4

c. Name : Triangle
Number of vertices = 3
Number of sides = 3

d. Name : Circle
Number of vertices = 0
Number of sides = 0

e. Name : Cube
Number of vertices = 8
Number of edges = 12
Number of faces = 6

f. Name : Cuboid
Number of vertices = 8
Number of edges = 12
Number of faces = 6

g. Name : Sphere
Number of vertices = 0
Number of edges = 0
Curved face = 1

h. Name : Cylinder
Curved face = 1
Flat circles = 2

i. Name : Cone
Number of vertices = 1
Curved face = 1
Flat circle = 1

2. a. 4 vertices, 4 sides
b. 8 vertices, 12 edges or 6 faces

3. a. → ii b. → v c. → i d. → iv
e. → iii

Exercise 7.3

1. square 2. 6 3. cylinder 4. 3
5. circle 6. 5 7. 12 8. square
9. cube 10. 8

Exercise 7.4

1. a.

b.

c.

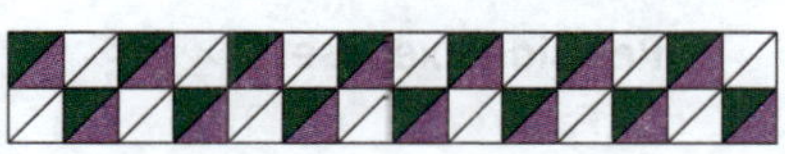

d.

2. a.

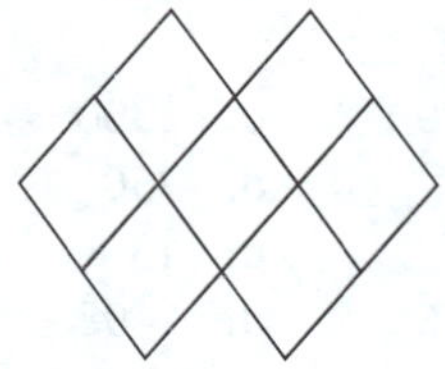

c.

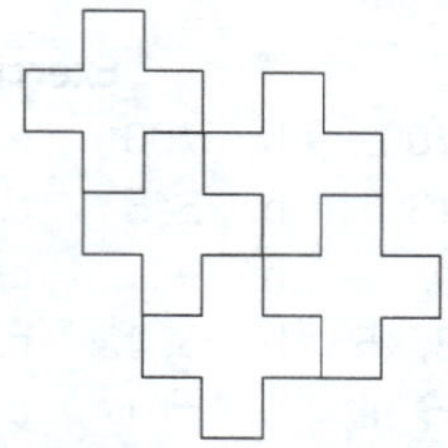

Exercise 7.5

1. a.

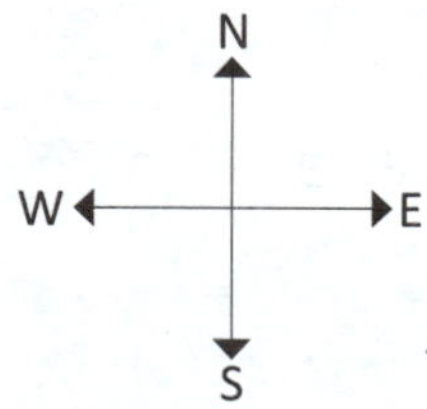

b.

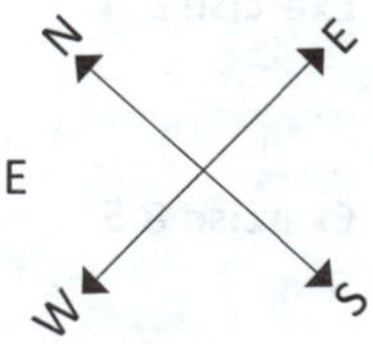

c.

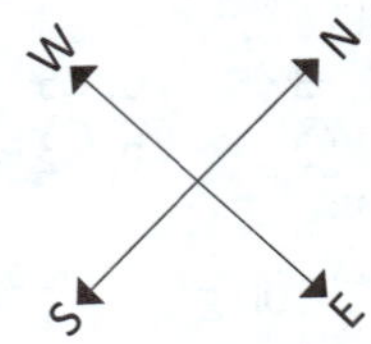

2. a. Park b. Hospital c. School
d. Alice's house e. Party house
f. Diya's house g. West h. North
i. South j. Park, Diya's house

Revision Exercise

1.

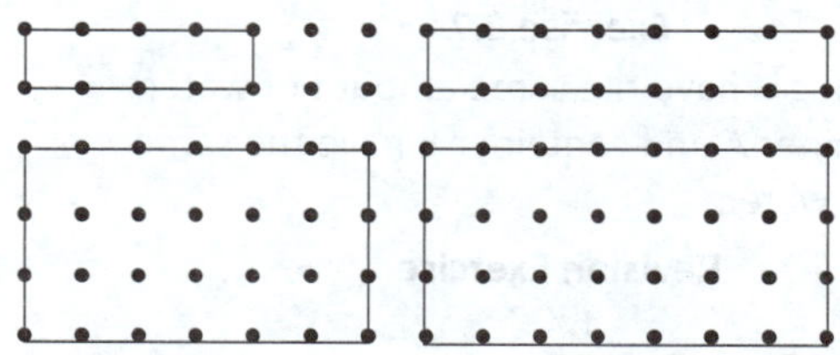

2. a. ✗ b. ✓ c. ✓ d. ✗
e. ✗ f. ✗

3. a. → iii b. → iv c. → v d. → ii e. → i

4. a. point x b. line AB c. ray XY
d. Line segment MN

5. Number of corners: 4
Number of sides: 4

6. a. Triangle, 3, 3 b. Cuboid, 8, 12, 6

7. a. 0, 0 b. 8, 5

8. a. North b. East c. City d. West

Chapter – 8

Exercise 8.1

1. Longest → Kilometre, Shortest → centimetre
2. Height of a house, Height of a door
3. a. cm b. km c. m d. cm
e. m f. m g. cm h. km

Exercise 8.2

1. a. 9 b. 8 c. 5 d. 7
2. a.

b.

c.
d.
e.
f.

3. a. 2 cm b. 3 cm c. 4 cm
   d. 6 cm

Exercise 8.3

1. a. 200 b. 700 c. 1100 d. 1300
2. a. 130 b. 545 c. 215 d. 750
3. a. 4 b. 9 c. 7 d. 13
4. a. 3, 15 b. 5, 42 c. 2, 76 d. 1, 98
5. a. → iii b. → iv c. → i d. → ii
   e. → v
6. a. < b. < c. = d. >

Exercise 8.4

1. a. 3 b. 5 c. 2
2. a. 2 b. 3 c. 5 d. 5 e. 3

Exercise 8.5

1. a. 100 g b. 9 kg
2. a. kg b. g
3. a. 2 kg b. 10 g
4. a. g b. g c. kg d. kg

Exercise 8.6

1. a. 8 b. 5
2. a. 1 mℓ b. 5 mℓ c. 200 mℓ
   d. 250 mℓ e. 200 mℓ

Exercise 8.7

1. Jug A and Jug B have the same amount of water.
2. Both container A and container B have the same amount of water.

Revision Exercise

1. a. ______ b. ______
2. a. cm b. m c. km
3. a. 4500 b. 375
4. a. 3, 0 b. 6, 25
5. a. (✓) b. (x) c. (x) d. (✓)
   e. (✓) f. (✓)
6. a. grams b. grams c. grams d. kilograms
   e. kilograms
7. Syringe, Tea cup, Ink, Bucket, Overhead tank
8. a. jug b. spoonfuls c. bottle
   d. cups

Chapter – 9

Exercise 9.1

1. a. 4:30 or half past 4
   b. 9:15 or quarter past 9
   c. 6:45 or quarter to 7
   d 8:45 or quarter to 9
2. a. b. c. d.

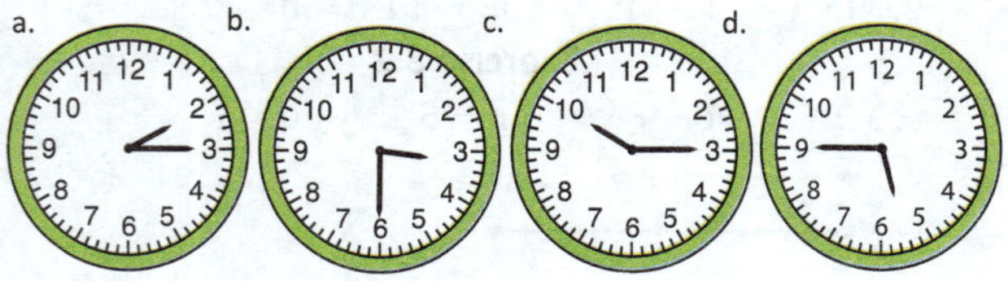

2:15 3:30 10:15 5:45

3. a. 10 minutes b. 15 minutes c. 25 minutes
   d. 40 minutes e. 55 minutes f. 60 minutes
4. a. 8:20 or 20 minutes past 8
   b. 1:45 or quarter to 2
   c. 4:50 or 50 minutes past 4
   d. 4:40 or 40 minutes past 4
5. a. b. c.

7:25 9:10 5:55

6.

A

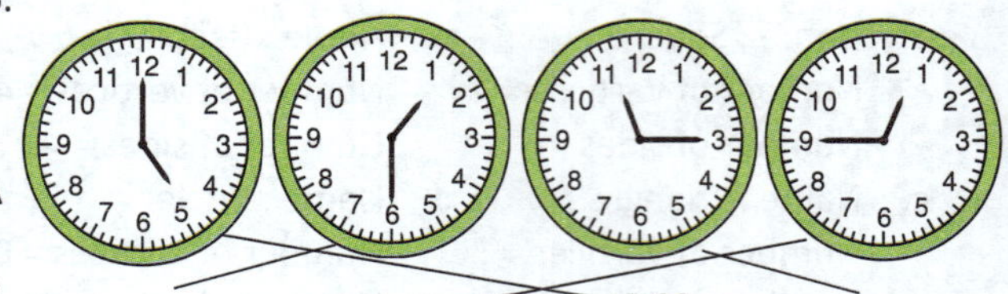

B

1:30 12:45 5:00 11:15

Exercise 9.2

1. a. 5:00 a.m. b. 7:00 p.m. c. 2:00 p.m.
   d. 11:00 a.m. e. Midnight f. Noon
2. 3 3. 45 4. 1 hour 15 minutes
5. 2 hours 25 minutes 6. 3 hours 15 minutes
7. 25

Exercise 9.3

1. a. 1:00 a.m. b. 6:00 a.m. c. 10:00 a.m.
   d. 10:45 a.m. e. Noon f. 12:30 p.m.
   g. 1:15 p.m. h. 3:20 p.m.
2. a. 1445 hours b. 1200 hours c. 0630 hours
   d. 1220 hours e. 1955 hours f. 2245 hours
3. a. 1:50 a.m. b. 10:40 a.m. c. 2:30 p.m.
   d. 12:10 p.m. e. 10:25 p.m. f. 12:59 a.m.
   g. 4:30 p.m. h. 1:00 p.m.

Exercise 9.4

1. a. 72 b. 120 c. 168 d. 240
   e. 27 f. 53 g. 74 h. 148
2. a. 180 b. 300 c. 360 d. 480
   e. 65 f. 127 g. 303 h. 495

Exercise 9.5

1. a. Rajdhani Express
   b. Rajdhani Express
   c. 16 hours 55 minutes
   d. Lohit Express
2. a. Apple pie and potato chips
   b. Plum cake
   c. 1 hour 10 minutes
   d. Plum cake
   e. 45 minutes

Revision Exercise

1. a. True b. False c. True
   d. False e. False f. True
   g. True h. False

2. a. 1:45 or Quarter to 2
   b. 7:10 or 10 minutes past 7
   c. 4:50 or 50 minutes past 4
3. 25 minutes
4. a.

11:30 or Half past 11

b.

6:40 or 40 minutes past 6

5. 1 hour 15 minutes   6. 2 hours 40 minutes
7. a. 6:00 a.m.   b. 10:00 a.m.   c. 9:00 p.m.
   d. Noon   e. 3:00 p.m.   f. Midnight
8. a. 1815 hours   b. 0705 hours   c. 0030 hours
   d. 2345 hours
9. a. 3:15 p.m.   b. 12:10 p.m.   c. 11:25 p.m.
   d. 8:20 a.m.
10. a. 216   b. 288   c. 135   d. 252
11. a. 540   b. 660   c. 186   d. 395

Chapter – 10

Exercise 10.1

1. a. i. 20   ii. 30   iii. 35   iv. 10
      v. 15
   b. Wednesday   c. Thursday   d. Tuesday
2. a. 14 students   b. 8 students   c. Pineapple
   d. Red velvet
3. a. 28   b. 24   c. Swimming
   d. Pottery making   e. 16 students

Exercise 10.2

1. a. i. 2 cakes   ii. 5 cakes   iii. 7 cakes
      iv. 1 cake
   b. Wednesday   c. 7 cakes   d. 6 cakes
2.
   a. i. 12 shells   ii. 14 shells
      iii. 10 shells   iv. 16 shells
   b. Preeti   c. 28 shells   d. 4 shells

Revision Exercise

1. a. David   b. Shyam   c. ₹120
   d. ₹30
2. a. 90   b. 60   c. Scooter   d. Bus
3.

Vegetable Name	Tally marks	No. of vegetables
Onion	||||	4
Pumpkin	||||	4
Potato	~~||||~~	5
Tomato	~~||||~~ |	6
Capsicum	||||	4
Carrot	|	1

a. Tomato   b. Carrot   c. 4   d. 6

4.

Ornaments in Udita's jewellery box		
Ornament type	Tally marks	No. of ornaments
Necklaces	~~||||~~ ~~||||~~ ||	12
Earring Pairs	~~||||~~ ~~||||~~ ~~||||~~ ~~||||~~ |||	23
Bracelets	~~||||~~ ||	7
Finger rings	||||	4

Ornaments in Udita's jewellery box	
Ornament type	No. of ornaments
Necklaces	OOOOOO
Earring Pairs	OOOOOOOOOOO(
Bracelets	OOO(
Finger rings	OO

a. 3   b. 46   c. 11   d. 5   e. 17

Chapter – 11

Exercise 11.1

1. a.

b.

2. a.

b.

c.

d.

3. a.

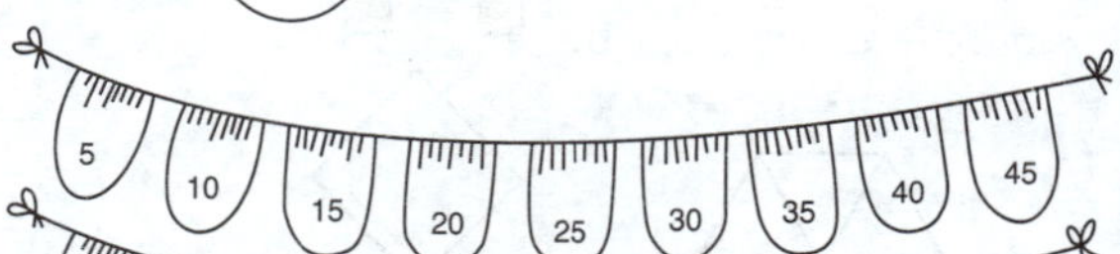

b.

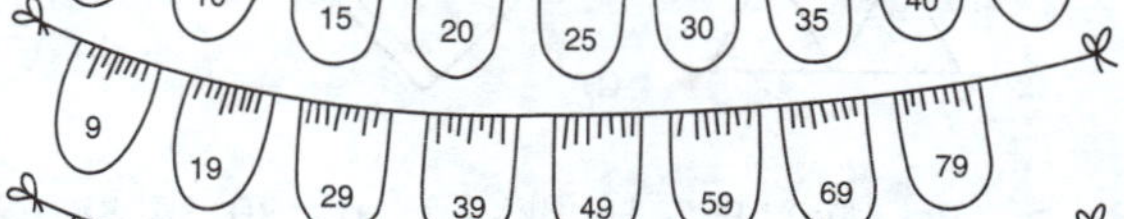

c.

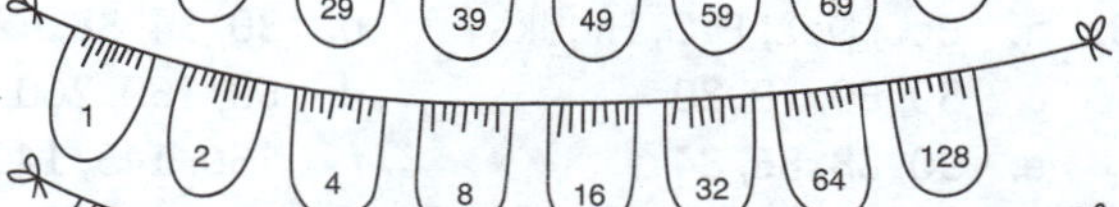

d.

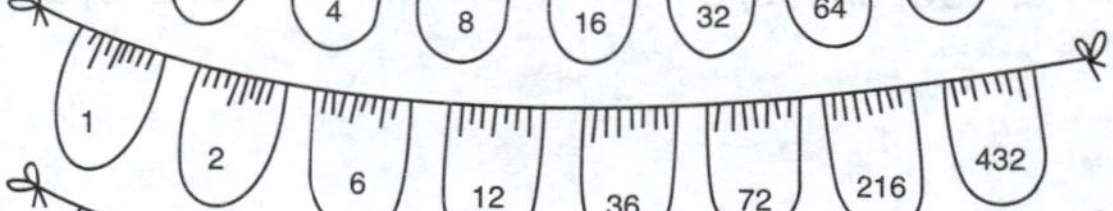

e.

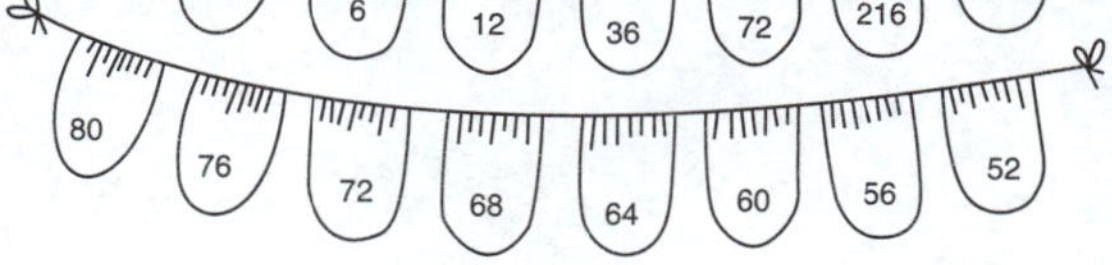

4.

a. 

b. 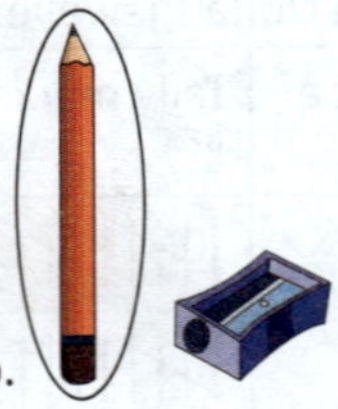

c. 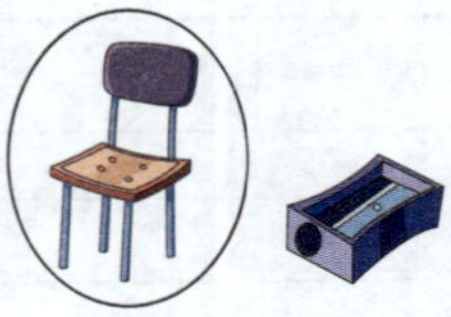

d. 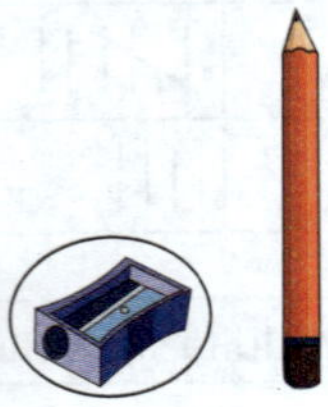

e. 

Exercise 11.2

1. 

2. 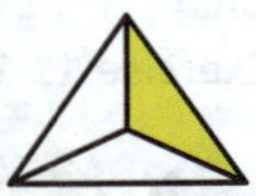

3. 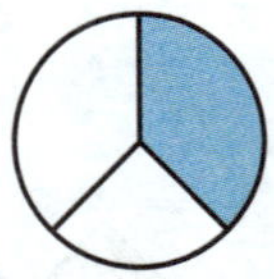

4. 

5. 

Revision Exercise

1. a.

b. 61, 71 c. 81, 243 d. w, w, v, v
e. T, N f. ABCDE, ABCDEF

2.

a. 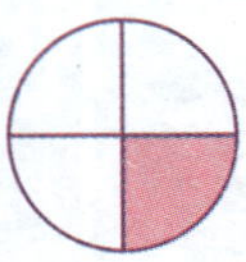

b. 

c. 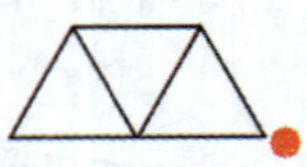

d. 

3. a. BcC, DeE, FgG, HiI, JkK b. 30, 34, 38, 42
c. 50, 60, 70, 80 d. 60, 160, 260, 360
e. 90, 88, 86, 84 f. 150, 145, 140, 135

Chapter – 12

Exercise 12.1

1. a. $\frac{1}{2}$ b. $\frac{1}{3}$ c. $\frac{1}{4}$

2. a. $\frac{1}{3}$ b. $\frac{1}{4}$

Exercise 12.2

1. 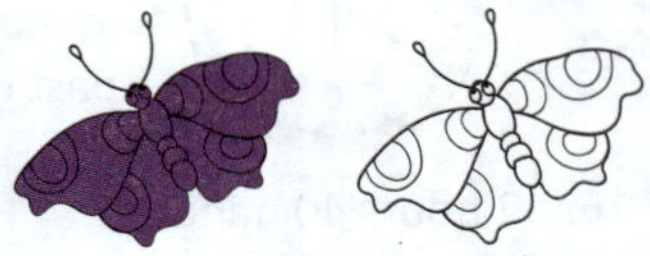

2. 

3. 

Revision Exercise

1. a. → iii b. → i c. → ii

2. a. i. 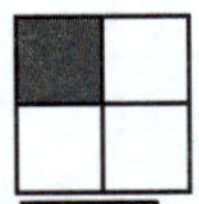

ii. 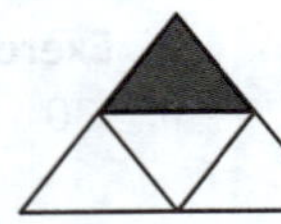

iii. 

iv. 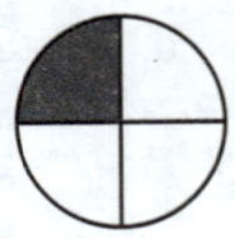

b. i. 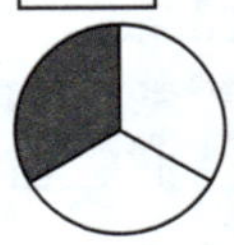

ii. 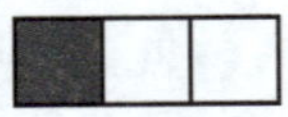

iii. 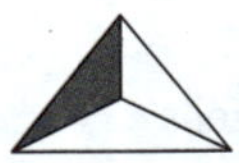

iv. 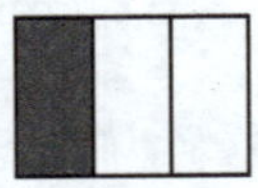

c

i. 

ii. 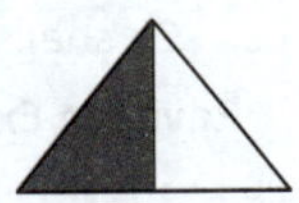

iii. 

iv. 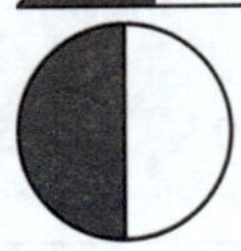

v. 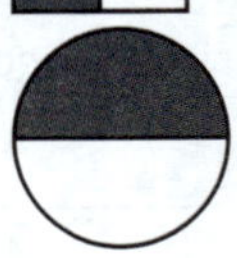